U0660178

1982年，陈振诚与妻子方舍梅（右）、女儿陈昕合影

1987年，Х. А.Рахматулин院士的另一位学生И. И. Поручиков教授来北京大学学术交流，到陈振诚家访问（自左到右陈昕、方舍梅、陈振诚、И.И.Поручиков教授、陈旸〈陈振诚的儿子〉）

1991年，在丽水市南明山陈振诚（左）与宣平县县长陈仿尧合影

1992年，在浙江宣平华塘村陈振诚（后排中）和大姐陈兰英（左一）、兄长陈振唐（左二）、嫂嫂吕宝苏（右二）、妹妹陈瑟英（右一）与父亲陈发新（时年93岁）合影

1986年9月，陈振诚（右一）在日本东京参加第三届亚洲流体力学学术讨论会

1985年，陈振诚（中）在南京与南京大学教授陈金全（右）参观菊花展览

1985年，陈振诚（中）与陈金全教授（右）、傅美娟副教授合影

1　发明船艇630（长6.3米）艇的船底构造

2　630敞篷船艇实船实航照片

1

2

1　630有篷船艇实船实航照片

2　1600（长16米）快艇的航行照片

1

2

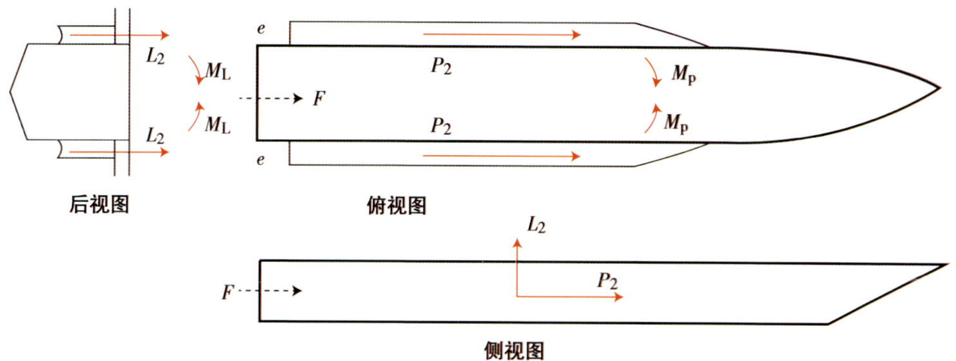

发明船艇大吨位单体船在直线前进时的受力示意图

发明船艇大吨位单体船在直线前进时的示意图

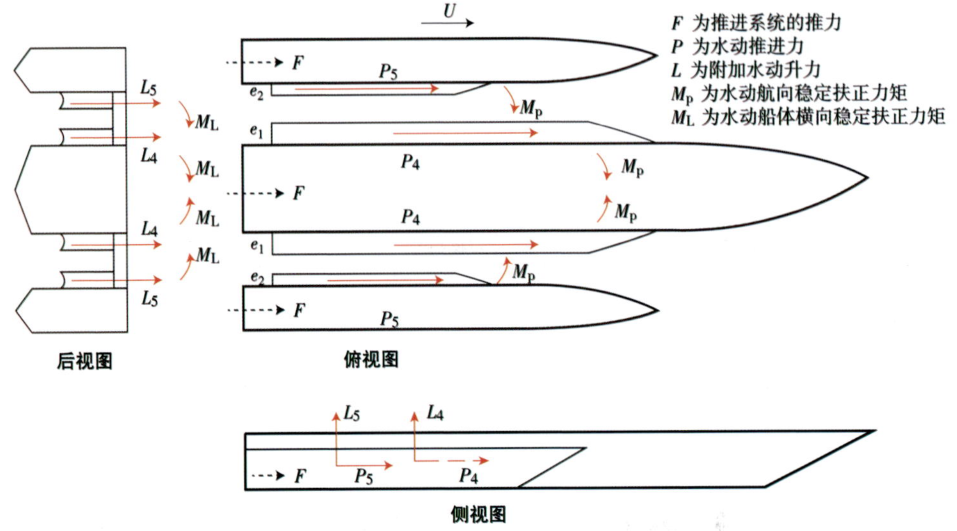

发明船艇三体船在直线前进时的受力示意图

发明船艇三体船航母在直线前进时的航态图

总 序

吴阶平　杨福家　吴文俊　袁隆平
孙家栋　陈清泉　刘国光　汝　信

中华民族，为其自身的文明发展与人类的社会进步，在数十个世纪的奋斗历程中，不断地作出了重要的贡献。

中华民族历来十分注重科学的进步与创新。古代曾有过火药、指南针等诸多重大的科学发明与创造，为人类的进步发展起到了重大而持续的推进作用。在受到很多侵害与打击的历史时期，中华民族也从未放弃与间断过教育的发展与科学的创造。中华学人在全民族人民的坚定支持下，为探求中华科学的重新辉煌、为推进人类的和平发展，进行了长时期前仆后继的艰苦奋斗。

当代中华的广大学人及其从他们当中成长出来的著名科学家们，坚持发展教育与科学，顽强拼搏、艰苦奋斗，有勇气有毅力为加速提高中华科学的自主创新能力、为攀登世界科学高峰做出一番事业。在他们身上集中体现了中华民族自强不息、敢于创新、和平友善的优良传统。他们的人生志向、科学思维、科学成就、优秀品格，是爱国主义、民族精神与科学精神的生动体现，是他们为中华民族与人类社会创造的宝贵物质财富与精神财富。我们理当将这些宝贵财富传承下去、发扬光大，使之继续成为中华兴旺发达与人类社会进步的巨大推动力量。

《中华当代著名科学家书系》正是根据这种科学与经济社会发展的需要而编著出版的。“书系”将选录海峡两岸和海外的诸多最高层次的中华自然科学家、工程科学家、社会科学家。被选录的每一位科学家都将由编委会和出版社为其编著出版侧重于科学生涯的传记性图书一种。

“书系”是一套面向大众，能够被图书馆珍藏，能够向各界读者展现中华当代著名科学家们献身科学、追求真理、推进经济社会发展、为中华文明与人类文明贡献毕生精力的高品位读物。在这些读物中，将生动介绍科学家们的人生经历、不懈追求、科学成就、奋斗历程，着重展现他们为中华复兴而表现出来的勤奋拼搏、勇于创新和赤诚奉献的精神与品格，以榜样的力量激励人们奋发进取，为中华与世界的科学腾飞、经济发展和社会进步不断地再创辉煌。

“书系”将整体性地展现中华民族对世界科学与经济社会发展的重要贡献，将充分体现中华民族尊重知识、尊重人才、和平友善、精诚团结的优良传统，将激励中华民族努力攀登世界科学高峰，为人类进步发展争作更大贡献的决心与信心；“书系”具有集锦科学成就、珍储科学史料的规模性系统性科学档案功能，并为长远的多方面的用途提供一批具有代表性与系列性的精要蓝本，具有很高的和久远的存用价值，定将流传百世；同时“书系”将在普及科学知识、弘扬科学精神、激励科学创新、推进科学发展方面发挥重要与深远的影响。

最高层次的著名科学家群体，是先进科学的领军群体。先进科学，是先进生产力的集中体现与主要标志。在当今世界，科学的发展将深刻地改变世界经济与人类社会的面貌。数十个世纪坚持科学进步与创新、不断为人类文明进步争做贡献的中华学人，定会站在时代的前列，传承民族精神，大力培养和造就科学人才、大力提高自主创新能力、努力攀登世界科学高峰，为创造更高的科学成就，为中华的未来与人类的进步发展，作出更大的贡献。

2012年9月

中华当代著名科学家书系
永久编著出版委员会

主　编	吴阶平	杨福家	吴文俊	袁隆平
	孙家栋	陈清泉	刘国光	汝　信
执行主编	唐廷友	唐　洁	赵岩青	刘忠勤
	柳　静	赵震平	王遂德	杨宗谷
副主编	单天伦	张　维	马京生	马胜云
	王　霞	王建蒙	王庭槐	彭洁清
编　委	（以姓氏笔画为序）			
	马京生	马胜云	马　越	马　兰
	马　进	马新生	山　立	王　霞
	王建蒙	王庭槐	王遂德	王增藩
	孙家栋	卢毓明	汝　信	刘国光
	刘忠勤	吴文俊	吴阶平	陈　弘
	陈清泉	张　维	李大耀	李忠效
	宋兆法	杨宗谷	杨福家	杨照德
	孟　佳	单天伦	郑绍唐	柳　静
	柳天明	赵岩青	赵震平	唐　洁
	唐廷友	顾迈男	袁隆平	常甲辰
	谢长江	曾先才	曾庆瑞	彭洁清
	谭邦治	熊延岭		
书系策划	唐廷友	唐　洁	赵岩青	刘忠勤
	柳　静	赵震平	王遂德	杨宗谷
	单天伦	钱海峰	张　维	马京生
	马胜云	王　霞	王建蒙	王庭槐
	彭洁清			

中华当代著名科学家书系
执行编著出版委员会

执行主编 唐廷友 唐 洁 赵岩青 刘忠勤

副 主 编 单天伦 张 维 马京生 马胜云 王 霞 王建蒙 王庭槐 彭洁清

编 委 马京生 马胜云 马 越 马 兰 马 进 王 霞 王建蒙 王庭槐 刘忠勤 李忠效 张 维 孟 佳 单天伦 赵岩青 唐 洁 唐廷友 曾庆瑞 彭洁清

见人之所常见，思人之所未思。

为学既要博大，更要高深。

努力为祖国、为中华民族、为世界多做有益的贡献。

——陈振诚

陈振诚简介

陈振诚，生于1929年2月24日，浙江省宣平县华塘村人。1956年8月毕业于上海同济大学。1956年9月—1958年2月，在北京中国科学院力学研究所为研究实习员。1958年3月—1958年11月，在北京俄语学院留苏预备部学习俄语、哲学。1958年12月，到莫斯科苏联科学院力学研究所为研究生，攻读流体动力学专业。研究生毕业后，于1961年回国，在北京中国科学院力学研究所为助理研究员，从事流体动力学、气体动力学以及相关的应用数学课题的研究工作。1968年，在中国人民解放军0912部队从事流体、气体动力学课题的研究工作。1974年，在北京中国科学院国家天文台担任副研究员。1988年，担任研究员，跨学科从事流体动力学（船舰流体动力学）、宇宙气体动力学（星系结构）、电磁流体力学（太阳活动区磁场、黑子、耀斑）以及相关的应用数学课题的研究工作。1991年，兼任北京飞鳐水面航行技术开发中心主任，飞鳐系列研制专家组长，水面航行器总设计师。

跨学科应用基础理论研究，取得的主要科研成果有：

1. 流体动力学领域

（1）研究并找到了地震激起而作用于水坝迎水面上的水动压力。为在地震区建造既节省费用又能抵抗地震的剧烈震动而安全可靠的水坝，提供科学依据。

（2）找到了高坝水闸闸下自由出流或淹没出流时，作用于水闸闸门浸湿面上的水动压力。为设计安全可靠的高坝闸门，提供科学依据。

（3）用他自己创建的陈振诚积分变换方法，找到了考虑三维效应和重力影响的水动浮力、水动推进力、水动离心力、水动反冲击力定量值的解析表述式。从而为原创性的重大发明建造水面航行器奠定了坚实可靠的科学基础。用这项发明，建造的实船实航卫星跟踪的GPS系统，实测显示的数据证实了：众所周知船舰运行时推进系统输出的功率，一部分克服水阻力推船前进做有用功，而另一部分则被船行激起的水流波浪运动所耗散成为无用能量。创造发明的新型船舰称为水面航行器，它的船底浸湿面外形结构能够把携带被耗散无用能量的水流引入船底，在此处转化为水动推进力，推动船舰加速前进而做有用功。也就是说，本发明的船舰，在流场中，体现了物理学中的能量守恒原理，把无用能量转化为水动推进力，做有用功。于是能使630艇，长630厘米、宽210厘米、型深80厘米，推进功率200马力舷外机，空船排水量1吨，乘员8人（相当于排水量1.5吨）时，航速36.15节。乘员16人（相当于排水量2吨）时，航速37.15节，也就是提高航速约22.4%，节能约33.3%。为我国的造船业带来重大的经济效益、社会效益和国防效益。

2. 电磁流体力学和宇宙气体动力学方面

（1）依据观测事实，研究并找到了太阳活动区光球及其上空的磁场。导出了计算太阳大气中磁场位形的表述式，以此为依据进一步研究了黑子浮现、演化、磁能凝聚、爆发耀斑的物理机制，从而得到了预言太阳耀斑爆发的判据。可为发射地球人造卫星以及航天器时提供高空环境情报。为捕捉高能粒子、发现新元素提供理论依据。

（2）依据观测事实研究了宇宙中的星系结构，对棒旋星系的形成演化作出了分析。

3. 应用数学方面

建立了不同于Fourier积分变换，也不同于Laplace积分变换的能解决上述积分变换解决不了的边值问题的应用数学方法，可称之为陈振诚积分变换。它有自己不同于前人积分变换中的积分核、积分环路和逆变换的反演定理，并且对定理做出了严格的证明。用它找到了水动浮力、水动推进力、水动离心力、水动反冲击力定量值的解析表述式，是提高船舶性能设计的有效工具。用它也找到了太阳活动区光球及其上空磁场的解析表述式以及星系的棒旋结构。

4. 创造发明方面

依据发明技术设计建造的630艇，见1-（3）中列述的实船实航数据显示：对比现有技术的快艇，想提高其3% 的航速都很难做到。那么630快艇能提高22.4% 的航速的原因何在？唯一的原因就是本发明技术的船底浸湿面外形结构造成了水动力流场中出现足够强大的水动推进力和相应的水动升力。其结果是航速提高约22.4%，节能约33.3%。

本发明获得了中、美、英、日、韩、德、意大利等22个造船先进国家知识产权局的发明专利授权。

主要学术论著有：

1. 在上述三个学科领域，把跨学科研究取得的成果，用中、英、俄、德、法、意大利、西班牙、日本、朝鲜、挪威、波兰等多国文字撰写发表论文100余篇。代表作有：《地震激起而作用于水坝迎水面上的水动压力》《船舰运营中激起的水动浮力》《水动推进力》《太阳活动区光球及其上空的磁场》《预言太阳耀斑爆发的判据》《星系的棒旋结构》。发明专利论文《水面航行器》《一种水面交通运输工具》等。

2. 出版专著：《陈振诚积分变换及其应用》。

关于船舰水动推进力的发明设计简要说明

船舰水动推进力是陈振诚对船舰运营中的水动力流场做了长期研究后提出的原创性发明。其内涵是：船舰运动时推进系统输出的功率，有一部分克服水阻力推船前进做有用功；另一部分激起水流波浪运动被耗散而成为无用能量。但是，可以设计优异的船底浸湿面外形，把那一部分携带着无用能量的水流波浪引入有优异外形设计的船底浸湿面，在这里迫使携带着无用能量的水流对船底浸湿面顶部形成足够强大的法向压力。法向压力的水平方向分量与船行方向一致，即为名副其实的推船加速前进的水动推进力。法向压力的垂向分量即为水动升力，使船舰吃水深度减小而提高航速。一对水动推进力对船舰重心构成航向稳定扶正力矩，迫使船舰不偏离既定目标而高速前进。一对水动升力对船舰重心构成横向稳定扶正力矩，克服船体横摇摆动。同时，对船舰重心构成纵向稳定扶正力矩，克服船舰的纵摇拍击，从而大幅度提高船舰的整体性能。

把携带无用能量的水流引入船底浸湿面，使它转化为水动推进力而做有用功，完全符合物理学中的能量守恒原理。

依据这项原创性发明，建造长6.3m、宽2.1m、型深0.8m的快艇，空船排水量1吨，用200马力的舷外机推进，乘员8人（实际排水量1.5吨）时航速为36.15节。把乘员增加一倍为16人（实际排水量2吨）时航速非但不下降，反倒增加1节达到37.15节。

现有技术的快艇对载重变化的响应特别敏感，载重量每增加2人航速下降1.7节，如果增加8人，航速下降4×1.7节=6.8节。可见本发明在推进功率没有任何添加，仍为200马力时，却有增加航速6.8节的功效，完全是来自被耗散的无用能量转化为水动推进力而做推船加速前进的有用功的具体表现。

这个具体的事实表现，证明陈振诚原创的船舰水动推进力的发明设计是切实可行的，将为船舰突破水的速度障而建成60节、70节、80节，甚至更高航速的快艇，从而为科学研究和生产实践奠定坚实的基础，为建造民用或军用的船舰打开广阔的前景。因而创造了重大的经济效益、社会效益和国防效益。

按照同样的原理，对大吨位的单体船、双体船、三体船，在水线处设置压浪导流挡板，把被波浪水流运动耗散的无用能量转化为水动推进力和相应的水动升力，从而克服水的阻力峰，将大幅度提高航速并能大力增强其稳定性和耐波性。用这种创新技术建造集装箱船、滚装船、大型船舰、航空母舰，必能为我国创造重大的经济效益、社会效益和保卫我国领土完整和海洋主权的国防效益。

著者　陈　昕

2016年12月

目 录

第一章

从童年到青年

1.1

童年时代的农村生活

华塘村的山水景观

陈振诚1929年出生在浙江省宣平县华塘村，该村有100多户人家，村前有一条小溪，溪流由北向南流经2000米，被小山挡住，称为水口山；改道向西流约2500米，又被另一座小山挡住，这座山叫上珠；再改道向南流到下珠，这里有一道水堰，叫龙江堰；继续向南流到宣平县治所在地柳城镇，再向南流到处州府丽水市流入瓯江，汇入东海。

在小溪的东岸，也就是华塘村的东面是一片水稻田，还有山上的梯田。水稻田和梯田用村东山上流出的泉水灌溉，种植水稻、麦子、油菜。山坡上不能辟成梯田之处，大片平坦地叫大坪，种植茶树、油茶树，还有大片的松树林。茶叶是高价值的经济作物，可出口多个国家。油茶树产的茶油是营养价值很高的食用油。山上有双剑峰耸立，人站在峰顶上能看到十里内外的农村景观和宣平县治柳城镇的全貌。

华塘村的南边就是被小溪围成的一片良田，种植水稻、宣平莲子。宣平莲子始种于唐朝显庆年间，到清朝嘉庆六年（1802年）被列为皇家贡品。宣莲是宣平的名优特产，也是我国三大莲子品牌之一。

拦截溪流向西转弯的水口山，山不高，像一条龙，把华塘南面围成一大片能种植水稻、宣莲的良田。龙头的右边使小溪再向南流的小山像一颗龙珠，称它为上珠。离上珠向南1000米处，出现的一座小山被称为下珠，构成“一龙戏两珠”的景观。小山上长满松树林，森林覆盖率达80%左右。

春季，黄色的油菜花、粉红色的紫云英花争奇斗艳；夏季，水塘边开满荷花；秋季盛开香满全村的桂花；而冬季有不怕寒冷的腊梅花。

晴天当风吹过，你会听到如波涛般的松涛声，空气清新，气候宜人，倍感舒爽。

华塘村的人文景观

村中有100多户人家，只有两家姓黄，三家姓涂，陈姓是主要的姓氏，建有两座陈氏宗祠。在清朝，陈振诚的曾祖父陈以忠是贡生，在门前竖旗杆。他在华塘村办私塾，招生遍及整个宣平县乡村。学生到丽水处州府乡试可考廪生。

辛亥革命后，废科举办小学、中学、大学。当年宣平县全县有三个中心小学，分别是柳城区中心小学、宣平南乡的曳岑区中心小学和华塘中心小学。因华塘中心小学的师资和校风较好，几十里以外的村民都送孩子到这里就读。这所学校毕业的学生在升学考试时，考入省立中学、国立大学的人不少。

陈振诚就出生在华塘村，在那里度过了童年时代的农村生活。后来他考入浙江省省立处州中学，之后在上海同济大学就读，大学毕业后，在苏联科学院力学研究所攻读研究生。

1.2

勤奋好学的青少年时代

少年时代的农村家庭环境和学习生活

陈振诚的曾祖父陈以忠，字玉琼，号菊谿，是清朝的贡生。祖父陈子顺，字逢时，号师杜，是清朝的廪生。父亲陈发新是农民，母亲邹兴环是农民。1929年2月24日（农历正月十五日）陈振诚出生时，曾祖父、曾祖母已经过世，当时家中有祖父、祖母、父亲、母亲、姐姐陈兰英、哥哥陈振唐。陈振诚于1935年入华塘中心小学一年级就读。父亲务农，祖父种桑养蚕。祖父对孙子很关怀，对陈振诚影响深远，从不打骂孩子，而是根据孩子的爱好加以启发诱导，促使他勤奋学习。上小学后，祖父告诉陈振诚：在大门外竖立的一对旗杆，石墩上刻有“贡生陈以忠”之名，就是曾祖父的成功标志。此外，正屋悬挂的中堂梅花和过春节时两厢悬挂的几幅花鸟条幅是宣平县贺知县到任时请他的侄子画好赠送给曾祖父的，以表彰曾祖父办私塾的贡献。

这几幅画作非常美丽，引起了陈振诚的兴趣，一有空他就去看这些画，揣摩怎样画出它的意境。祖父看出了陈振诚的兴趣，就买了《芥子园画谱》，以便陈振诚学习国画中的花鸟、梅花画法。但同时要求，陈振诚必须高度自觉地学好每门功课，并在期末考试中取得第一名。

到小学五年级，因哥哥外出做工，祖父就要求陈振诚在学习之余，帮助父亲放牛、砍柴。

在小学学习期间，对陈振诚帮助最大的除祖父外，还有班主任宣平少妃人王凤勋，柳城人王昌明、林泽普，他们对这位勤奋好学、每个学期都得第一名的学生，大加赞扬和鼓励，并常在家访时，对祖父说：“您的孙子大有前途，可报考中学的公费生，得到学校学杂费用的支持。”

1941年考入因杭州被日寇侵占而迁入宣平县桃溪镇西塘村的清华中学

清华中学师资水平高，对公费生的要求是入学考试时的前五名，主要科目为语文、数学、物理，三科均须在85分以上。入学后的每一个学期，都要保持这个水平，才能免缴学习费用和每个月的伙食费。为了取得公费生的资格，陈振诚更加努力地学习。1943年，陈振诚初中毕业，毕业考试再获第一名。

在初中学习阶段的暑假两个月、寒假一个月里，祖父教陈振诚读《孟子》，上午读书画画，下午放牛。1942年寒假，陈振诚画了一幅水墨梅花，

图1-1　陈振诚初中毕业照

祖父给该画题咏梅诗：岁末百花都消息，独有寒梅逞姿色。不与桃李斗芳春，冰姿玉骨质自持。并且给陈振诚起字"明远"。他说，"振诚"是"振兴诚信"之意。诚以致明，明而远之，所以可以起字"明远"。

在初中学习阶段，清华中学的校长屈家楠、姐姐陈兰英、姐夫沈世训对陈振诚的帮助也很大。

1944年，陈振诚考入浙江省省立浙东第二临时中学高中部。当时浙江省境内，被日寇侵占的县市很多，只有宣平县因山多未被占领。因此，省立二临中设在宣平县曳岑区。在班上有来自敌占区义乌、诸暨、浦江、金华等县市的学生。在教师中有一位北京大学物理系毕业的物理课老师敖彤凤，很是赞扬陈振诚的学习态度，建议他投考北京大学物理系。1945年抗日战争胜利后，陈振诚考入浙江省立处州中学高中部学习，它是浙江省的11个名牌中学之一。

1947年1月，陈振诚在浙江省省立处州中学高中毕业。请见图1-2陈振诚高中毕业全体同学留影纪念照片。

陈振诚（前排右七）、班主任数学教师姜子骥（前排左九）。这位教师对数学课的讲解令人入迷，更加激发陈振诚对数学的兴趣，为其后来在科学研究中，巧妙地运用数学方法解决物理难题打下基础。

在高中学习阶段，对陈振诚提供经济以及其他帮助的有潘昌燕、郑钧、陈倜、陈俊、陈豪、陈祥云。1944年暑期，金华人国画家何雪融教陈振诚学国画中的人物、花鸟画法，使他进一步提高对美术的兴趣和作画能力，为以后考入中央美术学院华东分院打下基础。

陈振诚高中毕业时18岁，正是精力旺盛的青年时期。他渴望考入大学，进一步深造，可是父母亲没有经济实力供他读大学，于是他决定先找个工作积累资金，作为考入大学后的费用。同时利用业余时间复习并加强语文、数学、物理课的基本功，争取考得奖学金和助学金。1949年6月宣平解放，陈振诚进入宣平中学担任数学、美术、英语教师。1951年陈振诚考入在杭州

图1-2　处州中学1947年高中毕业班排序

前排（自左至右）

吴芝寿　刘玉云　傅宗元　俞稽汤　金景龙　楼仁修　任金法　叶万源　姜子骥（教师）　郑祖德　单学渔　陈振诚　俞纪坤　王陈谟　毛仁麟　董万春　王德奎　刘岳琜

后排（自左至右）

梁瑞生　俞孟嘉　潘金来　刘兴明　丁　煜　周华昌　宗乘浪　骆有节　俞凤源　扬发申　胡泽民　温茂榕　蒋和鸣　曾渭俊　陈振贤　程博文　杨瑞环　陈心中

的中央美术学院华东分院实用美术系建筑学专业。1952年院系调整，陈振诚转入上海同济大学建筑结构系。

1950年11月，陈振诚在宣平中学工作期间，参加以宣平县委宣传部长耿旭东为领队的宣平县竹客乡土改工作队。

1951年2月，陈振诚完成土改工作后，担任宣平县柳城中心小学校长。在此期间得到史银香、黄丽仙、陈凤菊的帮助。在耿旭东的大力支持下，陈振诚于1951年8月考入中央美术学院华东分院，期间也得到新民主主义青年团宣平县委书记张凤群的支持。陈振诚在中央美术学院华东分院学习期间，1951年11月到1952年2月到皖北霍邱县参加土改工作。1952年3月回杭州继续在美术学院学习。在此期间学习素描、水彩画、建筑学制图。

图1-3　陈振诚高中毕业照

图1-4　班主任数学教师姜子骥

图1-5　2005年在浙江丽水市丽水中学（原浙江省立处州中学）建校百年庆典时，陈振诚（右二）与俞孟嘉（左二）合影。

图1-6　2005年在浙江丽水市丽水中学（原浙江省立处州中学）建校百年庆典时，陈振诚（中）与俞孟嘉（右二）、蒋和鸣（左一）合影。

1952年9月，陈振诚开始在同济大学学习。当年同济大学全面学习苏联大学的教学方法。每天上午教六节课，教完第四节课时，已经是11：30，食堂送来两个包子或花卷，吃完后继续上课；上完六节课后，吃中午饭。下午不上课，集中精力复习上午的上课内容；晚上也是复习先前没有复习完的内容。当时考试采用五分制记分。考试时笔试、口试一起进行，每一个房间有一位老师主考。考生一个人进入房间后，抽出一份试卷，在教师的面前笔试答题，交上笔试题后，口试开始，回答教师提出的问题。笔试答题全对，教师口试时全正确，得五分，是优秀。笔试答题有部分小错误，口试答题有部分小错误，得四分，是优良。如果笔试答题有部分错误，口试答题有部分错误，得三分，是及格。如果笔试答题有大错误，口试答题有大错误，得二分，是不及格。一位考生考完后，另一位考生进入房间接受教师的笔试和口试。这种考试方法最大的特点，是杜绝考试作弊，能准确判定考生的成绩。

图1-7　陈振诚考入中央美术学院华东分院时的照片

在大学学习时，陈振诚每个学期每门功课的考试都得五分。《同济大学学报》上刊登表扬优秀学生陈振诚，授予优秀学生奖章，在大学毕业文凭上印上红色的“成绩优等”字样。

在同济大学学习期间，陈振诚担任大班班长，一个大班分六个小班，总共120人。陈振诚还担任学生科学技术协会主席。为了学好每门功课，上午上课时，他专心听讲，并且做好听课笔记。下午除因担任班长、主席而必须参加的会议的时间外，集中全部力量复习上午的听课笔记，如时间不够，就动用晚上的时间复习。当时晚上九时就寝，陈振诚就十时就寝，早上六时起床。这样其他同学能睡九个小时，陈振诚只能睡八个小时。在这样的作息时间安排下，再加上他充沛的精力和高度自觉的学习精神，才能取得每门考试功课都得五分的成绩。

在同济大学学习期间，朱保华教授、赵清澄教授、王达时教授的讲课深

图1-8 同济大学毕业照

刻有感染力。在教中国建筑史时，陈从周教授带领全班到苏州园林观摩学习，深刻体会了中国园林艺术的高深创造力，在一块面积有限的地域中，通过曲径、假山、水榭、楼台亭阁创造出深远的景观意境。与西方的园林布局对比，实在是高明许多。同学中，纽宏、吴泉世对陈振诚帮助很大。在互相学习交流中，沈荣芳、颜德姮、崔德宁、曹国敖、赵居温、余涵、管奕等与其互相帮助。

陈振诚在1956年7月的毕业论文答辩中获得五分，等次优秀，大学顺利毕业。1956年中国科学院建立力学研究所，所长钱学森，副所长钱伟长，党支部书记晋曾毅，办公室主任赵景森。研究所派出专人到同济大学挑选两名优秀毕业生，陈振诚因成绩优秀被选中，1956年9月到北京中国科学院力学研究所报到。刚成立不久的力学研究所有员工100多人，其中行政后勤约40人。

1.3

知识和能力来源于不断扩大知识面的学习和高度自觉的多方面学习，超过先前的自我和超越他人的前进中

1956年9月，陈振诚进入力学研究所时被安排在弹塑性力学组，被指定当黄茂光研究员的助手。黄先生安排他继续学习，到北京大学物理系、清华大

学数学力学系听专题讲课，以便进一步提高数学物理功课的水平。

1957年陈振诚继续听专题讲课。这一年他对复数、复变函数、留数理论、数学物理方程的学习收获很大。为今后做基础理论研究打下了扎实的基础。1958年力学研究所在全国“大跃进”的形势下成立了多个研究室，还成立了工厂，共约1800人。通知在大学本科毕业的人中，挑选9个人经政治审查合格，可参加留学苏联科学院力学研究所的研究生选拔。经层层考试，陈振诚、陈海韬合格。四月到北京俄语学院留苏预备部学习俄语、哲学。苏联科学院认可北京俄语学院哲学考试成绩，到苏联科学院就不必参加研究生的哲学学习和考试。当时每星期除两节哲学课外，全部是俄语课，学习口头会话、发音及严格的语法，陈振诚的俄语水平迅速提高。与在同济大学每星期两节俄语课，学两年，能在字典的帮助下会笔译相比有天壤之别。1958年11月他通过俄语、哲学考试，于1958年12月乘北京到莫斯科的专列到达莫斯科。

在北京中国科学院力学研究所的两年中，陈振诚的知识和能力在不断扩大知识面的学习和高度自觉的多方面学习中，超越先前的自我、超越他人的前进中得到了很大提高，为进入今后的科学研究工作储备了扎实的基础和能力。

黄茂光研究员在美国有15年的大学教学与研究工作的经历，他安排陈振诚去北京大学、清华大学听专题课程，深入地学习复变函数、偏微分数学物理方程。这段时间，陈振诚在业务上有黄茂光大力帮助和指导，政治上有晋曾毅书记、办公室赵景森主任的帮助。

第二章

走在科学研究的道路上

2.1

从留学苏联开始，踏上了科学研究之路

1958年，陈振诚进入苏联科学院力学研究所为研究生时，导师是Х.А.Рахматулин院士。该导师在力学研究所担任波和流体动力学研究室主任，在莫斯科大学担任空气动力学教研室主任，还在军事工程科学院担任研究室主任。他每个星期一下午和星期三下午到力学研究所上班，指导研究工作，解答助手们提出的疑难问题。他在力学研究所的主要助手是И.К.Сомов和А.И.Бабичев。他们给陈

图2-1　导师Халил Ахмедович Рахматулин 院士50岁寿辰，从事科学研究和教学工作25周年的留影

图2-2 1959年，陈振诚（中）与导师的助手И.К.Сомов讨论研究工作时的合影。

振诚的安排是：从星期一到星期六，每天都到力学研究所波和流体动力学研究室上班。头三个月看复变函数、流体动力学、弹塑性动力学方面的书刊。

图2-3 1959年，陈振诚（右）与导师Халил Ахмедович Рахматулин院士讨论研究工作时的留影

根据导师秘书的安排，每星期一、星期三下午，导师到力学研究所上班时，第一个就叫陈振诚到导师办公室检查学习进度，解答疑难问题，指导其进一步的学习和研究工作。第六个月就给陈振诚研究课题：等同长度及不同长度及两个弹塑性杆件在相对强力撞击时，在杆内激起的弹塑性波的传播和反射，寻求弹塑性应力的定量值。导师对陈振诚说："根据前六个月对你的学习答题能力的考查，我看到你有很扎实的数学物理功底。所以我相信通过你的努力，能在年底前找到这个课题的答案，并写出研究报告，届时提交讨论会讨论你的研究结果。"1959年12月，在导师主持的力学研究所波和流体动力学研究室的学术讨论会上，陈振诚做了研究结果的学术报告。经与会的研

究工作人员的讨论、答辩，认为解题方法正确、严谨，得到的结果可信。导师依据讨论的结果和他自己对学术水平的衡量，认为这篇论文达到该课题的国际先进水平。于是推荐送苏联科学院主办的《苏联科学院科学通报》上发表，这个刊物是苏联国家级的而向全世界发行的期刊。导师对陈振诚的研究工作很满意，于是在1960年1月，给陈振诚另一个课题：地震时地面波动所激起而作用于水坝迎水面上的流体动压力。开始做这个课题的工作时，陈振诚做了调查研究，发现从1933年开始，有苏联、美国、日本、中国等国的学者做过这方面问题研究并发表了研究结果。

但是他们的研究都假定：地震时只沿着河流的方向有地面运动发生。这样一来，在数学计算方面就简化为一个二维的平面问题，解题就简单得多。但是在现实的生活中，地震时地面运动是各个方向都会有的地面三维运动，而且还包括地面起伏波动。陈振诚把此情况向导师介绍后，导师指出最终要解决的是三维的空间问题。研究地面各个方向的运动从数学计算方面比二维的平面问题会有更多的困难。但一个个方向分开研究，最后综合研究各个方向的同时运动所发生的水动压力就能解决难题。依据这个思路，陈振诚开始研究工作。有了第一个课题研究成功的启发，陈振诚全力以赴，入迷地投入第二个课题的研究工作。在研究工作中更熟练地应用复变函数、留数理论、环路积分。1960年9月写出研究结果的报告，导师看后很满意。

这个课题的第一次学术报告是在导师主持的报告会上。随后，导师推荐陈振诚到莫斯科大学Л.Н.Сретенский院士主持的学术讨论会上作报告。Л.Н.Сретенский院士认为，问题的提法专业，解决问题的方法严谨，得到的结果可信，是一篇изящное произведение（优秀的作品）。两位院士推荐给苏联科学院主办的、向世界发行的期刊《Прикладная математика и механика》（《应用数学和力学》）上发表。1961年2月第一期发表。1961年8月第四期发表另一篇论文。导师很赞赏陈振诚所取得的学术成果，称其为Талантливый ученик（有才华的学生）。并且当面说："Тебе везёт（你走运）。有的人知道这个难题，但没有能力解决，而你知道这个难题又有能力巧妙地解决，并且得到可信的研究结果。"1961年，陈振诚研究生毕业回国。发表在苏联刊物上的文章列于附录F—2·2和F—2·3的“陈振诚部分科学论著”中。

导师在送别时对陈振诚说：“我已把你带入科学研究工作领域。你已能依据客观现实和观测数据建立数学物理模型和相应的数学物理方程以及边界条件，运用你已掌握的数学物理方法解决难题，取得可信的研究结果。希望你今后在科学研究的道路上不断超越自我、超越他人，取得丰硕的科学研究成果。”

陈振诚开始踏上了科学研究之路，为今后的研究工作打下了坚实的基础。在苏联留学期间，沈燮昌、许孔时、曾庆存同学对陈振诚有许多帮助。

2.2

1961年回国后，仍回力学研究所工作

1961年，陈振诚回国。此时，黄茂光研究员已调到合肥中国科学技术大学任教。陈振诚除参加定向爆破的研究工作之外，继续在苏联留学期间的研究工作，考虑地面波动、河床运动等激起作用于水坝迎水面上的流体动压力。于1963年取得了三维效应，也就是包括各个方向运动的结果，写出论文《地震波所激起而作用于水坝迎水面上的流体动压力——论抗震坝型最优纵断面》。

陈振诚参加了中国力学学会第一次流体力学学术讨论会。1975年11月，发表在《中国科学》第六期上的《地面波动所激起而作用于水坝迎水面上的流体动压力》文章中（见附录F—2.4），表1是P_η，P_η'沿坝面分布图表，把各P_η，P_η'值与第（一）项相比较：（一）$P_{1max}=0.74$，（二）$P'_{1max}=0.20$，（三）$P_{3max}=0.74$，（四）$P_{4max}=0.74$，$P'_{4max}=0.20$，$P'_{3max}=0.83$，（五）$P_{4max}=0.74$，$P'_{4max}=0.20$，$P'_{3max}=1.83$，（六）$P_{2max}=0.76$，（七）$P_{2max}=0.42$。总和$P_\eta+P_\eta'$

=0.74+0.20+0.74+0.74+0.20+0.83+0.74+0.20+1.83+0.76+0.42=7.4。也就是说，前人只是知道沿河流方向震动的0.74，而陈振诚找到了各个方向都震动的7.4，10倍大于一个方向运动水动压力的定量值。张光斗院士对此的评价是“重大突破”。

图2-4　1961年，陈振诚（后排右二），从苏联留学毕业回国，回家乡浙江宣平华塘村合家团聚合影

1963年9月，中国力学学会第一次流体力学学术讨论会在上海锦江饭店举行。陈振诚的报告内容是三维流体动力学的科研成果，吸引了702所所长方文钧上校和他带领的科研团队参加这场如何解决三维难题的报告的讨论。陈振诚在会上宣读了研究论文，经过热烈讨论后，中国科学院院士钱令希给予“重要成果”的评价，并指出进一步的工作方向。当天晚上，702所研究团队邀请陈振诚座谈，并探讨如何解决船舰流体动力学中的三维难题。他们702所有着亚洲最先进的水池：长475米，试验段中间宽度14米，两头宽度7米，水深7米。行船速度20米/秒~15米/秒，也就是72公里/小时~54公里/小时，即38.88节~29.16节。他们用量纲分析法计算水动升力、阻力等，用水池实验测得无量纲升力系数C_L和速度U。水动升力L=C_L。其中ρ为水密度，B为船舰宽度。量纲分析

$$L=\frac{\text{kg秒}^2}{m^4}\cdot\frac{m^2}{\text{秒}^2}\cdot m^2=\text{kg}.$$

众所周知，希腊科学家阿基米德于公元前212年以前发现，一个静态物体在水面或水下承受的水静浮力，其定量值等于被该物体的体积所排开的水的重量，通常称为排水量。但是在水面或水下对水平面保持某一攻角θ运动的物体能激起水动浮力，由于缺乏有效的数学物理方法，还没有人找到令人信服的定量值。

702所用水池试验测得升力系数C_L，再用量纲分析得到升力L，表面看

来，量纲L（kg）似乎相似，但实际上可能相差不少。因为从物理定性来看，水动浮力（升力）的激起与运动物体对水平面的攻角密切相关，与运动物体的速度，尺度大小，吃水深度，与体现重力场对流场作用的重力加速度有关。如果用数学解析式来表达水动浮力，它应该是攻角θ，尺度大小a、b，运动物体的速度U，重力加速度g，运动物体的吃水深度δ，水的密度ρ的函数。但是升力系数C_L所表述的升力L中没有出现θ、δ、g，其中不出现θ是最不符合物理实际的。因为θ=0，就不可能激起水动浮力L。

如果吃水深度δ=1米，那么水静浮力（阿基米德浮力）$L'=\rho g\delta^3=102.06685\times 9.797500365\times 1^3=1000$kg。这就是众所周知的阿基米德原理。静水在重力场$L'$中有重力加速度g。动水在重力场中，动水浮力$L'$中也必然有重力加速度g。见附录F—2·8《中国科学》2012年第42卷第12期式21页中，可以看到ρ、δ、g、a、b、U、θ显示各物理量对水动浮力的贡献和相互制约的关系。实船实航的试验证实了式（21）符合实际。

在水池中做试验的船模是把实船按比例缩小而成。可是固定在地面上的水池不可能把重力加速度g缩小。所以测得的数据用于放大的实船上，其正确性值得疑虑，可能要引入重力修正系数才能纠偏。

座谈会上讨论后，大家认为应开展这方面的研究工作。可是要解决这个问题难在用前人建立的Fourier积分变换、Laplace积分变换得不到合乎物理实际的结果，只有另辟蹊径建立能解决此难题的数学物理方法。对此陈振诚着手探索应用数学的研究，但要经过长期的努力才有可能取得好结果。

2.3

1965年接受研制地对空导弹“红眼鱼”的空气动力学计算~541项目的任务

采用苏联提供的计算方法，得不到方法上的创新。1966年，“文化大革命”开始，“红眼鱼”的研究任务暂停，大字报铺天盖地。陈振诚只得替别人抄写大字报，但不起草自己的大字报，以免被人利用。在抄写大字报的间隙，陈振诚继续应用数学的创新研究。1968年—1972年间，陈振诚充分利用节假日以及替别人抄写大字报的间隙，深入研究了不同于前人的数学物理方法。功夫不负有心人，他终于在1972年建立了陈振诚积分变换的定理1。

1968年—1973年，中国科学院力学研究所怀柔分部被划归国防科工委的中国人民解放军0912部队，研究项目是空气动力学。1973年，在0912部队政治部主任王珍和中国科学院国家天文台的闫凤高的帮助下，陈振诚回归中国科学院。

2.4

1974年陈振诚进入中国科学院国家天文台工作

陈振诚在苏联留学期间，他的导师在苏联科学院力学研究所担任波和流体动力学研究室主任，有力学所的研究课题，有研究生和研究工作团队。同时，他还在莫斯科大学担任空气动力学教研室主任，有教学任务，有另外一个研究团队。可是，在中国，在两个单位担任职务是不可能的。

陈振诚回中国科学院后，到国家天文台任职，在一般人看来，他应该转行，只研究天文方面的课题。但是陈振诚当时在苏联学的是流体动力学，回国后在力学研究所也是从事流体、气体动力学和相关的应用数学方法的研究工作。他有18年的相关经历，并且有雄厚的力学、数学功底，开展跨学科的研究工作完全胜任。而且后来的事实证明：在跨学科的研究工作中，他在力学研究中建立了陈振诚积分变换定理1的基础上，因研究太阳活动区光球及其上空的磁场的需要而建立了陈振诚积分变换的定理2、定理3、定理4、定理5、定理6、定理7、定理8，回过头来又建立了定理9，从而创建了一套完整的陈振诚积分变换的应用数学方法，也解决了考虑三维效应和重力影响的水动浮力、水动推进力、水动离心力、水动反冲击力等问题，找到了这些力的解析表述式并且解决了太阳活动区及其上空的磁场问题，找到了计算磁场强度定量值的解析表述式，找到了星系棒旋结构的解析表述式。上述成果能创造重大的效益。

不过，人们的就职观念给开展研究工作的陈振诚造成了各种麻烦。因有科学院数理化局天文处的李荣镜、唐庭友，干部局的石廷俊，数学物理学部的章综以及天文台的王旭发、闫凤高等的帮助，困难逐个解决，陈振诚得以继续前进，取得各项工作的成功。

在此期间，他跨学科研究宇宙气体动力学中的星系棒旋结构，用陈振诚积分变换的定理1解决了问题，写出学术论文《星系的棒旋结构》。同时，陈振诚也做了流体动力学课题中的应用数学研究工作。

1966—1976年间，在“文化大革命”中，做基础理论研究工作，写文章，投稿发表论文会被批有着“名利思想”。陈振诚投稿了《力学学报》，学报编辑让力学研究所12研究室的党支部组织委员王永德把稿件退还。退稿的理由是陈振诚有“名利思想”。王永德进一步说明：文章发表了就会有名，有名就会带来利，所以叫名利思想。

为了减轻这种压力，1974年，陈振诚写信给当时主持中国科学院工作的胡耀邦，希望他支持自己的科学研究工作。想不到胡耀邦看了信件后接见了陈振诚，并且亲自批示“能潜心做深入的研究工作，应该得到表扬。”还把陈振诚写的研究报告《论水上飞船》批转当时担任中国科学院秘书长的钱三强同志所主持的学术报告会上发表。1975年9月，钱三强邀请了数学家吴新谋，力学研究所的郑哲敏、谈镐生，天文台的王绶琯等专家出席，听学术报告，并展开讨论。讨论过程中提出不少建议，并肯定是好的研究结果，指导继续完善内容。

2.5

1981年开始研究太阳活动区光球及其上空的磁场

1981年，陈振诚开始研究太阳活动区光球及其上空的磁场这一课题。这是电磁流体力学的课题。关于这个问题，前人做了不少研究工作，但他们都

图2-5　1982年，陈振诚与妻子方舍梅（右）、女儿陈昕合影

图2-6　1980年，陈振诚与儿子陈旸（左）合影

图2-7　陈振诚在书房写作时休息片刻

图2-8　1987年Х.А.Рахматулин院士的另一位学生И. И. Поручиков教授来北京大学作学术交流，到陈振诚家访问

自左到右：陈昕、方舍梅、陈振诚、И. И. Поручиков教授、胡晓青（陈振诚的儿媳）

假定，在人为地划定约40万公里有黑子浮现的太阳活动区之后，太阳黑子的N极和S极的磁力线都回到这个划定的区域内，区域外的磁场恒等于零。但是，事实的情况是区域外的磁场逐步衰减，在很远处才趋向于零。为什么要做这样不符合实际情况的假定呢？因为用Fourier积分变换或Laplace积分变换来解题，得到的结果必然会出现区域外的磁场恒等于零的结果。所以前人做出这个假定以便达到自圆其说的目的。如果解题时采用陈振诚积分变换就能得到合乎实际情况的结果。所以陈振诚在定理1的基础上，继续应用数学的研究工作。建立了定理2乃至定理9。1982年写出报告。

北京大学吴林襄教授认为陈振诚能用自己建立的数学物理方法

解决这个难题，实属难得。当年11月，陈振诚参加了在云南天文台召开的国际天文学会学术报告会，与会的各国专家认为这项研究成果是重要的科研结果。

图2-9　自左到右：陈昕、方舍梅、陈振诚、陈旸

在太阳活动丰年时，观测太阳黑子浮现、演化、磁能凝聚，爆发太阳耀斑等，就能依据太阳活动区光球及其上空的磁场解析表述式计算出重大的磁能将带电粒子加速抛向地球，穿透地球高空磁层进入大气层对无线电通信等造成干扰，对发射地球人造卫星造成干扰的强弱程度。所以这项研究取得的结果，给人们发射地球人造卫星和其他航天器提供了高空环境情报，为捕捉高能粒子、研究新元素提供了理论依据。既解决了电磁流体力学方面的问题，同时验证和充实了陈振诚积分变换在应用数学方面的可靠和可用性。学术论文发表在国际太阳物理学会的刊物《Solar Physics》（《太阳物理》），1989年，第119期，第279~299页。其中定理1的中文稿发表在中国科学院刊物，《科学通报》1980年，第18期第829~834页，请见本书的附录F—2.7和F—2.8。

图2-10　自左到右：方舍梅、陈振诚、И. И. Поручиков教授、陈昕

2.6

运用陈振诚积分变换找到了原创性的重大发明专利“水面航行器”中的水动推进力、水动离心力、水动反冲击力等

这里应该特别提到的是，该发明的核心技术是船舰在运行中发动机输出的功率有一部分推动船舰克服水的阻力前进，做有用功；而另一部分激起水流波浪运动被耗散成为无用能量。把携带着无用能量的水流引入前低后高顶部有导流槽的船底浸湿面中，在这里携带着无用能量的水流对导流槽顶部造成足够强大的法向压力。法向压力的水平方向分量与船行方向一致，就是名副其实的水动推进力，推动船加速前进。法向压力的垂向分量就是水动升力，使船减小吃水的深度，因而减小水阻力而提高航速。

水动推进力的出现和它的足够强大，有严谨的定量值解析表述式可计算，并且经过实船实航，得到严谨的实测证明。船长6.3米，空船排水量1吨，推进功率200马力，乘员8人（相当于排水量1.5吨），航速36.15节；乘员增加一倍，为16人（相当于排水量2吨），航速非但不下降，反倒提高1节，到37.15节。现有技术的船艇对载重量增大的响应特别敏感，载重每增2人，航速下降1.7节。如果增加8人航速下降4×1.7=6.8节。

在船底浸湿面设置2条导流槽，在两边船舷设置2条压浪导流挡板，浸湿面积增大了不少。如果是当时技术的快艇必定是航速下降，再加上乘员大量增加，则降速更大。本发明船艇因造成强大的水动推进力，其结果是不但消除了因浸湿面积增大而增大的水的摩擦阻力，还使航速提高了6.8节。也就是与现有技术的快艇相比，航速提高了22.4%，节能33.3%。请见附录F—2.5第

一节和F—2.6第二节。如果对现有技术的快艇进行改进，想提高3%的航速都很难做到。

用陈振诚积分变换找到的船舰运行时激起的水动推进力定量值解析表述式，计算得到的具体数据与实船实航中测得的实际数据相符合。这就证实了水动推进力定量值表述式是可用并且可靠的。

2.7

建立陈振诚积分变换的应用数学研究工作

从1963年开始到1972年，陈振诚建立了积分变换定理1，也就是持续9年的大量工作初见成效。到1989年完成定理2~定理8。1998年，最后完成定理9的建立和各定理的证明，前后做了26年的应用数学的研究，才算全面完成了这项工作。

陈振诚积分变换与前人的积分变换不同之处，在于Fourier积分变换的积分核是三角函数，其逆变换的积分环路，在复平面中是没有支点割缝的上半平面或下半平面。与Laplace积分变换的不同之处，在于Laplace积分变换的积分核是指数函数，其逆变换的积分环路，在复平面中是没有支点割缝的左半平面或右半平面。但是陈振诚积分变换的积分核是指数函数，或正弦函数，或余弦函数，或双曲正弦函数，或双曲余弦函数，并且都带有平方根的分母，或三角函数并带有平方根的分母。它们的逆变换的积分环路在复平面中有两个支点，有有限长度的割缝，割缝的左岸、右岸有不同的幅角值，或割缝的上岸、下岸有不同的幅角值。环路积分遍及上半平面、下半平面和左半平面以及右半平面，包含了整个复平面中极点的留数。

正是由于这些不同之处，就会出现Fourier积分变换和Laplace积分变换在满足了所求问题的数学物理方程和边界条件后，为最后得到问题的确切答案而进行逆变换的积分时，难以得到相关的物理参数的解析表述式而只能获得数值积分的近似解。但是陈振诚积分变换在满足了建立物理模型时所有的数学物理方程和边界条件后，为最后得到问题的确切答案，采取的逆变换中，由于积分核带有平方根的分母，积分环路遍及上、下、左、右整个复平面，从而包含了整个复平面中极点的留数，使其必然能够得到相关物理参数间的清晰的解析表述式。这就是陈振诚积分变换的积分核和积分环路的巧妙构思所带来的结果。这种清晰的相关的物理参数的解析表述式，使得基础理论研究工作者能一目了然地洞察各物理参数间的变化趋势，从而依据需要选择哪一个参数予以加强而更有利于工程或产品的竞争优势，或哪一个参数予以削弱而更有利于突出某个论点的优势。这就是陈振诚积分变换的巧妙构思所造成的最大优异之处。

在科学研究工作的道路上，前一个阶段，陈振诚从1958年在苏联科学院力学研究所在导师的指导下开始做研究工作，到1961年回国，在中国科学院研究所独立研究流体动力学。1965年他开始做541任务，地对空导弹的气体动力学研究计算，期间从1963年开始利用业余以及节假日时间进行相关的应用数学积分变换的研究，1968年开始全力研究舰船水动力学以及相关的应用数学研究，建立全新的积分变换方法用来解决水动力学中的难题。后一个阶段，从1974年进入中国科学院国家天文台，开始跨学科的研究工作。研究星系结构和太阳活动区光球及其上空的磁场。前者是宇宙气体动力学，后者是电磁流体力学的研究工作。同时，船舰水动力学的研究工作继续深入，为解决这些难题的应用数学积分变换继续深入研究。1991年，他开始进入原创性发明专利“水面航行器”的研究开发。1958年—1991年，陈振诚33年的科学研究工作使他付出了全部精力，克服种种困难，最后取得的成果有：

（1）得到地震激起而作用于水坝迎水面上的水动压力定量值的解析表述式。

（2）得到高坝的水闸闸门开启时，水流自由出流或淹没出流的情况下作用在闸门浸湿面上的水动压力的定量值解析表述式。

（3）找到了水动浮力定量值的解析表述式。

（4）得到船舰前进时激起的水动推进力和水动升力定量值的解析表述式。

（5）得到了船舰转弯时激起的水动离心力、水动助回转力矩、水动抗船体向心倾覆扶正力矩的定量值解析表述式。

（6）找到了船舰在迎浪前进时的水动反冲击力和水动升力定量值的解析表述式。

（7）找到了船舰在风浪中转弯时激起的水动离心力、水动助回转力矩、水动抗船体向心倾覆扶正力矩的定量值解析表述式。

（8）找到了星系棒旋结构的解析表述式。

图2-11　1989年，陈振诚在苏联莫斯科

图2-12　1990年，陈振诚在苏联列宁格勒（现圣彼得堡）的沙皇冬宫室内参观

图2-13　1990年，陈振诚在苏联列宁格勒（现圣彼得堡）的沙皇冬宫外广场

图2-14　1990年，陈振诚在苏联莫斯科大剧院外广场

图2-15 1990年，陈振诚在苏联列宁格勒沙皇的夏宫游览

（9）得到了太阳活动区光球及其上空磁场的解析表述式。

（10）求得了预言太阳耀斑爆发的判断依据。

（11）建立了可跨学科解决难题的陈振诚积分变换。

由于应用严谨的数学物理方法解题而得到了各种定量值的解析表述式，避免了近似的计算会带来含糊不清的缺点。

在33年的科学研究中，他把研究成果用中文、俄文、英文发表为学术论文，丰硕成果是付出艰辛努力的回报。跨学科研究工作的学术论文发表后，得到苏联、日本、芬兰等国家有关学术交流的邀请，赴苏联КРАСНОЯРСК大学宇宙物理系、苏联基辅（现为乌克兰首都）、苏联克里米亚天文台、雅尔塔、日本东京等地进行学术交流。

在赴芬兰赫尔辛基的途中，陈振诚经过列宁格勒（现为圣彼得堡），晚上9时，乘船过程中太阳挂在天空，没有夜晚的感觉，在午夜零时，一轮红日从北偏西方向降落到地平线，当时海而上、天空中出现红色光辉的晚霞，数分钟后，一轮红日又从北偏东方向的海平面升起，水面、天空布满红色光辉的朝霞。海鸥在船边飞舞，因此称之为白夜。

第三章

走在建立原创性重大发明并进入开发实施的实践中

前述的科学研究成果只是重要的学术结晶。在这个基础上做出可以看得见的有实用价值的产品，才算得上是发明而可以申请国家专利。经国家知识产权局审查批准后，才能获得发明专利授权，受国家法律保护。

3.1

从1991年开始起草发明专利论文《水面航行器》

在现有技术的船舰上加以改进，想提高3%速度都很难做到。对于小吨位的船艇，当加大推进功率，航速大于50节之后，就会出现稳定性危机，如果再加大推进功率，则不但航速上不去，还会出现失去稳定性，导致倾覆的危险。可以把它视为水动力流场中的水的速度障。因此，现有技术的

图3-1　1985年，陈振诚（中）在南京与南京大学教授陈金全参观菊花展览

图3-2　1985年，陈振诚（中）与陈金全教授、傅美娟副教授合影

图3-3　1986年9月，在日本东京陈振诚（右一）参加第三届亚洲流体力学学术讨论会

快艇，除运动赛事用的小赛艇外，世界上没有航速等于或大于60节的快艇。对于大吨位的排水型船舰在运行中会出现水的阻力峰，在船速达到32节左右，再加大推进功率，航速不会相应地提高。

要突破水动力流场中水的速度障，或水的阻力峰，就必须在船底浸湿面外形上下功夫，使流场中在没有添加推进功率的情况下出现足够强大的水动推进力和水动升力，推动船加速前进和减小吃水深度而进一步提高航速，同时增强稳定性，最后突破水的速度障和克服水的阻力峰。从而使快艇在加大推进功率时能相应地使航速达到或大于60节、70节、80节，甚至更高的航速，并且有高度的稳定性，使大吨位的排水型船舰相应地提高航速，达到33节、34节或更高的航速，并且有高度的稳定性。

写好发明专利论文《水面航行器》后，陈振诚于1994年8月向国家知识产权局提出发明专利申请。1999年经国家知识产权局审查后批准发明专利授权。美国、欧洲（包括英、法、意大利等11国）、日本、韩国、新加坡、波兰、挪威、巴西等22个国家的国家知识产权局经审查后批准给予陈振诚发明专利授权。

图3-4　1991年，在丽水市南明山陈振诚（左）与宣平县县长陈仿尧合影

图3-5　1992年，在浙江宣平华塘村，陈振诚（后排中）与大姐陈兰英（左一）、兄陈振唐（左二）、嫂嫂吕宝苏（右二）、妹妹陈瑟英（右一）、父亲陈发新（时年93岁）合影，身后远处是双剑山峰

3.2

1995年和浙江杭州东风造船厂，702研究所合作进行船模试航

1995年，陈振诚和浙江杭州东风造船厂、702研究所合作，进行船模试航。下图中，红色的船模由东风造船厂出资，白色的船模由陈振诚出资，在天然的水池中试航。设置涌浪导流槽，船艏已不见水波，水流都被导流槽导向船尾向后喷流。黄色船模在702所的水池中试航，因没有设置导流槽，水流向后斜向上喷溅。从这3个船模试航可以看出涌浪导流槽的优势。

在杭州期间，在船模制作、试航和建造、试航630艇的过程中，吴兴南、陶慰椿和吴逸民给陈振诚很多帮助。

图3-6　红色船模

图3-7　白色船模

图3-8　黄色船模

3.3

参照这三个船模试航，依据发明的论述建成实船试航

参照这三个船模试航，很快，大家依据发明的论述建造实船，欲进行试航。发明人设计了长4.5米，乘员8人，推进功率40马力的快艇在千岛湖水面上试航，与现有技术的快艇做对比。发明快艇航速超越了现有技术的快艇。1998年，发明人又设计了长6.3米、宽2.3米、型深0.9米的快艇在富春江上试航，用185马力的舷外机推进，乘员8人时和乘员4人时航速相同，证实水动推进力足够强大。

2001年11月，陈振诚和德清海鹰玻璃钢厂的厂长赵和中合作，总结了多次实船实航的实验结果，自己动手在现有技术的船模上设置涌浪导流槽和两

图3-9　1996年，陈振诚（右三）在浙江柳城镇政府与叶余刚（右二）、镇长雷玉林（右一）、陈金全教授（左一）、吴兴南（左三）合影

图3-10　1996年，陈振诚在黄山迎客松旁

图3-11　1997年，陈振诚在浙江千岛湖为630艇试航

舷设置压浪导流挡板。船长6.3米，宽2.1米，型深0.8米，槽宽0.2米，挡板宽0.15米，槽和挡板的末端高0.3米，从船艏开始∠α=0°，0.5°，1°，3°，5°，在离船末端的1/3长度处∠α=11°，向后延伸α=5°，α=1°到后端点。在这样的前低后高布局下做成的玻璃钢快艇，空船排水量1吨。请见附录F—2.5第一节和F—2.6第二节。

该艇于2002年2月12日在杭州钱塘江试航，玻璃钢艇建造由赵和中厂长出资。东风造船厂用9.8万元购买了200马力的舷外机，卫星跟踪的GPS系统实测显示下列数据：

图3-12　陈振诚与试航助手余成瑶（右）

图3-13　陈振诚与试航驾驶员陈道道（右）

图3-14　1997年，陈振诚在千岛湖为630艇试航

图3-15　1998年，陈振诚在北京大观园

图3-16　1998年，在杭州东风造船厂码头上合影，陈振诚（左一）、试航驾驶员左中文（左二）、702所高级工程师邢圣德（中）、东风造船厂总工程师张华甫（右一）

图3-17　1999年，陈振诚（中）与东风造船厂总工程师张华甫（左一）、助手桑品红（右一）合影

第一次试航乘员8人（相当于排水量1.5吨）。

逆水流行驶航速为35.8节，顺水流行驶航速为36.5节。平均航速为36.15节。

第二次试航乘员增加一倍为16人（相当于排水量2吨）。

逆水流行驶航速为36.9节，顺水流行驶航速为37.4节。平均航速为37.15节。

航行过程中航态好，没有出现纵摇拍击，也没有出现横摇摆动，两侧的水流飞溅很少。被扰动的水流集中在尾迹中，从两个涌浪导流槽和两个压浪导流挡板出流的水流在尾迹中的远处汇合于一点。即使达到了37.4节的高速，仍没有出现纵摇拍击现象，航向、横向、纵向高度稳定。

记录数据证明：在一定范围内，大幅度增加载重量，航速非但不下降，

图3-18　1994年陈振诚在嵩山少林寺

反倒增大1节到37.15节。

逆水流行驶，乘员8人时航速35.8节，乘员16人时航速36.9节。增速1.1节。

顺水流行驶，乘员8人时航速36.5节，乘员16人时航速37.4节。增速0.9节。

这是因为逆水流行驶时，导流槽和压浪挡板与水流之间的相对运动速度大于顺水流时的相对运动速度造成的结果。

现有技术的滑行艇对载重量变化的响应特别敏感，如果增加两位乘员，航速下降1.7节，如果增加8人，航速会下降4×1.7=6.8节。37.15节-6.8节=30.35节。（37.15-30.35）/30.35=22.4%，也就是航速提高22.4%。（2吨-1.5吨）/1.5=33.3%，也就是节能33.3%。可以看到，发明的核心思路是正确的，按发明核心思路设计船底浸湿面外形，确实形成了足够强大的水动推进力和水动升力。请见附录F—2.5第一节和F—2.6第二节。

在杭州东风造船厂船模陈列室，至今还陈列着当时的船模。

在附录F—2·5第一节中，图1~图8分布的力确实存在而且足够强大。在船艇转弯时能激起水动离心力、水动助回转力矩、水动抗船体向心倾覆扶正力矩，

图3-19　1994年陈振诚在嵩山少林寺

图3-20　1995年陈振诚在浙江杭州东风造船厂

迫使船艇以很小的回转半径迅速平稳地转弯而不会出现倾覆的危险，请见图9，附录F—2·1（1）。

这些力和力矩的定量值以速度U的3次方增大，所以本发明船艇具有越快速越安全稳定的独特性能。在加大推进功率时能够突破水的速度障而达到或大于60节、70节、80节，甚至更高的航速，并且有高度的稳定安全性。

依据国家船舶检验单位、浙江省船检局高级验船师李建新参加试航时记录的数据，经报送浙江省船检局审核，批准允许批量生产630艇，投放市场销售。请见浙江省船舶检验局的批文复印件，F—2·1。请见附录F—2·1（1）中图1至图8。

在630艇的基础上依据相似律放大设计的1600（长16米）艇，卧舱机2300马力，乘员13人，航速62节，用于缉私、救援、巡逻、边防、公安等工作的快艇。请见附录F—2.5第一节图7、图8。

3.4

对于大吨位吃水较深的单体排水型船舰，开展克服水动力流场中水的阻力峰的研究

例如集装箱船，又例如舰长156.5米，型宽17.2米，型深15米，吃水6.5米，满载排水量8520吨，主机功率2×5万马力=10万马力，最高航速32节，巡航速度18节。请见附录F—2·1（2）中图10、图11。

用10万马力使航速达到32节之后，再加大推进功率时，因出现水的阻力峰，无法克服，因此航速不会相应地得到提高。只有采用本发明技术在两船舷的水线处设置压浪导流挡板，挡板的顶线前低后高对船底基面形成倾角α。挡板的横剖面为圆弧形。当船舰前进时，船舷外侧的水流被导入压浪导流挡板中，因挡板前低后高的顶部曲面，水流对曲面造成了足够强大的法向压力，该法向压力的水平方向分量与船行方向一致，推动船加速前进，就是名副其实的水动推进力。法向压力的垂向分量，就是水动升力，它能减小船的吃水深度，从而减小水阻力而提高航速。水动推进力和水动升力的定量值都以航速U的3次方增大。从而在推进功率增大时能克服水的阻力峰而大幅度提高船速。一对水动推进力对船舰的重心构成航向稳定扶正力矩，一对水动升力对船艇重心构成横向稳定扶正力矩，它们都以U的3次方增大。于是使船舰的航向、横向、纵向的稳定性，耐波性大力增强。

美国企业号核动力航空母舰，满载排水量93970吨，主尺度：总长342.3米，舰体宽40.5米，长宽比342.5/40.5=8.45。吃水11.9米。飞行甲板长331.6米，宽76.8米。动力4台蒸汽轮机28万马力，航速33节。

图3-21　2008年在香港陈振诚（中）与徐诚（左）、张子桐合影

美国小鹰级航空母舰，满载排水量81123吨，主尺度：总长323.6米，舰体宽39.6米，长宽比323.6/39.6=8.17。吃水11.4米。飞行甲板长318.8米，宽76.8米。动力28万马力，航速32节。

再加大推进功率，因水的阻力峰无法克服，航速不可能相应地提高。只有采用本发明技术，在两船舷的水线处设置压浪导流挡板，从而在水动力流场中产生水动推进力、水动升力，才能克服水的阻力峰。于是在加大推动功率时才能相应地大幅度提高航速，同时增强其稳定性、耐波性。

3.5

双体船的研究

现有技术的双体船水下部分由两个对称平行于整船纵向中心线的侧体组成。在水面上的某一高度处用连接桥把两个侧体连成一体而成为双体船。侧体为细长的排水型船体，长宽比介于12~16之间。使得其在高速航行时显著降低了水的兴波阻力，从而提高航速。连接两个侧体的连接桥能提供足够的总纵强度，并且构成宽阔的甲板平面，为各种实际需求提供场地。

横摇摆动和纵摇拍击是船艇在波浪中最容易发生的运动航态，而且横摇在各种摇荡运动中幅值最大。

为了提高双体船的航速和稳定耐波性能，本发明提出在两个侧体的内侧船舷水线处设置压浪导流挡板，挡板的横剖面为圆弧形，而纵剖面的顶线前低后高，对船底基面形成倾角 α 。当船体前进时，波浪水流被导入压浪导流挡板中，因其纵剖面顶部前低后高的布局，使波浪水流对挡板的顶部产生足够强大的法向压力。该法向压力的水平方向分量与船行方向一致，推动船加速前进，即为名副其实的水动推进力。法向压力的垂向分量，即为水动升力。它能减小船艇的吃水深度，而减小水阻力，航速会进一步提高。对称平行于整船中心线的一对水动推进力对船艇重心构成水动航向稳定扶正力矩，迫使船艇不偏离既定目标高速前进。一对水动升力对船体重心构成水动横向稳定扶正力矩，削弱或消除幅值最大的横摇摆动。水动升力也构成纵向稳定扶正力矩，克服船艇的纵摇拍击。这些力和相对应的力矩的定量值以航速U的3次方增大，因此不但大幅度提高了航速，同时大大加强了船艇的稳定性和耐波性能。请见附录F—2· 1（3）图12、图13。

现在已建成的铝合金双体船，长45米，宽12米，吃水深度1.65米，推进功率4×2180kW，排水量241吨。因减小了水的兴波阻力，航速能达到40节，但稳定性和耐波性差。如果采用本发明技术，水动力流场中就会出现如附录F—2· 1（3）图12、图13所示的水动推进力和相对应的水动力矩，水动升力和相对应的水动力矩。那么航速还可大幅度提高，并且大大加强舰艇的稳定性和耐波性能。

3.6

三体船的研究

近年来，三体船引起了人们的广泛关注。民用方面，澳大利亚于2003年设计建造了长126米的三体高速客船“Benchijigua Express”号，该船运营于Canery群岛。军用方面，英国海军于2000年建成了长98.7米的实验舰“RV-Triton”号，并在该舰下水后，进行了一系列实船试验。此后，美国海军提出濒海战斗舰计划。目前第一艘三体濒海战斗舰“独立号”已建成并开始服役。“自由号”濒海战斗舰将进驻新加坡港口。

三体船水下部分由中体和对称于中体的两个侧体，共三个细长的排水型船体组成。两个侧体用连接桥与中体连接成一个整体。中体为超细长的排水型船体，长宽比介于12~18之间，使其在高速航行时能显著降低水的兴波阻力，从而提高其航速。两边的侧体也是排水型的浮体，它们减小了主体的吃水深度，从而减小水阻力而使整船的航速提高。

大多数高速三体船的侧体排水量占总排水量的10%以下，长度占船总长的1/3。能够提供稳定性以及较好的抗横摇性能。连接侧体和中体的连接桥能保证足够的总纵强度，并且形成宽阔的甲板平面，方便不同用途的各种布局。

但是现有技术的三体船横摇摆动和纵摇拍击是船艇在波浪中运行最容易发生的运动航态，而且横摇在各种摇荡运动中幅值最大。

为了增大三体船的航速和大力增强它们的稳定性和耐波性能，本发明提出在中体的两船舷水线处设置压浪导流挡板，在两侧体的内侧船舷水线处也设置压浪导流挡板。所有压浪导流挡板的横剖面为圆弧形，挡板的纵剖面顶线前低后高对船体基面形成倾角 α 。这种船底浸湿面的外形布局，当船前进时，船舷附近的波浪水流被导流挡板导入压浪挡板中，因其外形前低后高的顶部曲面，导致波浪水流对其顶部曲面产生足够强大的法向压力。该法向压力的水平方向分量与船行方向一致，推船加速前进，即为名副其实的水动推进力。法向压力的垂向分量即为水动升力，促使船体减小吃水深度，从而进一步提高航速。请见附录F—2· 1（4）图14、图15。图14中红色箭头所示的两对水动推进力P_4、P_5，它们对船艇重心构成航向稳定扶正力矩。确保船艇不会偏离既定目标而加速前进。红色箭头所示两对的水动升力L_4、L_5，它们对船艇重心构成船体横向稳定扶正力矩，克服船艇的横摇摆动。水动升力同时对船艇重心构成纵向稳定扶正力矩，克服船艇的纵摇拍击。这些力和力矩随着航速U的增加呈U^3比例迅速增大。因此它们使船艇迅速增加其航速的同时，稳定安全性和耐波性能迅速加强。

现有技术的三体船的船体浸湿面流场中不可能产生本发明的那些力和相对应的力矩。因此在推进功率没有添加的情况下，本发明的三体船的航速、稳定安全性、耐波性能会远远超过现有技术的三体船。

在发明专利的申请过程中方舍梅、陈昕给予经济上的大力支持。曾庆存、许孔时、方悴农、方菊如、闫晓春也给予许多帮助。

用本发明技术能建造更为强大的海军舰船，为捍卫我国的南海主权和海洋权益以及我国的国家领土完整做出应有的贡献。

在后续的研发工作中严俊、汪克敏给予陈振诚大力支持。

第四章

为祖国奉献
为捍卫中华民族南海的主权奉献

发明专利证书

发明名称：一种水面交通运输工具

发明人：陈振诚

专利权人：陈振诚

授权公告日：2015年09月02日

局长 申长雨

陈振诚所从事的科学研究工作中有流体动力学、气体动力学、宇宙气体动力学、电磁流体力学、应用数学等多方面跨学科的研究成果。在前面的几章中做了论述。在原创性发明方面，“水面航行器”是应用基础理论研究水动力流场的具体体现。他提出的船底浸湿面布局从根本上改变了船舰在运行中的水动力流场航态，出现了前所未有的水动推进力。从而不需要添加推进功率却能大幅度提高航速和整体性能。同时验证了其创建的积分变换能确切计算出相应的水动力和相对应的水动力矩。经实船实航，证实了发明的核心技术的正确、数据计算的可信。

4.1

为祖国奉献

在1991年撰写发明专利论文《水面航行器》时，中国科学院钱三强秘书长、周光召院长就支持这项研究工作。国家天文台科技处处长汪克敏写报告给数理化局获批25000元，与浙江杭州东风造船厂合作做船模试航。1994年，陈振诚自己花钱申请国家专利，和浙江杭州东风造船厂、德清海鹰玻璃钢船厂合作，由东风造船厂出资购买200马力的舷外机，厂长李仁鑫、总工程师张华甫大力支持这项原创性发明专利的开发。陈振诚出资建造450艇实船，630艇的建造由德清海鹰船厂厂长赵和中出资。试航都在杭州钱塘江进行。东风造船厂的16个工人作为乘员，吊车工人把船从码头上吊起放到江面上，试航完毕把船又从江面上吊起放回码头上。吊车工2人，乘员16人，总工程师1人，发明人1人，每次试航东风造船厂有19人参加。负责驾驶船艇试航的是钱江大桥护桥部队少校级的艇长和4名士兵。630艇试航时，德清海鹰船厂厂长赵和中、副厂长赵国民、李林福也参加。从1998年开始到2002年2月12日630

艇试航成功，得到确切的数据，参与单位投入了大量的人力和物力，最终开发成功，为祖国奉献出重大的原创性发明成果。

4.2

为捍卫中华民族南海的主权奉献

在我国南海分布着东沙群岛、西沙群岛、南沙群岛等，其中西沙群岛由我国大陆有效管辖，最大的大兴岛是三沙市的政府所在地。东沙群岛和南沙群岛中的太平岛现由台湾当局管辖。而太平岛是东沙、西沙、南沙群岛中自然面积最大而且唯一有淡水资源的天然岛屿，其战略地位也很重要。南海的全部群岛从来就是我国的固有领土。

但是现在周边一些国家，如越南、菲律宾等侵占了南沙群岛的一些岛礁，还强词夺理地提出主权要求。一些域外国家，如美国、日本，用所谓航行自由为借口，把舰船驶入我国的领海。面对这样的情形，海峡两岸的中华儿女应该奋起抗争，捍卫我国的领土主权，确保我国南海的祖产不被侵占，我国的领土一寸也不能损失。

陈振诚从1963年开始基础理论研究，经长期艰苦努力取得了重大的原创性发明。用这项技术建造的实船，经试航证明：各种吨位的舰艇在运行时的水动力流场中能激起足够强大的水动推进力、水动升力和相对应的水动力矩。用这种技术能建造强大的海军舰艇，用这种舰艇战胜侵占我国南海的任何人，从而开发与保护我国东海、南海的渔业资源和海底的石油矿产资源，具有重大的经济效益、社会效益和重大的国防效益。

建造航母战斗群，保卫我国的南海；驶向远洋，为保护我国的海外投资项目，以提高当地人民的经济效益和保卫世界和平做出重大的贡献。

第五章

学习、研究、治学的座右铭

5.1

在小学学习阶段

1935年，陈振诚7岁时进入浙江宣平县华塘中心小学一年级读书，开始小学的学习生活，当时的农村没有幼儿园，所以进小学才开始识字。陈振诚白天在学校里学习，晚上回到家里，由祖父指导复习功课，背诵当天语文课的课文，训练自己的记忆力，算术会演算，并且牢牢记住公式。到小学三年级就形成了对学习的浓厚兴趣，得到教师的表扬，取得了名列前茅的成绩。

5.2

在中学学习阶段

在中学阶段，陈振诚已经对科学文化形成浓厚的求知兴趣，学好功课是生活的第一要务。将每门课的基本概念学深、学透；语文课能写出好文章，数理化课能记住基本法则，牢记基本公式之外还学会推理，推导一些常用的公式，掌握其来龙去脉和应用发展，融会贯通。

5.3

在大学学习阶段

陈振诚对大学学习阶段的体验是：听课记笔记，其作用一是能专心听老师讲解；二是便于复习时进一步深入理解，并补充听课时没能记下的内容；三是如有疑问可以课后找老师解答，或找书本解答难题，对听课内容进一步深入地融会贯通。对计算式的推导必须举一反三，把书面上的东西变为离开书本后自己思想上的东西，而不需要死记硬背。因此考试时必然能对答如流，不出差错。他对每门功课深刻掌握基本概念，把书本由“厚”读到很“薄”。离开书本而形成自己的思路。除某些需要记住的东西外，基本原理清楚，需要时即可立即写出其推导过程。因此在大学学习的五年，每个学期的各门考试科目都获得5分，取得了优秀的成绩。因此，陈振诚能在1956年大学毕业时被推荐进入北京中国科学院力学研究所工作。1958年，陈振诚经过考试进入北京俄语学院留苏预备部学习俄语和哲学。通过考试合格后到苏联莫斯科，进入苏联科学院力学研究所进行研究生阶段的学习。

图5-1　1993年，在浙江杭州陈振诚（右二）与吴兴南（中）、陶慰椿（左二）合影

5.4

在科学研究工作阶段

1958年，陈振诚在莫斯科进入苏联科学院力学研究所，在苏联导师的指导下学习，并且开始科学研究工作。科学研究要解决的问题都是前人没有解决的难题。

虽然在小学、中学、大学学习阶段，陈振诚用自己的勤奋努力奠定了做研究工作的扎实基础，但是在研究工作中还是要不断努力充实并提高自己，在做基础理论研究工作中培养解决难题的能力。例如，在寻找地震时出现在水坝迎水面上的水动压力时，前人只做了假定地震时地面只沿河流方向有运动，而其他方向的运动不会发生。但是，实际上地震时地面的运动是各个方向都会发生的。地震只沿河流方向有地面运动，问题就简化为二维问题，用三角级数展开就能找到水动压力的定量值。但是各个方向都发生地面运动，问题就是三维立体，要解决三维问题，就必须深入研读Fourier积分变换与Laplace积分变换，不但要读深，读透，而且要巧妙地运用这两种积分变换，才能找到各个方向运

图5-2　2012年，同班毕业同学聚会于苏州穹窿山，在孙子著兵法塑像处纽宏（左）、陈振诚（中）、崔德宁（右）合影

图5-3 1995年，在同济大学陈振诚（中）与同学纽宏（左）、曹国敖（右）合影

图5-4 2002年，在浙江杭州陈振诚（左一）与同班毕业的女同学合影

动时出现在水坝迎水面上的水动压力定量值。不但难度大而且工作量也很大。在解题过程中要尝试各种途径，做了大量的尝试后才能找到一个正确无误的解答，准确的研究结果请见附录F—2·2，F—2·3，F—2.4。再例如要寻找船舰运行时激起的水动力流场中出现的水动浮力、水动推进力、水动升力、水动离心力、水动反冲击力，就是更难解决的问题，因为用现有的Fourier积分变换、Laplace积分变换找不到合乎物理实际图像的解答。只有建立完全不同于这两种积分变换方法的新积分变换方法才能找到前述水动力流场中的那些水动力和相对应的水动力矩。要建立全新的积分变换是一个应用数学的难题。要攻克这个难题，就要在积分变换的积分核和逆变换的积分环路上下功夫。陈振诚用了9年的时间探寻了各种途径，经过多次失败，在失败面前不气馁，坚韧不拔、愈挫愈勇，找出此路不通的原因，通过脚踏实地的艰辛努力，最后终于创建不同于前人的能解决实际问题的冠以“陈振诚”之名的

积分变换方法。从而能找到这个难题的解析表述式，该表述式中各相关物理因素之间的相互依赖和相互制约关系清晰可见。如用其他现有的积分变换方法不可能解决这些难题。

图5-5　2012年，陈振诚（前排中）在同济大学嘉定新校区与同班毕业的同学合影

现在来看前人对船舰运行时激起的水动力流场中出现的水动浮力、水动升力等是怎样演算的呢？众所周知，一个物体处于水面或水下不运动时它所承受的浮力，其定量值是被该物体所排开的水的重量，通常称为排水量。如果一个物体以某一个速度U，保持对水平面的攻角θ在水面或在水下运动就会激起水动浮力。从物理定性分析，水动浮力应该和物体运动的速度U，物体的尺度大小a，b，水的密度ρ，体现重力场对水动力流场作用的重力加速度g，物体的吃水深度δ密切相关。如果用解析式表述水动浮力物理定量值，那么水动浮力L是U，a，b，ρ，g，δ，θ的函数。

图5-6　2012年，陈振诚（第二排左三）在苏州穹窿山与同班毕业的同学合影

由于缺乏解决难题的数学工具，前人提出用量纲分析法求水动浮力

图5-7　2012年，陈振诚（右）与张子桐在苏州穹窿山合影

图5-8　2012年，在苏州陈振诚（左二）与沈荣芳（左一）、赵居温、纽宏（右一）合影

$L=C_L\frac{1}{2}\rho U^2B^2$ 式中，C_L为水动升力系数，无量纲，由水池试验中测出，$\frac{1}{2}\rho U^2$为动压头，B为船舰的宽度。这个式中只出现ρ，U，B，而没有θ，δ，g，a。物理参数中只出现3个，有4个没有出现，其中最说不过去的是没有出现θ。如果θ=0，则L=0；θ=1°，$sin1°$=0.01745；θ=3°，$sin3°$=0.05234；$sin3°$/$sin1°$=2.999≈3，θ=1°比θ=3°时的L值差3倍。此外，模型试验时，船舰的尺寸可以缩小，但水池在重力场中，重力加速度g无法缩小。所以用量纲分析法来计算水动浮力的正确性，很难令人信服。

运用陈振诚积分变换找到了水动浮力、水动升力、水动推进力、水动离心力、水动反冲击力的定量值解析表述式。各表述式中包含了U，a，b，ρ，g，δ，θ，与物理定性分析一致。用这些表述式设计的实船，经实航试验结果与物理实际完全吻合，令人确信其研究结果可靠。

5.5

将发明付诸市场

投放市场销售的全过程，这其中需要发明人：

（1）具备“见人之所常见，思人之所未思”的独到思考方式，并能把思考之所得严谨地用数学物理方法求得解析式以表述其定量值，从而建成实船试航，证明其定量值准确。人们所常见的船运行时发动机输出的功率有一部分用于克服水的阻力，推动船前进做有用功；而另一部分功率则激起波浪水流运动被耗散为无用能量。发明人正是想到其他人没有想过的，把这部分携带着无用能量的波浪水流引入自己设计的船底浸湿面特殊外形的布局中，在这里把无用能量根据特殊外形的作用而转化为水动推进力，从而推动船加速前进而做有用功。于是实现了不需要另外添加推进功率而能大幅度提高其航速、稳定性和耐波性能等整体性能。这就是该发明的核心技术。实船实航测到的数据证实该发明能取得重大效益。

（2）为了建成产品需要寻找造船厂家合作，陈振诚首先找到浙江杭州东风造船厂的李仁鑫厂长和总工程师张华甫。张华甫毕业于造船专业，陈振诚向他们讲

图5-9　1996年，在同济大学校庆学术报告会上陈振诚作报告

图5-10　2002年，在杭州西湖陈振诚（左三）与同班毕业同学合影

图5-12　1983年，陈振诚在北京中关村822楼前花园与陈昕、方舍梅合影

解了发明的核心技术和该技术会带来的经济效益，他们听后表示支持。经讨论后决定先做船模试航，经船模试航验证发明技术先进可靠。进一步建造长4.5米的实船，舷外机40马力，试航进一步证实发明技术的可靠。然后和德清海鹰船厂、东风造船厂合作，建造长6.3米、宽2.1米、型深0.8米的实船，主机200马力的舷外机推进，与现有技术的同类产品比较，发明技术的快艇航速提高22.4%，节能33.3%，试航完全成功。数据、图片如前所述，见附录F—2。经过8年时间，付出了大量人力、物力，经浙江省船舶检验局批准允许批量生产，投放市场销售。在此基础上进一步扩大发明技术的功效，建造长16米、宽4.3米、型深1.88米，排水量12.2吨，主机功率2300马力的用于缉私、救援、边防、公安工作的高速快艇，航速能达到62节。如果再加大推进功率，航速能达到70节、80节，甚至更高。但是现有技术的快艇，除运动赛事用的小赛艇外，没有达到或大于60节的航速，因为当现有技术的快艇航速达到50节之后就会出现稳定性危机，如果再加大推进功率，不但航

速上不去，还会出现失去稳定性造成倾覆的危险。因为现有技术的快艇没有能力突破水动力流场中水的速度障。

（3）进一步的工作是对大吨位的排水型单体船在两船舷的水线处设置压浪导流挡板，在双体船的侧体内侧船舷的水线处设置压浪导流挡板，在三体船的中体两船舷的水线处设置压浪导流挡板，在两侧体的内侧船舷设置压浪导流挡板。当船舰前进时就会激起水动推进力和水动升力以及相对应的水动力矩，它们能克服水动力流场中水的阻力峰，使航速大幅度提高以及船舰稳定性、耐波性大力加强。

5.6

治学的座右铭

（1）在学习阶段，养成对学习知识有浓厚兴趣的习惯，把它看成是生活中的第一需要。记住聪明来自勤劳，真知源于深入探究。语文课需多记住一些文采精美的句子，为自己今后的写作奠定坚实的基础。数理课需记住一些最基本的概念、最基本的公式，在此基础上理解和推导更多的关系式。把一本很厚的书读懂、读透，融会贯

图5-13　1991年，陈振诚在浙江宣平华塘村大坪茶园留影

通后变成自己的思想而成为很薄的书，离开此书而能独立思考。千万不要死记硬背各个章节而缺乏全面的理解和推理。为学既要博大，更要高深。

（2）在科学研究工作中，对工作入迷，要迎难而上，在中间环节遇到失败时要愈挫愈勇，百折不挠，坚信自己经过脚踏实地的艰苦努力一定能战胜困难，获得预期的理想成果。如果用前人的数学物理方法解决不了实际问题，就要自己创建新的数学物理方法解决实际难题。在研究工作中既要巧妙地运用现有的数学物理方法，又能在需要时创建新颖的数学物理方法解决用前人的方法不可能解决的难题。

（3）见人之所常见，思人之所未思。为了发明创新，既要深刻分析人们经常见到的现象，又要从人们经常见到的现象中找到别人没有想到的创新发明亮点，在亮点上建立原创性的发明核心技术。

图5-14 2016年，同济大学工业与民用建筑专业1956届毕业60周年纪念聚会，陈振诚（第二排左五）与同学们合影

图5-15　2009年8月，陈振诚（前排左四）在四川成都出席第九届全国水动力学学术会议暨第二十二届全国水动力学研讨会时与参会者合影，陈振诚在研讨会上宣读的学术论文《仿生研究导致的新发现（BIONICS RESEARCH RESULTING IN NOVEL DISCOVERY）》发表在论文集中

附　录

>>>

F-1

陈振诚生平活动年表

1929年

2月24日（正月十五日），出生于浙江省宣平县华塘村。

1935年2月—1940年12月

就读于浙江省宣平县华塘中心小学。

1941年2月—1943年12月

就读于浙江省宣平县西塘村杭州清华初级中学。

1944年2月—1945年12月

在浙江省宣平县曳岺区柳溪村浙江省立浙东第二临时中学就读高中一年级、高中二年级。

1946年2月—1947年2月

在浙江省丽水市浙江省立处州中学就读高中三年级。

1947年8月—1951年1月

在浙江省宣平县中学，担任数学、英语和美术教师。

1951年2月—1951年6月

在浙江省宣平县柳城区中心小学担任校长。

1951年8月—1952年8月

在浙江省杭州市中央美术学院华东分院实用美术系建筑学专业学习。

1952年9月—1956年8月

在上海同济大学建筑结构系学习。

1956年9月—1958年2月

在北京中国科学院力学研究所任实习研究员。

1958年3月—1958年11月

在北京俄语学院留苏预备部学习俄语、哲学。

1958年12月—1961年6月

在苏联莫斯科苏联科学院力学研究所研究生学习。

1961年7月—1964年5月

在北京中国科学院力学研究所第二研究室任助理研究员。

1964年6月—1968年6月

在北京中国科学院力学研究所第十二研究室怀柔分部，任541任务助理研究员。

1968年7月—1973年12月

在中国人民解放军0912部队任助理研究员。

1974年3月—1978年12月

在北京中国科学院国家天文台任助理研究员。

1979年1月—1987年12月

在北京中国科学院国家天文台任副研究员。

1988年1月—1991年1月

在北京中国科学院国家天文台任研究员。

1991年2月—2016年12月

在北京中国科学院国家天文台任研究员，兼任北京飞鳐水面航行技术开发中心主任、飞鳐系列研制专家组长、水面航行器总设计师。

F-2

用中文、俄文、英文发表在国内外刊物上的陈振诚的部分科学论著（部分为扫描原件图片）

F—2·1对于小吨位的船艇，现有技术的船艇如图1、图3、图5、图7所示，和发明技术的船艇，在运行中船底浸湿面出现的水动力和相对应水动力矩对比图。其中用红色箭头标出的是本发明技术船艇水动力和相对应的水动力矩，如图2、图4、图6、图8所示。图9是航迹对比图。

F-2·1（1）对于小吨位的船艇

<1>直线前进时能激起的水动力和水动力矩。

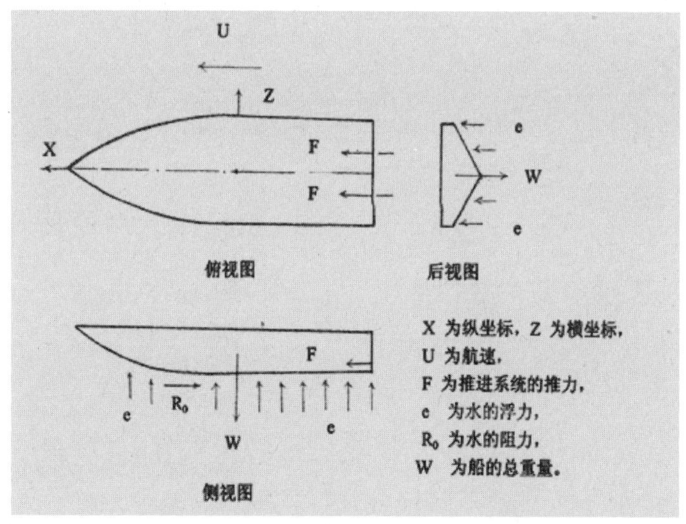

图1 现有舰艇直线前进时的受力示意图

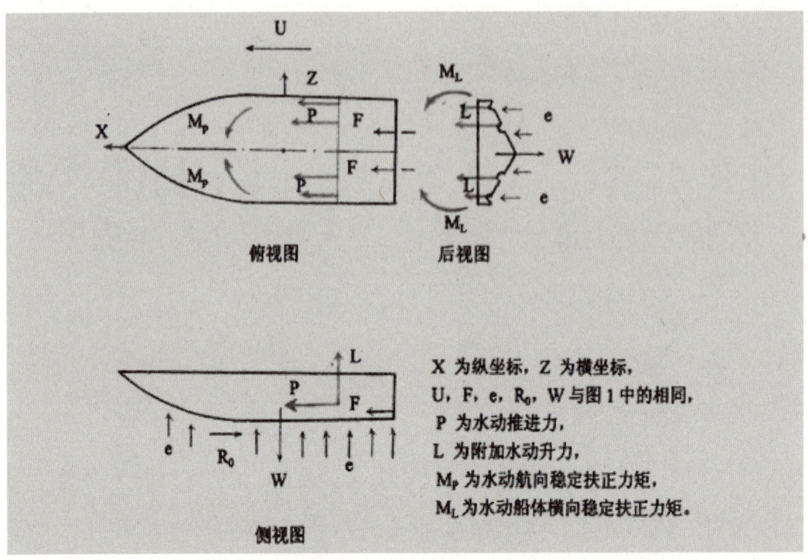

图2 本发明船艇直线前进时的受力示意图

<2>转弯时能激起的水动力和水动力矩。

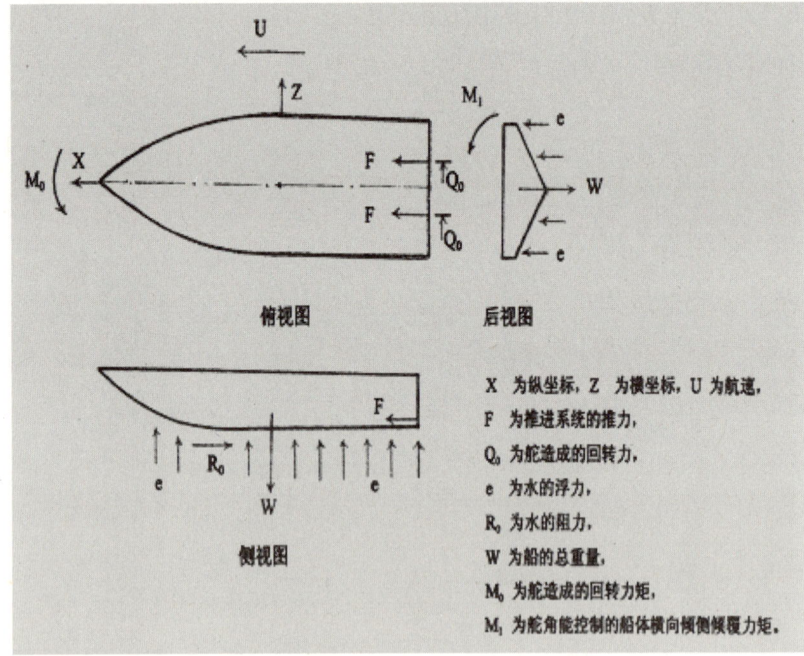

图3 本发明船艇回转时的受力示意图

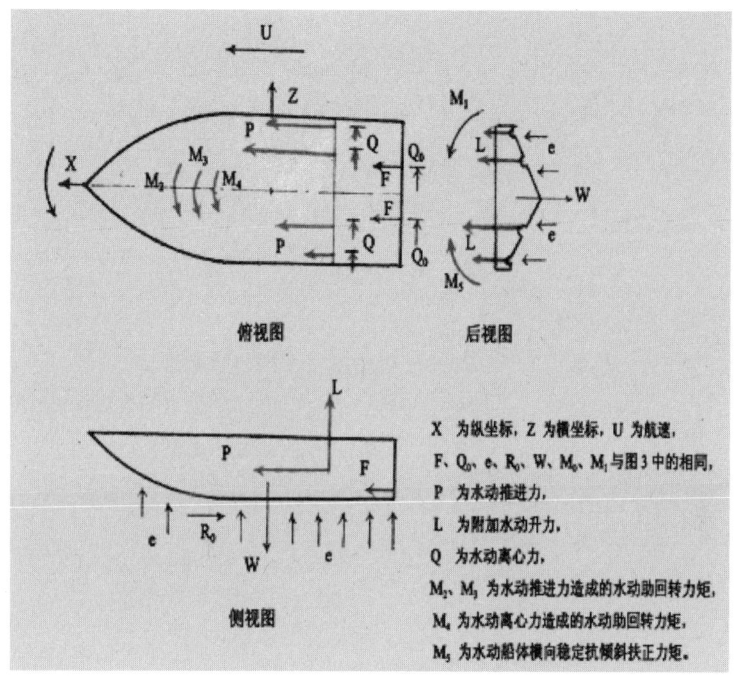

图4 本发明船艇回转时的受力示意图

<3>迎浪前进时能激起的水动力和水动力矩。

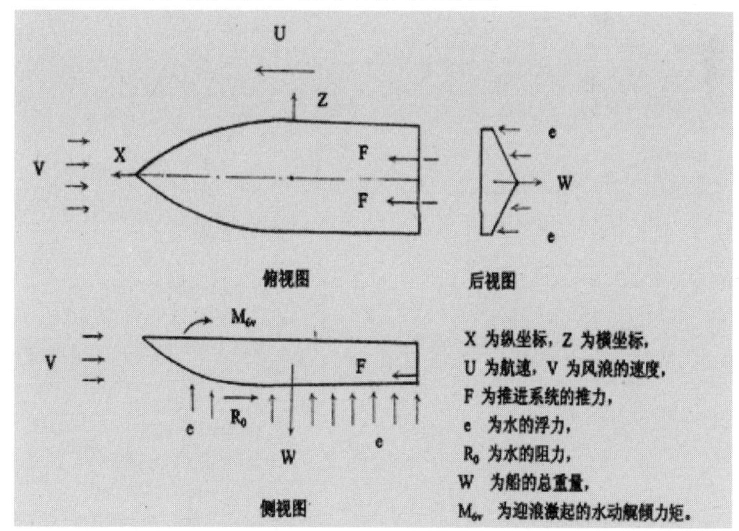

图5 现有船艇迎浪直线前进时的受力示意图

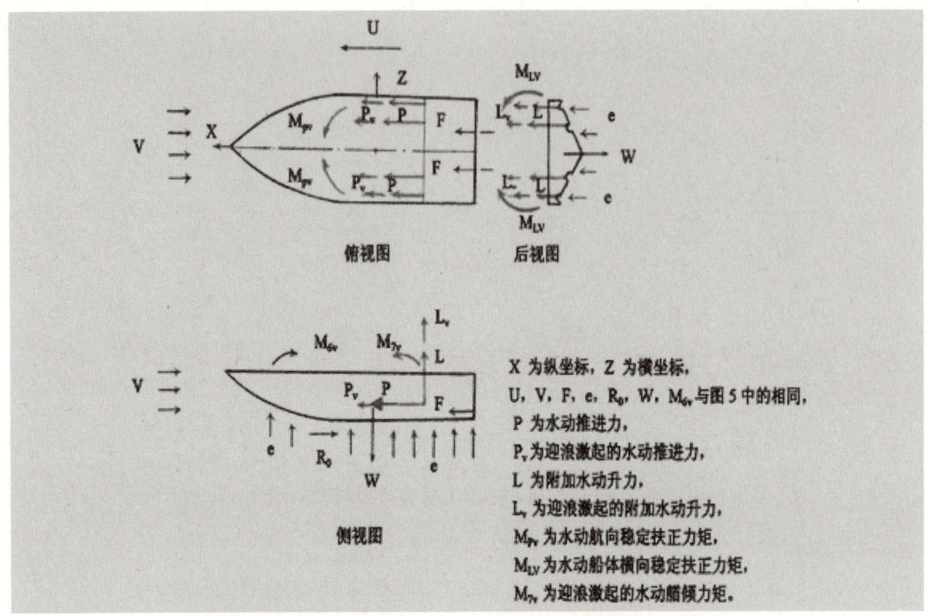

图6　本发明船艇迎浪直线前进时的受力示意图

<4>在风浪中转弯时能激起的水动力和水动力矩。

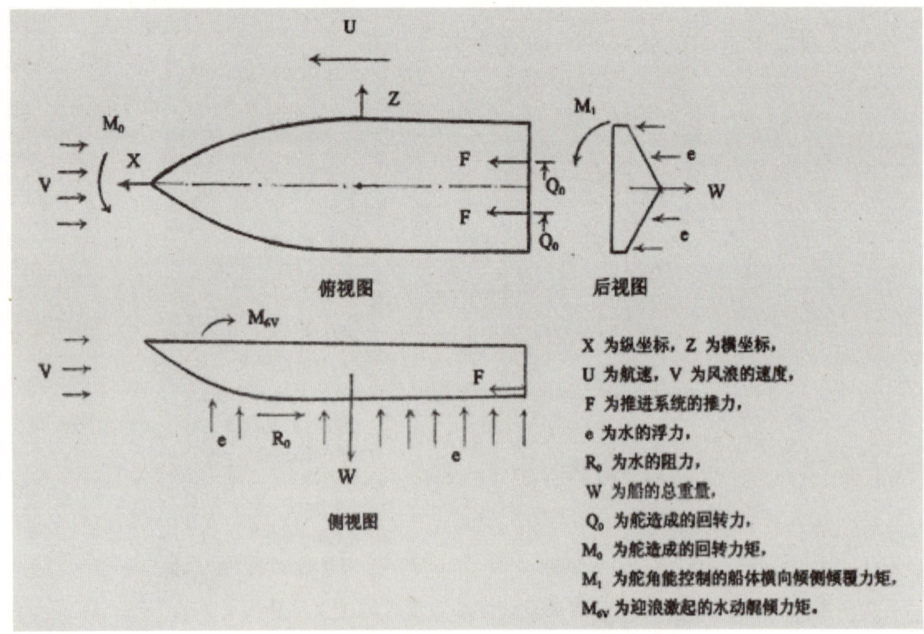

图7　现有船艇在风浪中回转时的受力示意图

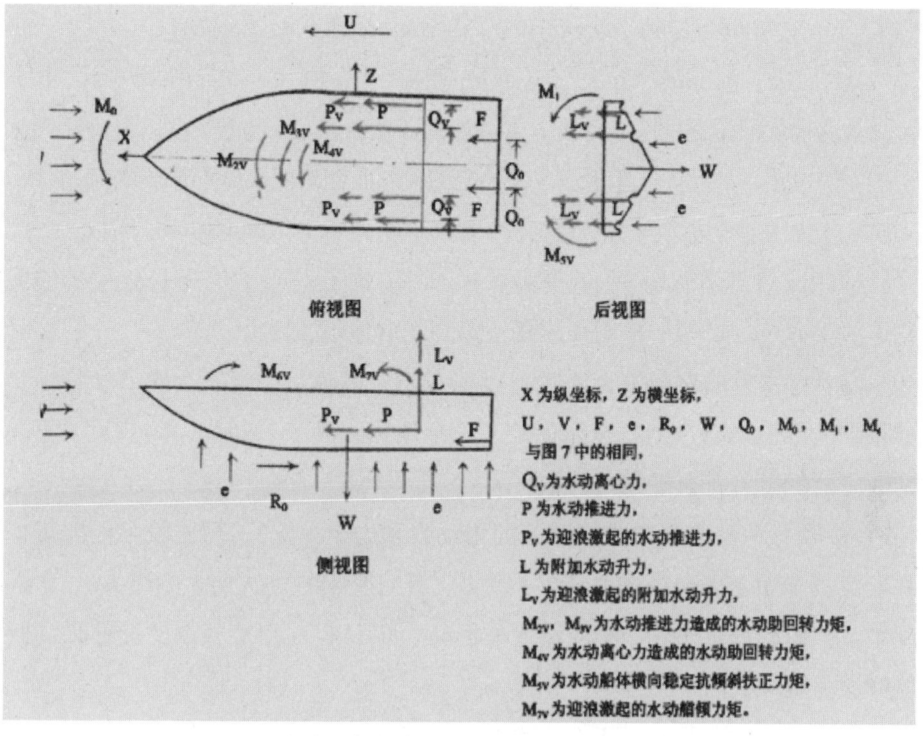

图8　本发明船艇在风浪中回转时的受力示意图

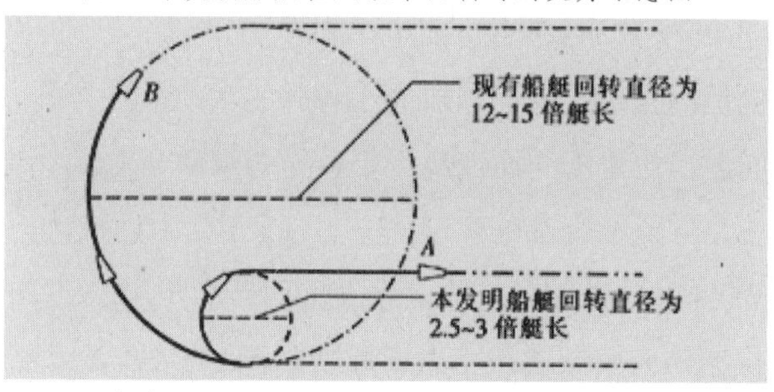

图9　本发明船艇和现有舰艇的回转直径、航迹比较图

在〈1〉中，图1：现有技术的船艇在船底浸湿面上出现推进系统的推力F，水的浮力e，水的阻力R_0，船的总重量W。

图2：发明技术的船艇，在船底浸湿面中除出现图1中有的F、e、R_0、W之外，还出现了因发明技术而特有的：

A.水动推进力P和相应的水动航向稳定扶正力矩M_P。

B.水动升力L和相应的水动船体横向稳定扶正力矩M_L。

$$P=48a^2 l\delta h\mathscr{Z}\mathscr{H}\eta\rho U^3\sin\alpha,\quad L=48a^2 l\delta h\mathscr{Z}\mathscr{H}\eta\rho U^3\cos\alpha \text{①}$$

式中$\mathscr{Z}=(\delta^2\sin\alpha-h^2\sin\theta)/\delta(\delta+h)$，$\mathscr{H}=[h(\delta^2-h^2)/g\delta(\delta^3-h^3)^3]^{1/2}$

δ为船底浸湿面的吃水深度，$2a$为船底长度，$2l$为导流槽宽度，θ为船底对水平面的攻角，U为船行速度，α为导流槽顶部曲面对船底基面形成的倾角（$\alpha>\theta$），h为水动推进力作用点的吃水深度，$0<\eta\leq1$，为无量纲的修正系数。

从P，L可见随着船速U的提高，P，L以U^3而迅速增大，于是M_p船的航向稳定扶正力矩，M_L船的横向稳定扶正力矩相应地迅速增大。

这就是本发明船艇突破水的速度障，越快速越是稳定安全的力学特性。如果加大推进功率，则航速能稳定、安全地达到60节、70节、80节甚至更高的速度而不会出现倾覆危险。

在〈2〉中迅速拐弯时能激起的水动力和力矩如图3，现有技术的船艇，在船底浸湿面上出现推进系统的推力F。船舵造成的力Q_0，水的浮力e，水的阻力R_0，船的总重量W。船舵造成的回转力矩M_0，舵角能控制的船体横向倾侧倾覆力矩M_1。

图4：发明技术的船艇，在船底浸湿中除出现图3中的F、e、R_0、W、M_0、M_1之外，还出现了因发明技术而特有的：

A.方向相同但因位置不同而造成大小各异的水动推进力P。

B.方向相同但因位置不同而造成大小各异的水动升力L。

C.主要集中在导流槽艉部的水动离心力Q。于是水动推进力造成了水动助回转力矩M_2、M_3，水动离心力造成了水动助回转力矩M_4，不同大小的水动升力造成了水动抗船体向心倾覆扶正力矩M_5。从图3的现有技术船艇转弯时船底浸湿而流场中出现的舵造成的回转力矩M_0、舵角能控制的船体横向倾侧倾覆力矩M_1、对比图4的本发明船艇船底浸湿面流场中出现的水动助回转力矩M_2、M_3、M_4，还有水动抗船体向心倾覆扶正力矩，就能清晰地看见$M_0+M_2+M_3+M_4$大于M_0、$M_5>M_1$，$M_0+M_2+M_3+M_4$迫使船艇快速稳定地转弯，$M_5>M_1$，迫使船艇不会出现向心倾覆的危险。在这些力和力矩的共同作用下，迫使船艇稳定安全地以很小的回转半径平稳迅速地转弯，并且不会出现向心倾覆的危险，其航迹的对比如图9所示。

在〈3〉中船艇迎浪前进时，能激起如图5、图6所示的水动力和相应的水动力矩。

在〈4〉中风浪中转弯时，能激起如图7、图8所示的水动力和相应的水动力矩。

为了激起<1><2><3><4>中的水动力和水动力矩，本发明船艇的船底浸湿面采取下列线型布局：

A.在船底中轴线两侧设置一对对称平行于中轴线的涌浪导流槽。槽的纵剖面顶线前低后高，对船底基面形成倾角α，α在船全长的1/3后段应为9°~12°，之后向前、向后逐渐减小到5°、3°、2°、1°。槽的顶部剖面为圆弧形。

B. 在两边船舷设置压浪导流挡板，挡板顶部的横剖面为圆弧形，纵剖面顶线前低后高形成倾角α，α的变化与导流槽相同。

在这样的布局下，当船艇前进时船艏附近的涌浪大部分被导流入槽，从而减小了水阻力，而船舷附近的涌浪被导入压浪导流挡板而减小了水阻力。在船底下面，被前进的船底推压的水流向两边挤入导流槽和压浪导流挡板，汇合从前面进入的水流共同导向艉部，顺畅地流出船尾。这时在导流槽和压浪导流挡板顶部因其前低后高的布局，给曲面造成足够强大的法向压力，法向压力的水平方向分量与船行方向一致，即为名副其实的水动推进力P_1，法向压力的垂直分量就是水动升力L_1，P_1、L_1的定量值解析表述式如前述①式所表述。

按上述线型布局设计建造的长6.3m、宽2.1m、型深0.8m的实船，空船排水量1吨，用推进功率为200马力的舷外机推进，在杭州钱塘江试航，用卫星跟踪的GPS系统实测显示，当乘员为8人时，排水量为1.5吨，航速35.15节。乘员16人时，排水量2吨，航速非但不下降，反倒提升到37.15节。如果是现有技术的快艇，对载重量的变化的响应特别敏感，载重量每增加2人航速下降1.7节，如果增加8人，就会下降4×1.7节=6.8节。乘员数量增加1倍，航速不降反倒提升1节，这就充分证明水动推进力是足够强大的，现有技术的船艇航速是37.15节–6.8节=30.35节。航速提高$\frac{37.15-30.35}{30.35}=\frac{6.8}{30.35}\approx 22.4\%$，节能$\frac{2-1.5}{1.5}=\frac{0.5}{1.5}\approx 33.3\%$。

从提高航速22.4%、节能33.3%，可以证实：发动机发出的推进功率一部分是克服水阻力推动船前进做有用功，另一部分功率激起水流运动向船的两边散开而消耗为无用能量，本发明船底浸湿面线型布局能把向两边散开的水流耗散的无用能量引入船底浸湿面转换为水动推进力而做加速推船前进的有用功。这完全符合物理学中的能量守恒原理。

该艇已获得浙江省船舶检验处批准，准许批量建造，投放市场销售。请见：

A. 浙江省船舶检验处的审查批准件（全国有效）

浙 江 省 船 舶 检 验 处

杭州 检验所

(ZHZ) 2003 审便字第007号

北京飞鸥水面航行技术中心：

关于贵单位送审的 6.3m高速封闭艇图纸，业经我处（所）审核，并已加盖审批章，图纸批准号为"ZHZ 2003007 号"。意见请见有关图纸／图纸审核意见书，编号为：(ZHZ) 审字2003007号。现随函退还，请查收。

图号及图名／详见退图清单。

退图清单与图纸送审目录同

附 注

日

B. 浙江省船检处的高级工程师、高级验船师李建新参加试航的实船实航记录。

飞鳐2号-1型艇实航记录

艇长6.3米，型宽2.1米，型深0.8米，主机为200马力水星机。艇体为玻璃钢质，自重800公斤，主机180公斤，加油箱等空船排水量为1吨。

试航地点：杭州钱塘江之江段。

试航时间：2002年1月12日下午1时55分开始，4时完成。

参加试航人员：张华甫、吴逸民、陈振诚、李建新、赵和中、李林富、赵国民、王文建、左中文、葛师傅、周师傅、阿强师傅、王师傅等共十九人。

驾驶员：左中文，试航数据记录：李建新，

读数：吴逸民、赵国民，测航速仪器：卫星跟踪GPS系统。

天气：晴

第一次试航：乘员8人，实测航速：逆水行驶为35.8节；顺水行驶为36.5节，平均航速为36.15节。

第二次试航：乘员15人，实测航速：逆水行驶为36.9节；顺水行驶为37.4节，平均航速为37.15节。

航行过程中航态好，两侧的水花飞溅很小，扰动水流集中在尾迹中，两涌浪导流设施中出流的水在尾迹中的远处会合于一点。即使达到37.4节的高速，仍没有出现拍击现象。

记录数据表明：在一定的范围内，大幅度增加载重量87.5%，航速非但不下降，反倒增加1节左右。

杭州东风船舶制造有限公司

二〇〇二年一月十六日

参加试航人员简介

张华甫：杭州东风船舶制造有限公司总工程师

副总经理、高级工程师

陈振诚：中国科学院研究员、飞鳐水面航行器总设计师

李建新：浙江省船舶检验局高级工程师、高级验船师

吴逸民：浙江省送变电工程公司工程师

左中文：武警之江艇班长

赵和中：杭州大运河玻璃钢厂厂长

赵国民：杭州大运河玻璃钢厂副厂长

李林富：杭州大运河玻璃钢厂副厂长

杭州东风船舶制造有限公司工人：

谭海荣师傅、周关校师傅、郑加祥师傅、黄勇师傅、徐世安师傅

俞良占师傅

以上的叙述充分验证了式①中的水动推进力P、水动升力L的足够强大，使原创性的本发明得以在实船实航中有这种优异的表现。

630艇（艇长6.3m）的船底浸湿面构造外形请见F—2.5第一节图4。

上列的数据和试航结果可以证实本发明的实航已成功。接下来应该研究大吨位单体船的水动力流场，以建造大吨位船舰和双体船以及三体船。

F-2·1（2）对于大吨位的单体船

把F-2·1（1）中的论述用到大吨位的船舰，例如排水量6600吨，满载排水量8520吨的集装箱船，巡洋舰、驱逐舰，长度156.5m，宽度17.2m，型深10~15m，高35.8m，吃水深度6.5m，这样的船推进功率为10万马力，又例如长300m，宽56m，排水量10万吨，吃水11m，推进功率28万马力的航空母

舰，航速只能达到32节左右，如果再加大推进功率，航速不会相应地提高。这就是水的阻力峰在起作用，要想提高航速，别无他法，只能用本发明技术，在两侧船舷的水线处设置压浪导流挡板，其结构外形是：导流挡板的顶部横剖面为圆弧形，其纵剖面的顶线前低后高对船底基面形成倾角α，导流挡板的宽度从零开始逐步增宽到1/8长度处，宽度定为e，向后延伸到挡板的尾端宽度不变。角α从0°，1°，2°，3°，5°，到长度中点处α =15°，α =20°，或α =25°，到后长度1/8处α逐步减小到5°，3°，2°，在挡板的终点α =1°，在这样的布局下，当船舰前进时水流向两边升起的涌浪，几乎全部进入压浪导流挡板中，顺畅地导向艉部流向船尾。这时在导流挡板的顶部造成足够强大的法向压力，法向压力的水平方向分量与船行方向一致，即为水动推进力，推动船加速前进，并且对船舰重心构成航向稳定扶正力矩。法向压力的垂向分量即为水动升力，能减小部分吃水深度从而减小水阻力而提高航速，并且对船舰重心构成水动横向稳定扶正力矩使船舰无法横摇摆动。见图10所示。

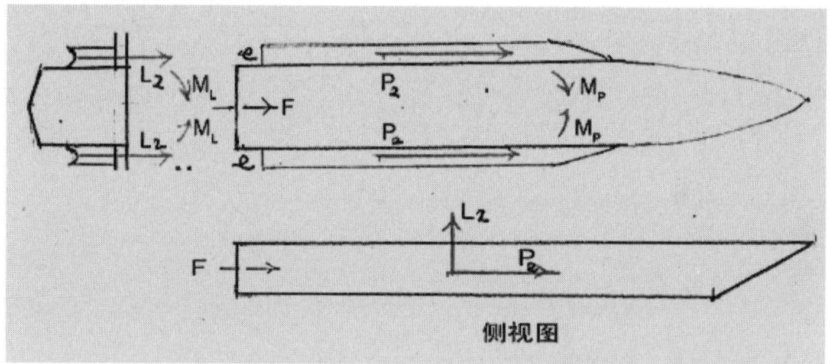

图10　发明船艇大吨位单体船在直线前进时的受力示意图

图11　发明船艇大吨位单体船在直线前进时的示意图

这就是说，那些被水流运动耗散带走的无用能量由于压浪导流挡板的作用转化为水动推进力而做推船加速前进的有用功。

水动推进力P_2、水动升力L_2的定量值表述式为：

$$P_2=\frac{a^2e}{\delta\sqrt{5gh}}\rho U^3\eta sinasina，L_2=\frac{a^2e}{\delta\sqrt{5gh}}\rho U^3\eta sinacosa \qquad ②$$

式中h为P_2，L_2为作用点的吃水深度，δ为船舰吃水深度。

F-2·1（3）对于双体船

见图12、图13。

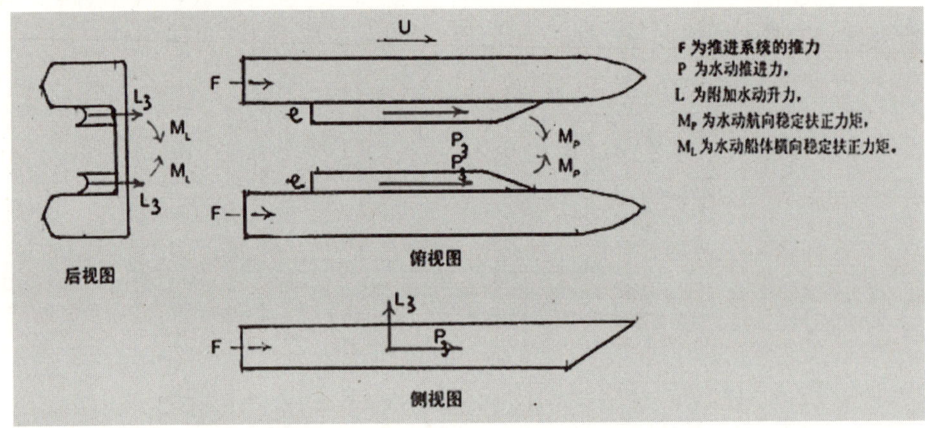
U
F
L3
ML
e
P3
MP
后视图
俯视图
侧视图
F 为推进系统的推力
P 为水动推进力，
L 为附加水动升力，
MP 为水动航向稳定扶正力矩，
ML 为水动船体横向稳定扶正力矩。

图12　发明船艇双体船在直线前进时的受力示意图

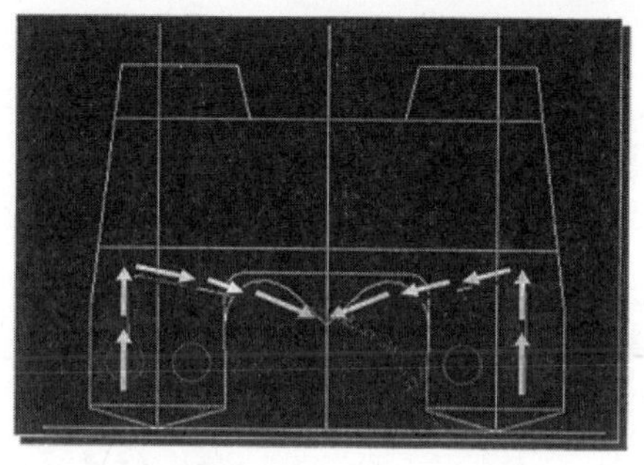

图13 发明船艇双体船在直线前进时的航态

为了降低水的兴波阻力，并获得更大的甲板平面，可采用由两个排水型侧体船组成的双体船，如我国已建成的长45m，两个侧体宽3m，侧体之间间隔6m，总宽度为12m的双体船，吃水深度1.65m，排水量241吨，推进功率4×2180kW，船速可达到40节，但耐波性、稳定性较差，亟待增强耐波性和稳定性。见图12和图13所示。

为了增强双体船的耐波性和稳定性，必须采用本发明的技术才能解决，具体措施是在两个侧体的内侧船舷，水线处设置压浪导流挡板，挡板的顶部横剖面为圆弧形，挡板的纵剖面顶线前低后高对船底基面形成倾角α，在挡板起点α=0°，随后α=1°，α=2°，α=3°，α=5°，到长度中点处α=15°，α=20°，或α=25°，到船后长度1/8处α逐步减小到5°，3°，2°，在挡板的终点α=1°，挡板的宽度在前端点处e=0，随后逐步增宽到1/8长度处，宽度定为e不变，向后延伸到挡板的尾端点处仍然是宽度为e。

有这样布局的内侧船舷压浪导流挡板，当船舰前进时，两侧体内船舷向后、向两边喷溅的水流被导入挡板，因其顶部前低后高的结构，水流在顶部造成足够强大的法向压力，水平方向分量与船行方向一致，即为水动推进力

P_3，推船加速前进，并且一对P_3对船舰重心构成航向稳定扶正力矩，迫使船不得左右摆动而向着既定目标直线前进。法向压力的垂向分量即为水动升力L_3，它能使船减小部分吃水深度从而减小水阻力而提高航速。并且一对L_3对船舰重心构成水动横向稳定扶正力矩，使船舰无法横摇摆动。并且构成纵向稳定扶正力矩，使船不得纵摇拍击，请看：

$$P_3=\frac{a^2e}{\delta\sqrt{5gh}}\rho U^3\eta sinasina，L_3=\frac{a^2e}{\delta\sqrt{5gh}}\rho U^3\eta sinacosa \qquad ③$$

式中P_3，L_3随着速度U的增加呈3次方增大，有这样强大的力和水动力矩，自然造成航速的进一步提高，耐波性、稳定性的大幅增强。h为P_3、L_3作用点的吃水深度，δ 为船舰吃水的深度。

F-2·1（4）对于三体船

见图14、图15。

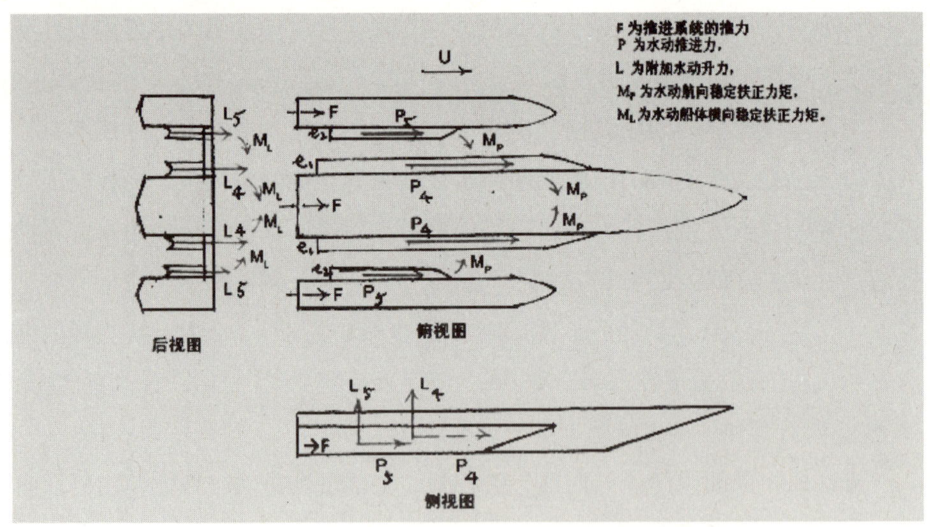
F 为推进系统的推力
P 为水动推进力，
L 为附加水动升力，
M_P 为水动航向稳定扶正力矩，
M_L 为水动船体横向稳定扶正力矩。
U
后视图
俯视图
侧视图

图14　发明船艇三体船在直线前进时的受力示意图

为了减小水的兴波阻力，可以建造三体船。军用方面，如英国海军于2000年建成的长98.7m的试航舰“RV-triton”号，并在该舰下水后进行了一系列实船试航。美国海军建成濒海战斗舰，独立号已建成并开始服役。自由号濒海战斗舰进驻新加坡港口。民用方面，澳大利亚于2003年设计建造了长126m的高速客船“Benchijigua Express”号，该船营运于Canary群岛。

图15 发明船艇三体船航母在直线前进时的航态图

三体船水下部分由中体和两个侧体对称地组成一体。两个侧体用连接桥与中体连结。中体为超细长的排水型船体，长宽比介于12~18之间，使其在高速航行时能显著降低兴波阻力，从而提高航速，两边的侧体也是排水型的浮体，它们减小了中体的吃水深度从而减小水阻力。大多数高速三体船的侧体排水量占总排水量的10%以下，长度约占船总长度的1/3，能够提供稳定性以及较好的抗横摇性能。连接中体和侧体的连接桥能保证足够强大的总纵强度，并且形成宽阔的甲板面积，方便不同用途的各种布置。但现有技术的三体船稳定性和耐波性能仍较差。

为了进一步增强其耐波性和稳定性，必须采用本发明的技术，使得其在流场中出现现有技术的三体船不可能有的水动推进力和相应的航向稳定扶正力矩，以及水动升力和相应的横向稳定、纵向稳定扶正力矩。请见图14所示。

具体的措施是：在中体的两侧船舷的水线设置压浪导流挡板，挡板的顶部横剖面为圆弧形，挡板的纵剖面顶线前低后高对船底基面形成倾角α，在挡板起点α=0°，从α=1°，2°，3°，5°，到长度中点处α=15°，α=20°，或α=25°，向后延伸到离船后端1/8长度处α逐步减小到α=5°，3°，2°，1°延伸到后端点。挡板的宽度在前端点处e_1=0，向后逐步增加到离前端点1/8长度处e_1= e_1，此后宽度定为e_1不变，向后延伸到挡板的尾端点处仍然是宽度为e_1。

在两个侧体的内侧船舷上的水线处设置压浪导流挡板，挡板的顶部横剖面为圆弧形，挡板的纵剖面顶线前低后高对船底基面形成倾角α，在挡板起点α=0，从α=1°，2°，3°，5°，到长度中点处α=15°，α=20°，或α=25°，向后延伸到离船后端1/8长度处α逐步减小到α=5°，3°，2°，1°延伸到后端点。挡板的宽度在前端点处$e_2=0$，向后逐步增加到离前端点1/8长度处$e_2= e_2$，此后宽度定为e_2不变，向后延伸到挡板的尾端点处仍然是宽度为e_2。

在上述的布局下，当船舰前进时，激起的波浪就被导流挡板导入挡板中，由于挡板顶部前低后高的结构，造成对其足够强大的法向压力，法向压力的水平方向分量与船行方向一致，即为水动推进力P，推动船加速前进，并且对船舰重心构成航向稳定扶正力矩M_p。迫使船不得左右摆动而向着既定目标直线前进。法向压力的垂向分量即为水动升力L，它对船舰重心构成水动横向稳定扶正力矩，使船舰无法横摇摆动。构成纵向稳定扶正力矩，使船不得纵摇拍击。中体两边船舷上的P_4，L_4为

$$P_4 = \frac{a^2 e_1}{\delta_1 \sqrt{5gh_1}} \rho U^3 \eta sinasina，L_4 = \frac{a^2 e_1}{\delta_1 \sqrt{5gh_1}} \rho U^3 \eta sinacosa \quad ④$$

两个侧体内侧船舷上的P_5，L_5为

$$P_5 = \frac{a^2 e_2}{\delta_2 \sqrt{5gh_2}} \rho U^3 \eta sinasina，L_5 = \frac{a^2 e_2}{\delta_2 \sqrt{5gh_2}} \rho U^3 \eta sinacosa \quad ⑤$$

式中h_1为中体，P_4，L_4作用点的吃水深度，δ_1为中体吃水深度。h_2为中体，P_5，L_5作用点的吃水深度，δ_2为侧体吃水深度。P_4，L_4，P_5，L_5随着速度U的增加呈3次方增大，有这样强大的水动力和水动力矩，必然促成航速的进一步提高，耐波性、稳定性的大力增强。

F—2 · 2

О ДИНАМИЧЕСКОМ ДАВЛЕНИИ ЖИДКОСТИ НА ПЛОТИНУ ПРИ ЗЕМЛЕТРЯСЕНИИ

Чень Чжень-чен (Москва, Пекин)

При расчетах плотин гидротехнических сооружений на действие землетрясений учитываются только напряжения, обусловленные собственными колебаниями плотины [1]. Очевидно, что при землетрясении вода также оказывает дополнительное динамическое давление на плотину. Попытка учесть этот фактор предпринята в работах [2,3], но в этих работах граничные условия удовлетворены приближенно, т. е. пренебрегалось поверхностной волной жидкости и не учитывалось смещение плотины при удовлетворении граничного условия на ней. Ниже задача об определении динамического давления исследуется более точно. Показывается, что нельзя пренебрегать наличием дополнительного динамического давления, которое в некоторых случаях превосходит величину гидростатического давления, особенно в верхних сечениях плотины.

* * *

Допустим, что в системе прямоугольных координат x, y, z в плоскости $x = U_0 \sin \omega t$ помещена плотина. Часть пространства, ограниченного условиями $x \geqslant U_0 \sin \omega t$, $-h \leqslant y \leqslant 0$, $-\infty \leqslant z \leqslant \infty$, заполнена жидкостью. Рассмотрим волновое движение и динамическое давление жидкости, вызванные тем, что в момент времени $t = 0$ вследствие землетрясения плотина мгновенно приобретает начальную скорость V_0, т. е. со стороны плотины на жидкость при $x = 0$, $t = 0$ действует ударный начальный импульс со скоростью V_0. Затем плотина совершает колебания $V = V_0 \cos \omega t$.

Очевидно, что при изучении волн жидкости и ее динамического давления влияние прогиба плотины является пренебрежимо малым. Поэтому, обозначая через $\varphi(x, y, t)$ потенциал скоростей жидкости и учитывая, что жидкость несжимаема и ее свободная поверхность первопокоящаяся, поставим начальные условия задачи

$$\frac{\partial \varphi (x, 0, 0)}{\partial t} = 0, \qquad \frac{\partial \varphi (0, y, 0)}{\partial x} = V_0 \tag{1}$$

и граничные условия

$$\frac{\partial \varphi}{\partial x} = V_0 \cos \omega t \quad \text{при } x = U_0 \sin \omega t \tag{2}$$

$$\frac{\partial \varphi}{\partial y} = 0 \quad \text{при } y = -h$$

$$\frac{\partial^2 \varphi}{\partial t^2} + g \frac{\partial \varphi}{\partial y} = 0 \quad \text{при } y = 0 \tag{3}$$

где U_0, V_0 — амплитуды смещения и скорости колеблющейся плотины соответственно.

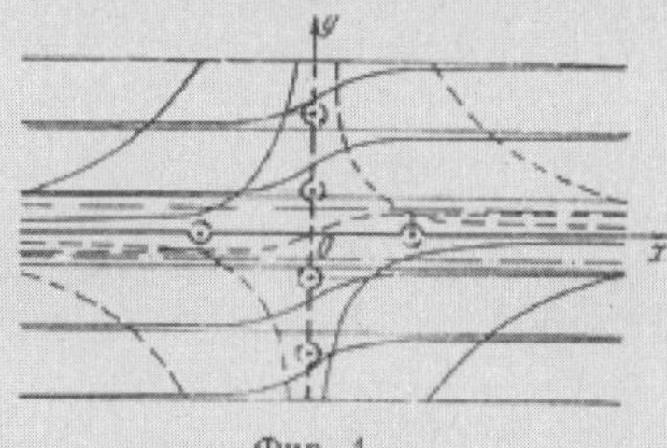

Фиг. 1.

Потенциал скоростей отыскиваемого решения задачи должен удовлетворять уравнению Лапласа $\Delta \varphi = 0$ и вышесказанным условиям. Представим потенциал скоростей $\varphi (x, y, t)$, удовлетворяющий уравнению Лапласа, в виде

$$\varphi (x, y, t) = \cos \omega t \left\{ \int_0^\infty [A (\alpha) \cos \alpha y + B (\alpha) \sin \alpha y]\, e^{-\alpha X} d\alpha + \right.$$

$$\left. + \iint_0^\infty [C (\alpha, k) \operatorname{ch} k (y + h) + D (\alpha, k) \operatorname{sh} ky] \cos kX \, d\alpha \, dk \right\} \tag{4}$$

Здесь

$$X = x - U_0 \sin \omega t$$

Произвольные функции $A (\alpha)$, $B (\alpha)$, $C (\alpha, k)$, $D (\alpha, k)$ — своих аргументов определяются посредством граничных и начальных условий. Условимся, что

$$\varphi = \varphi (x, y, t) \quad \text{при } x \geqslant U_0 \sin \omega t, \qquad \varphi = 0 \quad \text{при } x < U_0 \sin \omega t \tag{5}$$

Подставляя $\varphi (x, y, t)$ во второе граничное условие (3), получим

$$QA (\alpha) = \alpha B (\alpha) \quad (Q = \omega^2 / g) \quad (kg \operatorname{sh} kh - \omega^2 \operatorname{ch} kh)\, C (\alpha, k) = -kgD (\alpha, k) \tag{6}$$

удовлетворяя условию (2), получим интегральное уравнение

$$-\int_0^\infty \frac{B(\alpha)}{Q}[\alpha\cos\alpha y + Q\sin\alpha y]\,\alpha\,d\alpha = V_0 \tag{7}$$

Введя новые переменные $\lambda = (\alpha / Q)^2$, $y = -\nu$, перепишем уравнение (7) в виде

$$-\frac{\sqrt{2}}{\pi}\int_0^\infty \frac{\pi B(Q\sqrt{\lambda})\,Q^2(\lambda+1)}{2\sqrt{2}}\left[\cos\sqrt{\lambda}Q\nu - \frac{\sin\sqrt{\lambda}Q\nu}{\sqrt{\lambda}}\right]\frac{\sqrt{\lambda}}{\lambda+1}\,d\lambda = V_0\psi(\nu) \tag{8}$$

где

$$\psi(\nu) = 0 \quad \text{при } h < \nu < \infty \quad \text{и} \quad -\infty < \nu < 0; \qquad \psi(\nu) = 1 \quad \text{при } 0 \leqslant \nu \leqslant h \tag{9}$$

При $\theta = {}^1/_4\,\pi$, пользуясь известной формулой обращения

$$F_0(\lambda) = \int_0^\infty f_0(\varkappa)\left[\sin\theta\cos\sqrt{\lambda}\varkappa - \cos\theta\,\frac{\sin\sqrt{\lambda}\varkappa}{\sqrt{\lambda}}\right]d\varkappa$$

$$f_0(\varkappa) = \frac{1}{\pi}\int_0^\infty F_0(\lambda)\left[\sin\theta\cos\sqrt{\lambda}\varkappa - \cos\theta\,\frac{\sin\sqrt{\lambda}\varkappa}{\sqrt{\lambda}}\right]\frac{\sqrt{\lambda}\,d\lambda}{\lambda\sin^2\theta + \cos^2\theta} \tag{10}$$

и учитывая свойство функций $\psi(\nu)$, определим произвольную функцию

$$B(\alpha) = \frac{2V_0Q\,[Q(1-\cos\alpha h) - \alpha\sin\alpha h]}{\pi\alpha^2(\alpha^2+Q^2)} \tag{11}$$

Удовлетворяя первому условию (3), получим другое интегральное уравнение

$$\int_0^\infty\left[\int_0^\infty D(\alpha,\ k)\,k\,\mathrm{ch}\,kh\cos kX\,dk + \frac{2V_0}{\pi}G(\alpha)\,M(\alpha)\,e^{-\alpha X}\right]d\alpha = 0 \tag{12}$$

где

$$G(\alpha) = \pi B(\alpha) / 2V_0Q, \qquad M(\alpha) = \alpha(\alpha\sin\alpha h + Q\cos\alpha h)$$

Полагая выражение в квадратных скобках равным нулю, вводя новую переменную $\xi = X$, имея в виду характер функции $\varphi(x,\ y,\ t)$ и воспользовавшись интегральной формулой Фурье, имеем

$$\frac{\pi}{2}D(\alpha,\ k)\,k\,\mathrm{ch}\,kh + \frac{2V_0}{\pi}G(\alpha)\,M(\alpha)\int_0^\infty e^{-\alpha\xi}\cos k\xi\,d\xi = 0$$

Отсюда

$$D(\alpha,\ k) = -\frac{4V_0\alpha^2(\alpha\sin\alpha h + Q\cos\alpha h)}{\pi^2k(\alpha^2+k^2)\,\mathrm{ch}\,kh}G(\alpha) \tag{13}$$

Теперь все произвольные коэффициенты в (4) определены и полученный потенциал скоростей $\varphi(x,\ y,\ t)$ удовлетворяет начальным условиям (1).

Дифференцируя потенциал скоростей $\varphi(x,\ y,\ t)$ по t, при $x = U_0\sin\omega t$ имеем

$$\frac{\partial\varphi}{\partial t} = \frac{2V_0}{\pi}\omega\sin\omega t\left\{\frac{2}{\pi}\iint_0^\infty \frac{f(\alpha)\,\mathrm{sh}\,ky\,d\alpha\,dk}{k(\alpha^2+Q^2)(\alpha^2+k^2)\,\mathrm{ch}\,kh} - \int_0^\infty \frac{F(\alpha,\ y)}{\alpha^2(\alpha^2+Q^2)}d\alpha - \right.$$

$$\left. -\frac{2g}{\pi}\iint_0^\infty \frac{f(\alpha)\,\mathrm{ch}\,k(y+h)\,d\alpha\,dk}{(\alpha^2+Q^2)(\alpha^2+k^2)(kg\,\mathrm{sh}\,kh - \omega^2\,\mathrm{ch}\,kh)\,\mathrm{ch}\,kh}\right\} + \frac{2V_0^2}{\pi}\cos^2\omega t\int_0^\infty \frac{F(\alpha,\ y)\,d\alpha}{\alpha(\alpha^2+Q^2)} \tag{14}$$

где

$$N(\alpha) = [Q(1-\cos\alpha h) - \alpha\sin\alpha h], \qquad F(\alpha,\ y) = N(\alpha)(\alpha\cos\alpha y + Q\sin\alpha y)$$

$$f(\alpha) = N(\alpha)\,M(\alpha) / \alpha$$

При вычислении двойного интеграла (14) воспользуемся теорией вычетов. Сначала интегрируем по переменному α, при этом имеем на комплексной плоскости полюсы, лежащие на мнимой оси $\pm iQ$ и $\pm ik$. Затем при интегрировании по переменному k имеем полюсы, находящиеся на вещественной оси $\pm Q$ и для $\mathrm{ch}\,kh = 0$ на мнимой оси $\pm im\pi / 2h$, где $m = 1,\ 3,\ 5,\ \cdots,\infty$, а для трансцендентного уравнения $kg\,\mathrm{sh}\,kh - \omega^2\,\mathrm{ch}\,kh = 0$ имеем два корня, лежащих на вещественной оси $\pm\gamma_0$ и бесконечное число корней $\pm i\gamma_n$, где $n = 1,\ 2,\ 3,\ldots,$ на мнимой оси. Их можно найти, руководствуясь фиг. 1, посредством последовательных приближений, при этом может быть достигнута нужная степень. Решаем уравнение для вещественных корней $\gamma \operatorname{th} \gamma = Qh$ и для мнимых корней $\gamma \operatorname{tg} \gamma = -Qh$, где $\gamma = kh$.

Переходя к вычислениям, имеем

$$\int_0^\infty \frac{N(\alpha)(Q\cos\alpha h + \alpha \sin \alpha h)}{(\alpha^2+Q^2)(\alpha^2+k^2)}\, d\alpha = \frac{Q\pi R_0}{k^2-Q^2} + \frac{\pi}{2}\,\frac{[Q(1-\operatorname{ch} kh) + k \operatorname{sh} kh]}{k(Q-k)}\, e^{-kh} \quad (15)$$

Следовательно,

$$\iint_0^\infty \frac{f(\alpha)\operatorname{sh} ky\, d\alpha\, dk}{k(\alpha^2+Q^2)(\alpha^2+k^2)\operatorname{ch} kh} = \frac{\pi}{2}\int_0^\infty \frac{[Q(1-\operatorname{ch} kh)+k\operatorname{sh} kh]\, e^{-kh}}{k^2(Q-k)\operatorname{ch} kh} \operatorname{sh} ky\, dk +$$

$$+ Q\pi R_0 \int_0^\infty \frac{\operatorname{sh} ky\, dk}{(k^2-Q^2)\, k \operatorname{ch} kh} = \frac{\pi}{2}\int_0^\infty \frac{f(k)\sin ky\, dk}{k^2(k^2+Q^2)\cos kh} - i\,\frac{\pi^2}{2}\,\frac{R_0 \operatorname{sh} Qy}{Q \operatorname{ch} Qh} - \quad (16)$$

$$- \frac{\pi^2}{2}\sum_{m=1,3}^{\infty} \frac{(Q - C\sin C_\pi)(Q+iC)}{hC^2(Q^2+C^2)}\sin Cy - Q\pi^2 R_0 \sum_{m=1,3}^{\infty}\frac{\sin Cy \sin C_\pi}{hC(Q^2+C^2)} + iH$$

Здесь

$$f(k) = N(k)(Q\cos kh + k\sin kh), \qquad N(k) = [Q(1-\cos kh) - k\sin kh]$$

$$R_0 = (1-e^{-Qh})\, e^{-Qh}, \quad C = m\pi/2h, \quad C_\pi = m\pi/2$$

причем

$$H = \int_0^\infty \frac{N(k)(k\cos kh - Q\sin kh)}{k^2(k^2+Q^2)\cos kh}\sin ky\, dk \quad (17)$$

Вычислив таким же путем второй двойной интеграл в формуле (14) и подставив в нее найденные результаты интегрирования, получим при $x = U_0 \sin \omega t$

$$\frac{\partial\varphi}{\partial t} = -2V_0 Q h^2 \omega \sum_{n=1}^{\infty} \frac{C_n \cos[\gamma_n(y+h)/h]\sin\omega t}{[\gamma_n^2 - (1-Qh)Qh]\,\gamma_n \cos\gamma_n} - V_0^2\,[1 - 2(1-e^{-Qh})\,e^{Qy}]\cos^2\omega t \quad (18)$$

где

$$C_n = 1 - C_n', \quad C_n' = 2R_0\gamma_n^2/(\gamma_n^2 + Q^2h^2)\cos\gamma_n$$

Дальше продифференцируем $\varphi(x, y, t)$ по y; при $x = U_0 \sin\omega t$ имеем

$$\frac{\partial\varphi}{\partial y} = \frac{2V_0}{\pi}\cos\omega t\left\{\int_0^\infty \frac{N(\alpha)[Q\cos\alpha y - \alpha\sin\alpha y]}{\alpha(\alpha^2+Q^2)}\, d\alpha - \frac{2}{\pi}\iint_0^\infty \frac{f(\alpha)\operatorname{ch} ky\, d\alpha\, dk}{(\alpha^2+Q^2)(\alpha^2+k^2)\operatorname{ch} kh} + \right.$$

$$\left. + \frac{2g}{\pi}\iint_0^\infty \frac{f(\alpha)\, k \operatorname{sh} k(y+h)\, d\alpha\, dk}{(\alpha^2+Q^2)(\alpha^2+k^2)(kg\operatorname{sh} kh - \omega^2 \operatorname{ch} kh)\operatorname{ch} kh}\right\} \quad (19)$$

Проводя здесь аналогичные вычисления, получим при $x = U_0 \sin\omega t$

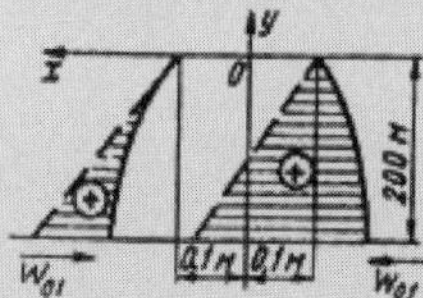

Фиг. 2

$$\frac{\partial\varphi}{\partial y} = -2V_0 Qh \sum_{n=1}^{\infty}\frac{C_n \sin[\gamma_n(y+h)/h]}{[\gamma_n^2 - (1-Qh)Qh]\cos\gamma_n}\cos\omega t \quad (20)$$

Как известно,

$$\frac{\partial\varphi}{\partial x} = V_0 \cos\omega t \quad (21)$$

Обозначая через ρ плотность жидкости, а через P^* ее динамическое давление, будем иметь формулу

$$\frac{P^*}{\rho} = -\frac{\partial\varphi}{\partial t} - \frac{1}{2}\left[\left(\frac{\partial\varphi}{\partial x}\right)^2 + \left(\frac{\partial\varphi}{\partial y}\right)^2\right] \quad (22)$$

Преобразуем формулу (18) к следующему виду:

$$\frac{\partial\varphi}{\partial t} = -2U_0 g \sum_{n=1}^{\infty}\frac{C_n\cos[\gamma_n(y+h)/h]}{\gamma_n[R_1 - (R_2 - 1)]\cos\gamma_n}\sin\omega t - V_0^2\,[1 - 2(1-e^{-Qh})\,e^{Qy}]\cos^2\omega t \quad (23)$$

$$(R_1 = (\gamma_n/Qh)^2, \; R_2 = 1/Qh)$$

Обозначим через $\varphi_y = \partial\varphi / \partial y$, $\varphi_t = \partial\varphi / \partial t$ (при $x = U_0 \sin \omega t$). Сопоставление формул (20) и (18) показывает, что если ωh велико, то φ_y представляет собой величину более высокого порядка. Из первого слагаемого под знаком суммы (23) мы видим, что для заданной амплитуды смещения U_0 при увеличении h или ω динамическое давление жидкости значительно увеличивается, ибо при этом $\gamma_n \to {}^1/_2\pi$ (фиг. 1) и в связи с этим $\cos \gamma_n \to 0$, причем $C_n \to 1$, $[R_1 - (R_2 - 1)] \to 1$. Отсюда следует, что числитель сохраняет некоторое конечное значение, а знаменатель быстро уменьшается и, следовательно, величина φ_t быстро возрастает. Следует отметить, что $\gamma_n \to n\pi$ с ростом числа n; ввиду этого $\cos \gamma_n \to 1$ (фиг. 1), а поэтому ряд, содержащийся в формуле (23), быстро сходится. Это позволяет легко получить распределение динамического давления P^* вдоль плотины. В качестве примера, взяв первые два члена суммы из (23), имеем на дне плотины при глубине жидкости, равной 200 *м*, максимальное значение.

1) $\varphi_t = 96720 U_0$ (для $\omega = 20$), если $U_0 \geqslant 0.021$ *м*, то динамическое давление $P^* = 2031\rho$ больше статического давления $P^\circ = 1960\rho$, 2) $\varphi_t = 11502 U_0$ (для $\omega = 10$), если $U_0 \geqslant 0.18$ *м*, то $P^* = 2070\rho$, 3) $\varphi_t = 5756 U_0$ ($\omega = 6$), если $U_0 \geqslant 0.35$ *м*, то $P^* \geqslant 2015\rho$. Сравнение 1) и 2) показывает, что при увеличении ω вдвое величина φ_t возрастает больше чем в 8 раз.

Из сейсмических законов знаем, что последний случай приближается к случаю разрушительного землетрясения. Очевидно, при этом дополнительное динамическое давление превосходит статическое, так как $\beta = 103$, 150 и 158% при $y = -h$, $-0.5h$ и $-0.1h$ соответственно, где β обозначает безразмерный параметр P^* / P°.

Во втором случае при $U_0 = 0.10$ *м* приближаемся к случаю сильного землетрясения, при этом имеем $\beta = 59\%$ ($y = -h$), $\beta = 84\%$ ($y = -0.5h$), $\beta = 92\%$ ($y = -0.1h$). При увеличении глубины жидкости до 300 *м* будем иметь $\varphi_t = 13470 U_0$ ($\omega = 10$) и $\varphi_t = 6740 U_0$ ($\omega = 6$). Исходя из вышеуказанного анализа, видно, что при разрушительном, а также и сильном землетрясении динамическое давление жидкости, вызванное колеблющейся плотиной, оказывает большое влияние на ее нагрузку, в особенности для верхних сечений плотины.

Подставляя (18), (20) и (21) в формулу (22), видим, что максимальное давление появится в тот момент времени, при котором колеблющаяся плотина, дойдя до $x = -U_0$, приобретает максимальное ускорение и двигается навстречу направлению движения жидкости, а минимальное давление возникает тогда, когда плотина, дойдя до $x = U_0$, двигается с максимальным ускорением от жидкости.

По заданным h, ω, U_0, V_0, нетрудно с помощью формул (18) — (22) построить графики распределения максимального давления жидкости вдоль плотины. В качестве примера в случае $h = 200$ *м*, $\omega = 10$, $U_0 = 0.1$ *м* и $\omega = 6$, $U_0 = 0.35$ *м* построим графики, изображенные на фиг. 2 и 3 соответственно, где пунктирная линия выражает статическое давление, а сплошная линия — дополнительное динамическое давление, W_{01}, W_{02} — максимальное ускорение плотины. Из фиг. 3 видно, что для этого случая при $x = U_0$ плотина подвергается отрицательной нагрузке, равной 4500 и 5500 *кг / м²* (при $y = -200$ и -10 *м* соответственно), но меньшей атмосферного давления 1×10^4 *кг / м²*.

Чтобы избежать возникновения разрушительного давления жидкости, или чтобы не позволить их максимальному значению превзойти некоторый предел, назначенный при проектировании, можно при известном ω уменьшать глубину жидкости h, чтобы γ_n не стремилось к ${}^1/_2\pi$, а сохраняло некоторое значение, соответствующее нашему назначенному значению. Зависимость γ_n от ω и h можно получить из уравнения $\gamma_n \operatorname{tg} \gamma_n = -Qh$ с достаточной степенью точности.

Теперь перейдем к рассмотрению волн жидкости. Уравнение, определяющее вид волновой поверхности, таково

$$\zeta(x, t) = -\frac{1}{g}\frac{\partial\varphi(x, 0, t)}{\partial t} = \frac{4V_0}{\pi^2}\iint_0^\infty \frac{\omega f(\alpha)\cos kX \sin \omega t \, d\alpha \, dk}{(\alpha^2 + Q^2)(\alpha^2 + k^2)(kg \operatorname{sh} kh - \omega^2 \operatorname{ch} kh)} +$$

$$+ \frac{2V_0}{g\pi}\omega \sin \omega t \int_0^\infty \frac{N(\alpha) e^{-\alpha X}}{\alpha(\alpha^2 + Q^2)} \, d\alpha \tag{24}$$

Обозначая через η двойной интеграл и сначала интегрируя его по переменному α, имеем соотношение (15). Подставив (15) в (24), получим

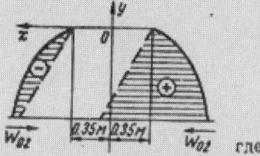

$$\eta = \frac{Q\pi R_0}{8i}\int_{-\infty}^{\infty}\frac{J(k, x, t)\,dk}{(k^2-Q^2)(kg\,\mathrm{sh}\,kh-\omega^2\,\mathrm{ch}\,kh)} - \tag{25}$$

$$-\frac{\pi}{8i}\int_{0}^{\infty}\frac{[Q(1-\mathrm{ch}\,kh)+k\,\mathrm{sh}\,kh]\,e^{-kh}J(k, x, t)}{k(k-Q)(kg\,\mathrm{sh}\,kh-\omega^2\,\mathrm{ch}\,kh)}\,dk$$

где

$$J(k, x, t) = \exp[i(\omega t + kX)] + \exp[i(\omega t - kX)] - $$
$$-\exp[-i(\omega t - kX)] - \exp[-i(\omega t + kX)]$$

Фиг. 3

Выбирая пути интегрирования, указанные на фиг. 1, где толстая сплошная линия есть путь первой интеграции (25), а пунктирная — путь второй интеграции, причем обход полюсов для первых двух слагаемых $J(k, x, t)$ указан сплошной линией, а для последних двух слагаемых обход указан стрелками (при таком выборе пути интегрирования обеспечивается уход волн от плотины на бесконечность [5]), и пользуясь теорией вычетов, вычислим η. После подстановки этих результатов интегрирования в (24), получим (при $t > 0$)

$$\zeta(x, t) = 2U_0Q^2h^2\sum_{n=1}^{\infty}\frac{C_n\exp(-\gamma_n X/h)\sin\omega t}{\gamma_n[\gamma_n^2-(1-Qh)Qh]} + \frac{2U_0Q^2h^2C_s\cos[(\gamma_s/h)(X-\omega ht/\gamma_s)]}{(\gamma_s-Qh)[\gamma_s^2+(1-Qh)Qh]\,\mathrm{ch}\gamma_s} \tag{26}$$

где $C_s = e^{-\gamma_s} - C_s'$, $C_s' = 2R_0\gamma_s/(\gamma_s + Qh)$. Формула (26) показывает, что вслед за движением плотины вблизи нее уровень жидкости периодически поднимается и опускается, вследствие чего образуемые прогресивные волны уходят от плотины на бесконечность со скоростью $\omega h/\gamma_s$, длина волн равна $2\pi h/\gamma_s$.

Замечание: При определении произвольной функции $D(\alpha, k)$ подынтегральная функция в (12) по переменному α полагалась равной нулю. Мы знаем, эта функция апериодическая (аргумент α изменяется от 0 до ∞), и поэтому, хотя интеграл по α тождественно равен нулю, но подынтегральная функция может быть равной нулю, но и может быть не нулем. Итак, представим второй член (4) однократным интегралом по переменному k. Удовлетворяя прежним условиям, получим функции $D(k)$ и $C(k)$, которые будут функциями k, умноженными на некоторые постоянные, являющиеся интегралами по α. Например,

$$D(k) = I(k)\int_0^{\infty}L(\alpha)\,d\alpha$$

Подставляя эти коэффициенты в $\varphi(x, y, t)$, получим прежний результат, поэтому в данном случае подынтегральная функция равна нулю.

Автор приносит глубокую благодарность Х. А. Рахматулину и Л. Н. Сретенскому за их ценные советы, а также и С. С. Войту, Н. И. Сомову за их помощь.

Поступила 3 X 1960

Институт механики АН СССР

ЛИТЕРАТУРА

1. Напетваридзе Ш. Г. Гидродинамическое давление при сейсмическом воздействии. Тр. Ин-та строит. дела АН ГрузССР, Тбилиси, 1955.
2. Лейбензон Л. С. О натуральных периодах колебаний плотины, подпирающей реку. Уч. зап. МГУ, 1935, № 2.
3. Уразбаев М. Т. Сейсмостойкость гидроупругих систем. Строительная механика и расчет сооружений, 1959, вып. 5.
4. Левитан Б. М. Разложение по собственным функциям линейного дифференциального уравнения. ГИТТЛ, 1950.
5. Сретенский Л. Н. О направленном излучении волн из области, подверженной внешнему давлению. ПММ, 1956, т. XX, вып. 3.
6. Войт С. С. Волны на поверхности жидкости, возникающие от перемещающейся периодической системы давлений. ПММ, 1957, т. XXI, вып. 1.
7. Черкесов Л. В. О волнах на поверхности жидкости. Изв. АН СССР. ОТН, Механика и машиностроение, 1959, вып. 2.

F—2 · 3

Прикладная математика и механика. Том XXV, 1961
Отделение технических наук Академии наук Союза ССР

О ГИДРОДИНАМИЧЕСКОМ ДАВЛЕНИИ НА ПЛОТИНУ, ВЫЗВАННОМ ЕЕ АПЕРИОДИЧЕСКИМИ ИЛИ ИМПУЛЬСИВНЫМИ КОЛЕБАНИЯМИ И ВЕРТИКАЛЬНЫМИ КОЛЕБАНИЯМИ ЗЕМНОЙ ПОВЕРХНОСТИ

Чень Чжень-чен
(Москва)

Рассматривается задача о распределении гидродинамического давления вдоль плотины, обусловленного ее апериодическими или импульсивными колебаниями и вертикальными колебаниями земной поверхности, находящейся под жидкостью. Из полученных результатов вытекает, что вертикальные колебания земной поверхности оказывают значительное влияние на нагрузку плотины как при сильном, так и при разрушительном землетрясении. Выводятся формулы для распределения динамического давления жидкости по плотине.

Задача о динамическом давлении жидкости на плотину, вызванном ее колебаниями по периодическому закону, например $V = V_0 \cos \omega t$, была рассмотрена в работах [1-4], где V_0 — амплитуда скорости колеблющейся плотины. Задача о поверхностных волнах жидкости, возникающих от периодической поверхностной или внутренней системы давлений была рассмотрена в работах [5-7].

§ 1. Исследуем задачу о динамическом давлении жидкости на плотину, обусловленном колебаниями земной поверхности со скоростью $V(t)$, которая лежит в плоскости x, y и наклонена под углом ϑ к горизонту.

Пусть в прямоугольных координатах x, y, z, в плоскостях $x = U_1(t)$, $y = U_2(t) - h$ помещаются плотина и земная поверхность соответственно. Часть пространства, ограниченного условиями $x \geqslant U_1(t)$, $U_2(t) - h \leqslant y \leqslant U_2(t)$, $-\infty \leqslant z \leqslant \infty$, заполняется жидкостью.

Предположим, что поверхность жидкости вначале покоится. Обозначая через $\varphi(x, y, t)$ потенциал скоростей жидкости, имеем начальные и граничные условия задачи

$$\frac{\partial \varphi(x, 0, 0)}{\partial t} = 0, \qquad \frac{\partial \varphi(0, y, 0)}{\partial x} = V_1(0), \qquad \frac{\partial \varphi(x, -h, 0)}{\partial y} = V_2(0) \quad (1.1)$$

$$\frac{\partial \varphi}{\partial x} = V_1(t) \quad \text{при } x = U_1(t) = \int_0^t V_1(\tau)\, d\tau \qquad (V_1(t) = V(t)\cos\vartheta) \quad (1.2)$$

$$\frac{\partial \varphi}{\partial y} = V_2(t) \quad \text{при } y = U_2(t) - h \quad (1.3)$$

$$\frac{\partial^2 \varphi}{\partial t^2} + g\frac{\partial \varphi}{\partial y} = 0 \quad \text{при } y = U_2(t) = \int_0^t V_2(\tau)\, d\tau \qquad (V_2(t) = V(t)\sin\vartheta) \quad (1.4)$$

Потенциал скоростей жидкости, который должен удовлетворять уравнению Лапласа $\Delta\varphi = 0$, возьмем в виде

$$\varphi(x, y, t) = \iint_0^\infty [B(\omega, k)\operatorname{ch} k(Y + h) + D(\omega, k)\operatorname{sh} kY] \cos kX \cos \omega t\, d\omega\, dk +$$
$$+ \iint_0^\infty A(\omega, \alpha) \sin \alpha Y e^{-\alpha X} \cos \omega t\, d\omega\, d\alpha \qquad \begin{pmatrix} X = x - U_1(t) \\ Y = y - U_2(t) \end{pmatrix} \quad (1.5)$$

Здесь функции $A(\omega, \alpha)$, $B(\omega, k)$ и $D(\omega, k)$ — произвольные, функция $\varphi(x, y, t)$ определяется так, чтобы

$$\varphi = \varphi(x, y, t) \quad \text{при } x \geqslant U_1(t) \ (-h \leqslant Y \leqslant 0), \qquad \varphi = 0 \quad \text{при } x < U_1(t)$$

Граничное условие (1.2) будет удовлетворено, если взять

$$-\iint_0^\infty \alpha A(\omega, \alpha) \sin \alpha Y \cos \omega t \, d\omega \, d\alpha = V_1(t) \tag{1.6}$$

Введем новую переменную $\zeta = Y$ и перепишем (1.6) в виде

$$-\iint_0^\infty \alpha A(\omega, \alpha) \sin \alpha\zeta \cos \omega t \, d\omega \, d\alpha = V_1(t) f(\zeta) \tag{1.7}$$

где

$$f(\zeta) = 1 \quad \text{при } -h \leqslant \zeta \leqslant 0, \qquad f(\zeta) = 0 \quad \text{при } -h > \zeta > 0$$

Пользуясь преобразованием Фурье, из интегрального уравнения (1.7) получим

$$A(\omega, \alpha) = \frac{4(1 - \cos \alpha h)}{\pi^2 \alpha^2} G_1(\omega) \qquad \left(G_1(\omega) = \int_0^\infty V_1(\tau) \cos \omega\tau \, d\tau\right) \tag{1.8}$$

В силу граничного условия (1.3) имеем

$$\int_0^\infty \left[\int_0^\infty D(\omega, k) k \operatorname{ch} kh \cos kX dk + \int_0^\infty A(\omega, \alpha) \cos \alpha h e^{-\alpha X} \alpha d\alpha\right] \cos \omega t \, d\omega = V_2(t) \tag{1.9}$$

Отсюда

$$D(\omega, k) = -\frac{2}{\pi} \int_0^\infty \frac{A(\omega, \alpha) \alpha^2 \cos \alpha h}{k(\alpha^2 + k^2) \operatorname{ch} kh} d\alpha + \frac{2}{\pi} \frac{G_2(\omega) \delta(k)}{k \operatorname{ch} kh} \tag{1.10}$$

Здесь

$$\delta(k) = \frac{2}{\pi} \lim_{l \to \infty} \frac{\sin kl}{k} \quad \left(\begin{matrix}\text{дельта-функ-}\\ \text{ция Дирака}\end{matrix}\right), \qquad G_2(\omega) = \int_0^\infty V_2(\tau) \cos \omega\tau \, d\tau$$

Из граничного условия (1.4) определим неизвестную функцию

$$B(\omega, k) = -\frac{kgD(\omega, k)}{kg \operatorname{sh} kh - \omega^2 \operatorname{ch} kh} - \frac{2g}{\pi} \int_0^\infty \frac{A(\omega, \alpha) \alpha^2 d\alpha}{(\alpha^2 + k^2)(kg \operatorname{sh} kh - \omega^2 \operatorname{ch} kh)} \tag{1.11}$$

После подстановки выражения (1.8), (1.10) и (1.11) в формулу (1.5) получаем искомый потенциал скоростей $\varphi(x, y, t)$.

1°. Для того, чтобы найти динамическое давление жидкости на плотину, вызванное ее апериодическими колебаниями, будем предполагать, что

$$V(t) = V_0 e^{-\lambda t} \qquad (\lambda = \xi + i\eta) \tag{1.12}$$

где V_0, ξ и η — вещественные постоянные. При этом скорости колеблющейся плотины $V_1(t)$ и земной поверхности $V_2(t)$, находящейся под жидкостью, соответственно будут

$$V_1(t) = V_1 e^{-\lambda t}, \qquad V_2(t) = V_2 e^{-\lambda t} \qquad (V_1 = V_0 \cos \vartheta, \ V_2 = V_0 \sin \vartheta) \tag{1.13}$$

$$U(t) = \int_0^t V(\tau) \, d\tau = U_0(1 - e^{-\lambda t}) \qquad \left(U_0 = \frac{V_0}{\lambda}\right)$$

Отсюда смещения плотины $U_1(t)$ и земной поверхности $U_2(t)$ будут

$$U_1(t) = U_1(1 - e^{-\lambda t}), \quad U_2(t) = U_2(1 - e^{-\lambda t}) \quad (U_1 = U_0 \cos\vartheta,\ U_2 = U_0 \sin\vartheta) \tag{1.14}$$

Из выражения (1.12), учитывая (1.8) и (1.10), находим

$$G_1(\omega) = \frac{\lambda V_1}{\lambda^2 + \omega^2}, \qquad G_2(\omega) = \frac{\lambda V_2}{\lambda^2 + \omega^2} \tag{1.15}$$

Введем обозначения

$$\Psi(\alpha, k, \omega) = (1 - \cos\alpha h) G_1(\omega) / (\alpha^2 + k^2)(kg \operatorname{sh} kh - \omega^2 \operatorname{ch} kh)$$

$$S_1 = \iiint\limits_0^\infty \frac{\cos\alpha h}{\operatorname{ch} kh} \Psi(\alpha, k, \omega) \operatorname{ch} k(Y + h)\, \omega \sin\omega t\, d\alpha\, dk\, d\omega$$

$$S_2 = \iiint\limits_0^\infty \Psi(\alpha, k, \omega) \operatorname{ch} k(Y + h)\, \omega \sin\omega t\, d\alpha\, dk\, d\omega \tag{1.16}$$

$$S_3 = \iiint\limits_0^\infty \frac{\cos\alpha h}{\operatorname{ch} kh} \Psi(\alpha, k, \omega)\, k \operatorname{sh} k(Y + h) \cos\omega t\, d\alpha\, dk\, d\omega$$

$$S_4 = \iiint\limits_0^\infty \Psi(\alpha, k, \omega)\, k \operatorname{sh} k(Y + h) \cos\omega t\, d\alpha\, dk\, d\omega$$

Дифференцируя $\varphi(x, y, t)$ по t при $t > 0$, $x = U_1(t)$, имеем

$$\frac{\partial\varphi}{\partial t} = \frac{8}{\pi^3} \iiint\limits_0^\infty \frac{(1 - \cos\alpha h)\cos\alpha h}{k(\alpha^2 + k^2)\operatorname{ch} kh} G_1(\omega) [\omega \sin\omega t \operatorname{sh} kY +$$

$$+ V_2 e^{-\lambda t} k \operatorname{ch} kY \cos\omega t]\, d\alpha\, dk\, d\omega - \frac{8g}{\pi^3} [S_1 - S_2 + V_2 e^{-\lambda t}(S_3 - S_4)] +$$

$$+ U_2 g(e^{-\lambda t} - 1) - \lambda V_2 Y e^{-\lambda t} - V_2^2 e^{-2\lambda t} -$$

$$- \frac{4}{\pi^2} \iint\limits_0^\infty \frac{(1 - \cos\alpha h)}{\alpha^2} G_1(\omega) [\omega \sin\omega t \sin\alpha Y +$$

$$+ \alpha(V_2 \cos\alpha Y - V_1 \sin\alpha Y) e^{-\lambda t} \cos\omega t]\, d\alpha\, d\omega \tag{1.17}$$

Начнем с рассмотрения S_1. Сначала интегрируем по переменному ω, при этом имеем

$$T = \lambda V_1 \int\limits_0^\infty \frac{\omega \sin\omega t\, d\omega}{(\omega^2 + \lambda^2)(kg \operatorname{sh} kh - \omega^2 \operatorname{ch} kh)} = \frac{\pi\lambda}{2} V_1 \frac{e^{-\lambda t} - \cos\sqrt{kg \operatorname{th} kh}\, t}{kg \operatorname{sh} kh + \lambda^2 \operatorname{ch} kh} \tag{1.18}$$

Введем обозначение $M_1 = \sqrt{kg \operatorname{th} kh}$. Подстановка (1.18) в выражение (1.16) для S_1 дает

$$S_1 = \frac{\pi\lambda}{2} V_1 (R_1 e^{-\lambda t} - R_2) \tag{1.19}$$

где

$$R_1 = \iint\limits_0^\infty \frac{(1 - \cos\alpha h)\cos\alpha h \operatorname{ch} k(Y + h)\, d\alpha\, dk}{(\alpha^2 + k^2)(kg \operatorname{sh} kh + \lambda^2 \operatorname{ch} kh)\operatorname{ch} kh}$$

$$R_2 = \iint\limits_0^\infty \frac{(1 - \cos\alpha h)\cos\alpha h \operatorname{ch} k(Y + h)\cos M_1 t}{(\alpha^2 + k^2)(kg \operatorname{sh} kh + \lambda^2 \operatorname{ch} kh)\operatorname{ch} kh}\, d\alpha\, dk$$

Так как интегралы (1.19) равномерно сходятся относительно α и k, то мы можем изменять порядок интегрирования, т. е. будем интегрировать сначала по k. Перепишем R_1 в следующем виде

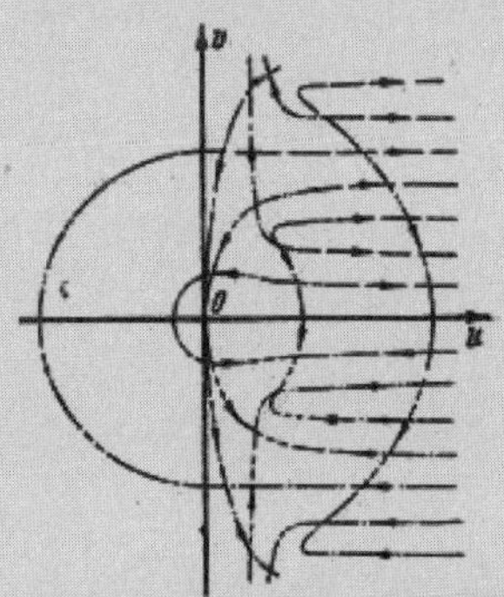

Фиг. 1

$$R_1 = \int_0^\infty (1 - \cos \alpha h) \cos \alpha h \, d\alpha R_1^* \tag{1.20}$$

$$\left(R_1^* = \int_0^\infty \frac{\operatorname{ch} k (Y + h) \, dk}{(\alpha^2 + k^2)(kg \operatorname{sh} kh + \lambda^2 \operatorname{ch} kh) \operatorname{ch} kh} \right)$$

Вычислим R_1^*, пользуясь теорией вычетов. На комплексной плоскости имеем два корня $\pm i\alpha$ и бесконечное число корней $\pm im\pi/2h$, где $m = 1, 3, 5, \ldots, \infty$ для уравнений $\alpha^2 + k^2 = 0$ и $\operatorname{ch} kh = 0$ соответственно. Чтобы найти корни трансцендентного уравнения $kg \operatorname{sh} kh + \lambda^2 \operatorname{ch} kh = 0$, введем новую переменную $kh = \gamma$ и преобразуем его к виду

$$\gamma \operatorname{th} \gamma = \mu \qquad (\mu = -\lambda^2 h / g = (\eta^2 - \xi^2 - i2\eta\xi) h / g) \tag{1.21}$$

Воспользуемся конформным отображением

$$w = f(z') = z' \operatorname{th} z' \qquad (w = u + iv, \; z' = x' + iy') \tag{1.22}$$

Отсюда

$$u = \frac{x' \operatorname{sh} 2x' - y' \sin 2y'}{\cos 2y' + \operatorname{ch} 2x'}, \qquad v = \frac{y' \operatorname{sh} 2x' + x' \sin 2y'}{\cos 2y' + \operatorname{ch} 2x'} \tag{1.23}$$

Из формулы (1.23) и фиг. 1,2 видно, что отображение (1.22) преобразует параллельные прямые $\pm n\pi/4$, где $n = 1, \ldots, 8$, на плоскости z' в кривые на плоскости w. При помощи этих фигур, при известном μ, найдем корни уравнения (1.21) на плоскости z', соответствующие точке μ на плоскости w. Кроме того, посредством последовательных приближений из формул (1.21) и (1.23) получим искомые γ с нужной степенью точности. Из фиг. 1,2 и формулы (1.23) видим, что уравнение (1.21) имеет следующие корни: при μ являющейся комплексной постоянной, — несколько комплексных корней (два, четыре и т. д.); при $\mu < 0$ — бесконечное число мнимых корней; при $\mu > 0$ — два вещественных корня и бесконечное число мнимых корней; при μ — мнимой постоянной — несколько комплексных корней. Последнему случаю соответствует $\xi = \eta$.

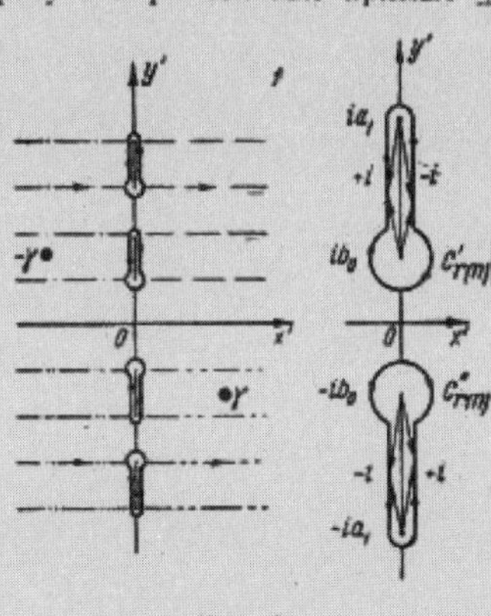

Фиг. 2

В качестве примера предположим, что $\xi < \eta$ и точка μ расположена, как указано на фиг. 1.

После ряда интегрирований находим

$$R_1 = -i\frac{\pi^2 h}{2}\frac{(1-\operatorname{ch}\gamma)\operatorname{ch}[\gamma(Y+h)/h]}{g[\gamma^2-(1+\mu)\mu]\operatorname{ch}^2\gamma}e^{-\gamma}+\frac{\pi}{2}\int_0^\infty\frac{(1-\cos\alpha h)\cos\alpha(Y+h)\,d\alpha}{\alpha(\lambda^2\cos\alpha h-\alpha g\sin\alpha h)}+$$

$$+\pi\int_0^\infty\sum_{m=1,3}^{\infty}\frac{\cos C(Y+h)\cos\alpha h}{gC(C^2-\alpha^2)h}(1-\cos\alpha h)\,d\alpha\qquad\binom{\gamma=p-iq}{C=m\pi/2h}\tag{1.24}$$

Здесь p, q — вещественные постоянные.

Возвращаясь к вычислению R_2, рассмотрим интеграл

$$R_2{}^*=\int_0^\infty\frac{\operatorname{ch}k(Y+h)\cos M_1 t\,dk}{(\alpha^2+k^2)(kg\operatorname{sh}kh+\lambda^2\operatorname{ch}kh)\operatorname{ch}kh}\tag{1.25}$$

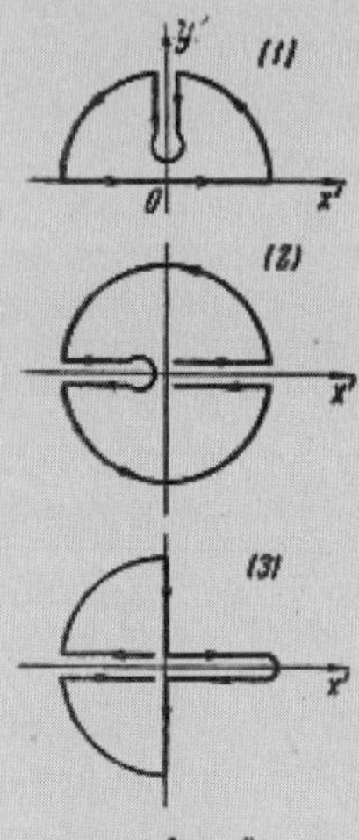

Фиг. 3

Для вычисления этого интеграла выберем три вспомогательные функции

$$F_1(z')=\frac{\operatorname{ch}z'(Y+h)\exp[iM_1(z')t]}{(\alpha^2+z'^2)(z'g\operatorname{sh}z'h+\lambda^2\operatorname{ch}z'h)\operatorname{ch}z'h}$$

$$F_2(z')=\frac{\cos z'(Y+h)\exp[-M_2(z')t]}{(\alpha^2-z'^2)(\lambda^2\cos z'h-z'g\sin z'h)\cos z'h}\tag{1.26}$$

$$F_3(z')=\frac{\cos z'(Y+h)\exp[M_2(z')t]}{(\alpha^2-z'^2)(\lambda^2\cos z'h-z'g\sin z'h)\cos z'h}$$

и соответствующие контуры, изображенные на фиг. 3, где контур (*1*) находится на плоскости *1* (фиг. 2), а контуры (*2*) и (*3*) размещаются на плоскости *1'* получающейся из плоскости *1* преобразованием (x', y') на $(-y', x')$ и поворотом на 90° по часовой стрелке. При этом имеем два корня $\pm i\gamma$ на преобразованной плоскости, соответствующего уравнению $\lambda^2\cos z'h - z'g\sin z'h=0$.

Прежде чем перейти к контурному интегрированию, изучим многозначные функции

$$M_1(z')=\sqrt{z'g\operatorname{th}z'h},\qquad M_2(z')=\sqrt{z'g\operatorname{tg}z'h}\tag{1.27}$$

Разложив $\operatorname{th}z'h$ и $\operatorname{tg}z'h$ в бесконечные произведения

$$\operatorname{th}\chi=\chi\prod_{n=1}^{\infty}\left(1+\frac{\chi^2}{n^2\pi^2}\right)\Big/\prod_{n=0}^{\infty}\left(1+\frac{4\chi^2}{(2n+1)^2\pi^2}\right)$$

$$\operatorname{tg}\chi=\chi\prod_{n=1}^{\infty}\left(1-\frac{\chi^2}{n^2\pi^2}\right)\Big/\prod_{n=0}^{\infty}\left(1-\frac{4\chi^2}{(2n+1)^2\pi^2}\right)\tag{1.28}$$

где $\chi = z'h$, получим

$$M_1(z')=z'C_0\sqrt{\frac{z'-ia_1}{z'-ib_0}}\sqrt{\frac{z'+ia_1}{z'+ib_0}}\sqrt{\frac{z'-ia_2}{z'-ib_1}}\cdots$$

$$M_2(z')=z'C_0\sqrt{\frac{z'-a_1}{z'-b_0}}\sqrt{\frac{z'+a_1}{z'+b_0}}\sqrt{\frac{z'-a_2}{z'-b_1}}\cdots\tag{1.29}$$

где C_0, b_0, a_1, b_1, a_2 — вещественные постоянные, причем $a_{n+1}=(n+1)\pi/h$, $b_n=(2n+1)\pi/2h$. Отсюда видим, что функция $M_1(z')$ имеет бесконечное число точек разветвлении, находящихся на мнимой оси, а $M_2(z')$ имеет такие же точки, но они находятся на вещественной оси.

Вырежем плоскость z', как указано на фиг. 2. После этого внутри соответствующего контура в многосвязной области функции $M_1(z')$ $M_2(z')$ будут однозначны. Положим

$$M_1^*(z') = M_1(z')/z'$$

Значениями аргументов будут соответственно на левом и правом берегах разрезов, находящихся на положительной мнимой оси

$$\arg M_1^*(z') = \tfrac{1}{2}\left[-\tfrac{1}{2}\pi - \left(\tfrac{1}{2}\pi - 2\pi\right) + 0 + 0 + \cdots\right] = \tfrac{1}{2}\pi$$

$$\arg M_1^*(z') = \tfrac{1}{2}\left(-\tfrac{1}{2}\pi - \tfrac{1}{2}\pi + 0 + 0 + \cdots\right) = -\tfrac{1}{2}\pi$$

Вследствие этого на левом и правом берегах функция $M_1^*(z')$ имеет соответственно $+i$, $-i$ перед корнем. Аналогичным путем определим $\arg M_1^*(z')$ на соответствующих берегах отрезков, помещающихся на отрицательной мнимой оси (фиг. 2).

Заметим, что при интегрированиях по контурам (*1*) и (*3*) обходы принимают направления, указанные стрелками на фиг. 2, а по контуру (*2*) — по часовой стрелке. Применяя теорему о вычетах, получаем

$$\oint_{(1)\,l} F_1(z')\,dz' = 2R_2^* + iN_1 + iN_2 + \sum_{n=0}^{\infty} \lim_{r\to 0} \int_{C'_{r(n)}} F_1(z')\,dz' = -iN^* e^{-\lambda t} + f_1^*(\alpha, Y, t) \tag{1.30}$$

$$\oint_{(2)\,l'} F_2(z')\,dz' = 2N_1 + 2N_2 + H_1 + \sum_{n=0}^{\infty} \lim_{r\to 0} \int_{C'_{r(n)}} F_2(z')\,dz' = N^*\left(e^{\lambda t} - e^{-\lambda t}\right) + f_2^*(\alpha, Y, t)$$

$$\oint_{(3)\,l'} F_3(z')\,dz' = -i2R_2^* + H_2 + \sum_{n=0}^{\infty} \lim_{r\to 0} \int_{C''_{r(n)}} F_3(z')\,dz' + f_3^*(\alpha, Y, t) = -N^* e^{-\lambda t}$$

Здесь

$$N_1 = \sum_{n=0}^{\infty} \int_{a_{n+1}}^{b_n} \frac{\cos k(Y+h)\exp(iM_2 t)\,dk}{(\alpha^2 - k^2)(\lambda^2 \cos kh - kg \sin kh)\cos kh}$$

$$N_2 = \sum_{n=0}^{\infty} \int_{b_n}^{a_{n+1}} \frac{\cos k(Y+h)\exp(-iM_2 t)\,dk}{(\alpha^2 - k^2)(\lambda^2 \cos kh - kg \sin kh)\cos kh}$$

$$N^* = \frac{2\pi\gamma h^2 \operatorname{ch}[\gamma(Y+h)/h]}{g(\alpha^2 h^2 + \gamma^2)\,\Gamma(\gamma, \mu)\operatorname{ch}^2\gamma}, \qquad M_2 = \sqrt{kg \operatorname{tg} kh}, \qquad \Gamma(\gamma, \mu) = \gamma^2 - (1+\mu)\mu$$

Здесь $f_\nu^*(\alpha, Y, t)$ — некоторые функции α, Y и t, где $\nu = 1, 2, 3$.

Очевидно, что все интегралы по дугам больших окружностей равны нулю при стремлении их радиусов к ∞. Рассмотрим интегралы под знаками сумм в формулах (1.30) и проинтегрируем их по малым окружностям $C'_{r(n)}$ и $C''_{r(n)}$.

При стремлении радиусов окружностей к нулю имеем

$$\sum_{n=0}^{\infty} \lim_{r\to 0} \int_{C'_{r(n)}} F_1(z')\,dz' = \tag{1.31}$$

$$= -i\sum_{n=0}^{\infty} C_n \lim_{r\to 0} \int_{\pi/2}^{-3\pi/2} \exp\left[-\frac{C_n^{(1)}}{\sqrt{r}}(1-i)\exp\left(\frac{-i\beta}{2}\right)\right]d\beta =$$

$$= -i2\sum_{n=0}^{\infty} C_n \lim_{r\to 0} \int_{\pi/2}^{-\pi/2} \exp\left[-\frac{C_n^{(2)}}{\sqrt{r}}(\cos\varkappa - i\sin\varkappa)\right]d\varkappa \to 0$$

Здесь C_n, $C_n^{(1)}$, $C_n^{(2)}$ — некоторые положительные постоянные, β, $\varkappa$ — аргументы. Равным образом можно доказать, что

$$\sum_{n=0}^{\infty} \lim_{r\to 0} \int_{C'_{r(n)}} F_2(z')\,dz' \to 0, \qquad \sum_{n=0}^{\infty} \lim_{r\to 0} \int_{C''_{r(n)}} F_3(z')\,dz' \to 0 \tag{1.32}$$

Заметим, что

$$H_1 = \sum_{n=0}^{\infty} \lim_{r\to 0} \int_{C''_{r(n)}} F_2(z')\,dz' = i2\sum_{n=0}^{\infty} C_n \lim_{r\to 0} \int_{\pi/2}^{-\pi/2} \exp\left[\frac{C_n^{(1)}}{\sqrt{r}}(\cos\varkappa - i\sin\varkappa)\right]d\varkappa$$

$$(1.33)$$

$$H_2 = \sum_{n=0}^{\infty} \lim_{r\to 0} \int_{C'_{r(n)}} F_3(z')\,dz' =$$

$$= -i\sum_{n=0}^{\infty} C_n \lim_{r\to 0} \int_{2\pi}^{0} \exp\left[i\frac{C_n^{(1)}}{\sqrt{r}}\exp\left(\frac{-i\beta}{2}\right)\right]d\beta = -H_1$$

Из системы уравнений (1.30) и соотношений (1.31), (1.32), (1.33) найдется искомый интеграл

$$R_2^* = -iN^* e^{\lambda t}/2 + f^*(\alpha,\ Y,\ t) \tag{1.34}$$

Подставив (1.34) и (1.24) в формулу (1.19) и произведя для R_2 интегрирование по α, получим

$$S_1 = i\frac{\pi^3}{2}\lambda h e^{-\gamma}V_1 \frac{(1-\operatorname{ch}\gamma)\operatorname{sh}\lambda t}{g\Gamma(\gamma,\ \mu)\operatorname{ch}^2\gamma}\operatorname{ch}\left[\frac{\gamma}{h}(Y+h)\right] + e^{-\lambda t}\int_0^{\infty} f_1(\alpha,\ Y)\,d\alpha +$$

$$+\int_0^{\infty} f_2(\alpha,\ Y,\ t)\,d\alpha + \frac{\pi^2}{2}\lambda e^{-\lambda t}V_1\int_0^{\infty}\sum_{m=1,\,3}^{\infty}\frac{\cos C(Y+h)\cos\alpha h}{gC(C^2-\alpha^2)h}(1-\cos\alpha h)\,d\alpha \tag{1.35}$$

Таким же путем найдем (1.36)

$$S_2 = i\frac{\pi^3}{2}\lambda h V_1 \frac{\operatorname{ch}[\gamma(Y+h)/h]}{g\Gamma(\gamma,\mu)\operatorname{ch}\gamma}(1-e^{-\gamma})\operatorname{sh}\lambda t + e^{-\lambda t}\int_0^\infty f_1(\alpha, Y)d\alpha + \int_0^\infty f_2(\alpha, Y, t)d\alpha$$

$$S_3 = -i\frac{\pi^3}{2}\gamma e^{-\gamma}V_1 \frac{(1-\operatorname{ch}\gamma)\operatorname{ch}\lambda t}{g\Gamma(\gamma,\mu)\operatorname{ch}^2\gamma}\operatorname{sh}\left[\frac{\gamma}{h}(Y+h)\right] + e^{-\lambda t}\int_0^\infty f_3(\alpha, Y)\,d\alpha +$$

$$+\int_0^\infty f_4(\alpha, Y, t)\,d\alpha + \frac{\pi^2}{2}e^{-\lambda t}V_1\int_0^\infty \sum_{m=1,3}^{\infty}\frac{\sin C(Y+h)\cos\alpha h}{gh(\alpha^2-C^2)}(1-\cos\alpha h)\,d\alpha$$

$$S_4 = -i\frac{\pi^3}{2}\gamma V_1 \frac{\operatorname{sh}[\gamma(Y+h)/h]}{g\Gamma(\gamma,\mu)\operatorname{ch}\gamma}(1-e^{-\gamma})\operatorname{ch}\lambda t + e^{-\lambda t}\int_0^\infty f_3(\alpha, Y)d\alpha + \int_0^\infty f_4(\alpha, Y, t)d\alpha$$

Подставив формулы (1.35) и (1.36) в (1.17) и вычислив остальные интегралы, окончательно получим

$$\frac{\partial\varphi}{\partial t} = i4\mu\lambda h V_1 \frac{\operatorname{ch}[\gamma(Y+h)/h]}{\gamma\Gamma(\gamma,\mu)\operatorname{ch}\gamma}\operatorname{sh}\lambda t - i4\mu e^{-\lambda t}V_1V_2\frac{\operatorname{sh}[\gamma(Y+h)/h]}{\Gamma(\gamma,\mu)\operatorname{ch}\gamma}\operatorname{ch}\lambda t -$$

$$-\lambda V_2 Y e^{-\lambda t} - (V_1^2+V_2^2)e^{-2\lambda t} + U_2 g(e^{-\lambda t}-1) \qquad (1.37)$$

при $t>0$, $Y<0$, $x=U_1(t)$. Таким же образом находим при $t>0$, $Y<0$, $x=U_1(t)$

$$\frac{\partial\varphi}{\partial y} = i4\mu V_1\frac{\operatorname{sh}[\gamma(Y+h)/h]}{\Gamma(\gamma,\mu)\operatorname{ch}\gamma}\operatorname{ch}\lambda t + V_2 e^{-\lambda t} \qquad (1.38)$$

Нетрудно найти

$$\frac{\partial\varphi}{\partial x} = V_1 e^{-\lambda t} \qquad (1.39)$$

Чтобы определить динамическое давление жидкости при $t=0$, обращаемся к формуле (1.17). Проинтегрировав по переменному ω, полагая $t=0$, имеем

$$\frac{\partial\varphi}{\partial t} = \frac{4}{\pi^2}\lambda V_1\iint_0^\infty \frac{(1-\cos\alpha h)\cos\alpha h}{k(\alpha^2+k^2)\operatorname{ch}kh}\operatorname{sh}kY\,d\alpha\,dk +$$

$$+\frac{4}{\pi^2}V_1V_2\iint_0^\infty\frac{(1-\cos\alpha h)\cos\alpha h}{(\alpha^2+k^2)\operatorname{ch}kh}\operatorname{ch}kY\,d\alpha\,dk -$$

$$-\frac{4g}{\pi^2}V_1V_2\iint_0^\infty\frac{(1-\cos\alpha h)k\operatorname{sh}k(Y+h)}{(\alpha^2+k^2)(kg\operatorname{sh}kh+\lambda^2\operatorname{ch}kh)}\left(\frac{\cos\alpha h}{\operatorname{ch}kh}-1\right)d\alpha\,dk - \lambda V_2 Y - V_2^2 - V_1^2 -$$

$$-\frac{2}{\pi}V_1\int_0^\infty\frac{(1-\cos\alpha h)}{\alpha^2}(\lambda\sin\alpha Y + V_2\alpha\cos\alpha Y)\,d\alpha \qquad (1.40)$$

Выполнив для первого двойного интеграла (1.40) интегрирование сначала по α, а для второго и третьего двойных интегралов — сначала по k, найдем при $t=0$, $y<0$, $x=0$

(1.41)

$$\frac{\partial\varphi}{\partial t} = -\frac{2\lambda}{h}V_1\sum_{m=1,3}^{\infty}\frac{\sin CY}{C^2} - i2\mu V_1V_2\frac{\operatorname{sh}[\gamma(Y+h)/h]}{\Gamma(\gamma,\mu)\operatorname{ch}\gamma} - \lambda V_2 Y - V_1^2 - V_2^2$$

9*

Отметим, что при вычислении $\partial\varphi/\partial y$ интегрируем все двойные интегралы вначале по k. Интегрирование дает

$$\frac{\partial\varphi}{\partial y} = i2\mu V_1 \frac{\operatorname{sh}[\gamma(Y+h)/h]}{\Gamma(\gamma, \mu)\operatorname{ch}\gamma} + V_2 \qquad \left(\frac{\partial\varphi}{\partial x} = V_1\right) \tag{1.42}$$

2°. Перейдем теперь к изучению динамического давления на плотину, образованного ее импульсивным действием на жидкость. Предположим, что

$$V(t) = V_0 e^{-\xi t} \tag{1.43}$$

Итак, действительно, после замены λ на ξ формулы (1.12) — (1.19) действуют и для этого случая. Отметим, что при вычислениях интегралов S_1, S_2, S_3, S_4 оба случая различны, так как в этом случае урав-

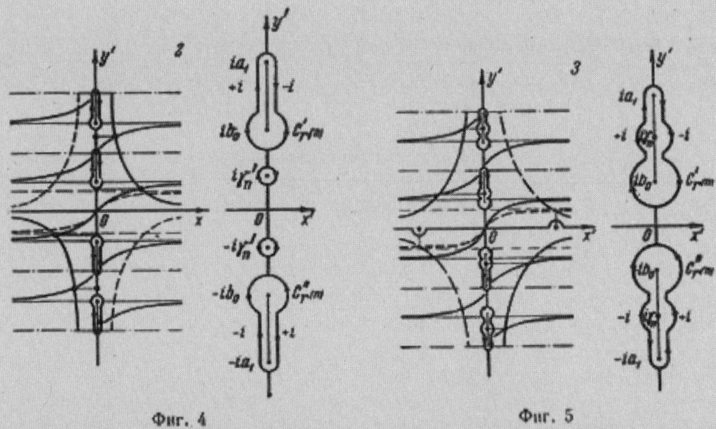

Фиг. 4 Фиг. 5

нение $kg \operatorname{sh} kh + \xi^2 \operatorname{ch} kh = 0$ имеет бесконечное число корней, γ_n', где $n = 1, 2, 3, \ldots$, лежащих на мнимой оси, как указано на фиг. 4.

Для вычисления R_2^* выберем те же вспомогательные функции и контуры интегрований, но при этом в выражениях (1.25) и (1.26) вместо λ будет ξ, причем контур (*1*) расположен на плоскости *2* (фиг. 4), а контуры (*2*) и (*3*) помещены на плоскости 2′, полученной из плоскости *2* преобразованием (x', y') на $(-y', x')$ и поворотом на 90° по часовой стрелке. Заметим эти свойства подынтегральных функций и приступая к интегрированию, имеем

$$\oint_{(1)2} F_1(z')\,dz' = 2R_2^* + iN_1 + iN_2 - L^* e^{-\xi t} + f_1^*(\alpha, Y, t) = 0 \tag{1.44}$$

$$\oint_{(2)2'} F_2(z')\,dz' = 2N_1 + 2N_2 + H_1 - iL^*(e^{\xi t} - e^{-\xi t}) + f_2^*(\alpha, Y, t) = 0$$

$$\oint_{(3)2'} F_3(z')\,dz' = -i2R_2^* + H_2 + iL^*(e^{\xi t} + e^{-\xi t}) + f_3^*(\alpha, Y, t) = 0$$

где N_1, N_2 — такие же обозначения, как в (1.30), но вместо λ будет ξ

$$L^* = 2\pi \sum_{n=1}^{\infty} \frac{\gamma'_{nh^2} \cos[\gamma'_n (Y+h)/h]}{g(\alpha^2 h^2 - \gamma'^2_n)\, \Gamma(\gamma_n', \sigma) \cos^2 \gamma'_n}$$

$$\left(\Gamma(\gamma'_n, \sigma) = \gamma_n'^2 + (1+\sigma h) h\sigma, \quad \sigma = \frac{\xi^2}{g}\right)$$

которое получено путем интегрирования по малым окружностям с центрами в точках γ_n' с радиусами, стремящимися к нулю.

Из системы уравнений (1.44) найдется R_2^*. После ряда соответствующих интегрирований получим

$$\frac{\partial \varphi}{\partial t} = 2\xi\sigma h^2 V_1 \sum_{n=1}^{\infty} \frac{\cos[\gamma'_n (Y+h)/h]}{\gamma_n' \Gamma(\gamma_n', \sigma) \cos \gamma_n'} e^{-\xi t} - 2\sigma h V_1 V_2 \sum_{n=1}^{\infty} \frac{\sin[\gamma'_n (Y+h)/h]}{\Gamma(\gamma'_n, \sigma) \cos \gamma_n'} e^{-2\xi t} -$$

$$- \xi V'_2 Y e^{-\xi t} - (V_2^2 + V_2^2) e^{-2\xi t} - U_2 g (1 - e^{-\xi t}) \qquad (1.45)$$

$$\frac{\partial \varphi}{\partial y} = 2\sigma h V_1 \sum_{n=1}^{\infty} \frac{\sin[\gamma_n' (Y+h)/h]}{\Gamma(\gamma_n', \sigma) \cos \gamma'_n} e^{-\xi t} + V_2 e^{-\xi t}, \qquad \frac{\partial \varphi}{\partial x} = V_1 e^{-\xi t}$$

при $t > 0$, $y < U_2(t)$, $x = U_1(t)$.

Для момента времени $t = 0$ имеем при $y < 0$, $x = 0$

$$\frac{\partial \varphi}{\partial t} = -\frac{2\xi}{h} V_1 \sum_{m=1,3}^{\infty} \frac{\sin CY}{C^2} - 2\sigma h V_1 V_2 \sum_{n=1}^{\infty} \frac{\sin[\gamma_n' (Y+h)/h]}{\Gamma(\gamma_n', \sigma) \cos \gamma_n'} - \xi V_2 Y - V_1^2 - V_2^2$$

$$\frac{\partial \varphi}{\partial y} = 2\sigma h V_1 \sum_{n=1}^{\infty} \frac{\sin[\gamma_n' (Y+h)/h]}{\Gamma(\gamma'_n, \sigma) \cos \gamma'_n} + V_2, \qquad \frac{\partial \varphi}{\partial x} = V_1 \qquad (1.46)$$

§ 2. Рассмотрим задачу о динамическом давлении жидкости на плотину, обусловленном начальными условиями

$$\varphi(x, y, 0) = 0, \qquad \frac{\partial \varphi(x, 0, 0)}{\partial t} = 0 \qquad (2.1)$$

и граничными условиями

$$\frac{\partial \varphi}{\partial x} = V_1 \sin \omega t \quad (V_1 = V_0 \cos \vartheta) \quad \text{при } x = -U_1 \cos \omega t \qquad (U_1 = U_0 \cos \vartheta) \quad (2.2)$$

$$\frac{\partial \varphi}{\partial y} = V_2 \sin \omega t \quad (V_2 = V_0 \sin \vartheta) \quad \text{при } y = -h - U_2 \cos \omega t \qquad (2.3)$$

$$(U_2 = U_0 \sin \vartheta)$$

$$\frac{\partial^2 \varphi}{\partial t^2} + g \frac{\partial \varphi}{\partial y} = 0 \qquad \text{при } y = -U_2 \cos \omega t \qquad (2.4)$$

Здесь V_0, U_0 — амплитуды скорости и смещения колеблющейся земной поверхности.

Возьмем потенциал скоростей $\varphi(x, y, t)$, который удовлетворяет $\Delta\varphi = 0$ в следующем виде

$$(2.5)$$

$$\varphi(x, y, t) = \sin \omega t \left\{ \int_0^{\infty} [B(k) \operatorname{ch} k(Y+h) + C(k) \operatorname{sh} kY] \cos kX\, dk + \right.$$

$$\left. + \int_0^{\infty} A(\alpha) \sin \alpha Y e^{-\alpha X} d\alpha \right\} + \int_0^{\infty} D(k) \operatorname{ch} k(Y+h) \cos kX \sin Mt\, dk \quad \left(\begin{matrix} X = x + U_1 \cos \omega t \\ Y = y + U_2 \cos \omega t \end{matrix}\right)$$

Здесь функции $A(\alpha)$, $B(k)$, $C(k)$ и $D(k)$ — произвольные.

Используя условия (2.1) — (2.4) при помощи интеграла Фурье, находим

$$A(\alpha)=\frac{2V_1}{\pi}\frac{(1-\cos\alpha h)}{\alpha^2},\qquad D(k)=-\frac{\omega}{M}B(k),\qquad M=\sqrt{kg\,\operatorname{th}kh}$$

$$C(k)=\frac{\delta(k)V_2}{k\operatorname{ch}kh}-\frac{4V_1}{\pi^2}\int_0^\infty\frac{(1-\cos\alpha h)\cos\alpha h}{(\alpha^2+k^2)\,k\operatorname{ch}kh}\,d\alpha \tag{2.6}$$

$$(kg\operatorname{sh}kh-\omega^2\operatorname{ch}kh)\,B(k)+kg\,C(k)=-\frac{2g}{\pi}\int_0^\infty\frac{A(\alpha)\,\alpha^2}{\alpha^2+k^2}\,d\alpha$$

Дифференцируя $\varphi(x,\ y,\ t)$ по t, при $x=-U_1\cos\omega t$ имеем

$$\frac{\partial\varphi}{\partial t}=\frac{4V_1}{\pi^2}\iint_0^\infty\frac{(1-\cos\alpha h)\cos\alpha h}{(\alpha^2+k^2)\,k\operatorname{ch}kh}\,(V_2k\operatorname{ch}kY\sin^2\omega t-\omega\cos\omega t\operatorname{sh}kY)\,d\alpha\,dk+$$

$$+\frac{4V_1}{\pi^2}\,g\,[\omega(S_5-S_6)-V_2(S_7-S_8)]+U_2g(\cos\omega t-1)+\omega V_2Y\cos\omega t-$$

$$-V_2^2\sin^2\omega t+\frac{2V_1}{\pi}\int_0^\infty\frac{(1-\cos\alpha h)}{\alpha^2}\,[\omega\cos\omega t\sin\alpha Y+ \tag{2.7}$$

$$+\alpha\sin^2\omega t\,(V_1\sin\alpha Y-V_2\cos\alpha Y)]\,d\alpha$$

Здесь

$$S_5=\cos\omega t\iint_0^\infty\Omega(\alpha,\ k)\operatorname{ch}k(Y+h)\,d\alpha\,dk$$

$$S_6=\iint_0^\infty\Omega(\alpha,\ k)\operatorname{ch}k(Y+h)\cos Mt\,d\alpha\,dk$$

$$S_7=\sin^2\omega t\iint_0^\infty\Omega(\alpha,\ k)\,k\operatorname{sh}k(Y+h)\,d\alpha\,dk$$

$$S_8=\omega\sin\omega t\iint_0^\infty\frac{\sin Mt}{M}\,\Omega(\alpha,\ k)\,k\operatorname{sh}k(Y+h)\,d\alpha\,dk$$

$$\Omega(\alpha,\ k)=(1-\cos\alpha h)(\cos\alpha h-\operatorname{ch}kh)\,/\,(\alpha^2+k^2)\quad(kg\operatorname{sh}kh-\omega^2\operatorname{ch}kh)\operatorname{ch}kh$$

Следует отметить, что при вычислении интегралов S_6 и S_8 сначала интегрируем по k, а все остальные двойные интегралы сначала по α. Приступая к вычислению S_6, рассмотрим интеграл

$$T^*=\int_0^\infty\frac{\operatorname{ch}k(Y+h)\cos Mt\,dk}{(\alpha^2+k^2)(kg\operatorname{sh}kh-\omega^2\operatorname{ch}kh)\operatorname{ch}kh} \tag{2.8}$$

Возьмем три вспомогательные функции, подобные (1.26), но вместо λ^2 будет $-\omega^2$. При этом для уравнения $kg\operatorname{sh}kh-\omega^2\operatorname{ch}kh=0$ имеем бесконечное число мнимых корней γ_n, попадающих на отрезки, указанные на фиг. 5, и два вещественных корня.

Выберем контуры интегрирований, изображенные на фиг. 3, таким образом, чтобы контур (*1*) находился на плоскости *3* (фиг. 5), а контуры (*2*) и (*3*) на плоскости 3′, которая получается из плоскости *3* преобразованием (x', y') на $(-y', x')$ и поворотом на 90° по часовой стрелке. По теореме о вычетах имеем

$$\oint_{(1)3} F_1(z')\,dz' = 2T^* - iN_3 - iN_4 + K_1^* - K_2^* + f_1^*(\alpha, Y, t) = 0$$

$$\oint_{(2)3'} F_2(z')\,dz' = 2N_3 + 2N_4 + i2K_1^* + H_1 + f_2^*(\alpha, Y, t) = 0 \qquad (2.9)$$

$$\oint_{(3)3'} F_3(z')\,dz' = i2T^* - i2K_2^* - iK_1^* + H_2 + f_3^*(\alpha, Y, t) = 0$$

где $N_3 = -N_1$, $N_4 = -N_2$, но вместо λ^2 будет $-\omega^2$,

$$K_1^* = 2\pi\gamma_s h^2 \frac{\operatorname{ch}[\gamma_s(Y+h)/h]\sin\omega t}{g(\alpha^2h^2+\gamma_s^2)\Gamma(\gamma_s, Q)\operatorname{ch}^2\gamma_s}$$

$$K_2^* = \frac{2\pi}{g}h^2\sum_{n=1}^{\infty}\frac{\gamma_n\cos[\gamma_n(Y+h)/h]\cos\omega t}{(\alpha^2h^2-\gamma_n^2)\Gamma(\gamma_n, Q)\cos^2\gamma_n}$$

$$\Gamma(\gamma_s, Q) = \gamma_s^2 + (1-Qh)Qh, \qquad \Gamma(\gamma_n, Q) = \gamma_n^2 - (1-Qh)Qh, \qquad Q = \omega^2/g$$

причем K_2^* получается путем интегрирования по малым полуокружностям с центрами в точках γ_n при стремлении радиусов полуокружностей к нулю (фиг. 5).

Из системы (2.9) находим

$$T^* = -\frac{\pi}{g}h^2\frac{\gamma_s\operatorname{ch}[\gamma_s(Y+h)/h]\sin\omega t}{(\alpha^2h^2+\gamma_s^2)\Gamma(\gamma_s, Q)\operatorname{ch}^2\gamma_s} + f^*(\alpha, Y, t) \qquad (2.10)$$

Подставив (2.10) в выражение S_6 и проинтегрировав по α, получим

$$S_6 = -\frac{\pi^2}{2g}Qh^2\frac{\operatorname{ch}[\gamma_s(Y+h)/h]}{\gamma_s\Gamma(\gamma_s, Q)\operatorname{ch}\gamma_s}\sin\omega t \qquad (2.11)$$

Аналогичным путем найдем

$$S_8 = \frac{\pi^2}{4g}Qh\frac{\operatorname{sh}[\gamma_s(Y+h)/h]}{\Gamma(\gamma_s, Q)\operatorname{ch}\gamma_s}\sin 2\omega t \qquad (2.12)$$

Вычислив остальные двойные интегралы и подставив их в (2.7) будем иметь при $t>0$, $Y<0$, $x=-U_1\cos\omega t$

$$\frac{\partial\varphi}{\partial t} = 2\omega Qh^2V_1\sum_{n=1}^{\infty}\frac{\cos[\gamma_n(Y+h)/h]}{\gamma_n\Gamma(\gamma_n, Q)\cos\gamma_n}\cos\omega t + \qquad (2.13)$$

$$+ 2QhV_1V_2\sum_{n=1}^{\infty}\frac{\sin[\gamma_n(Y+h)/h]}{\Gamma(\gamma_n, Q)\cos\gamma_n}\sin^2\omega t -$$

$$- 2\omega Qh^2V_1\frac{\operatorname{ch}[\gamma_s(Y+h)/h]}{\gamma_s\Gamma(\gamma_s, Q)\operatorname{ch}\gamma_s}\sin\omega t - QhV_1V_2\frac{\operatorname{sh}[\gamma_s(Y+h)/h]}{\Gamma(\gamma_s, Q)\operatorname{ch}\gamma_s}\sin 2\omega t +$$

$$+ \omega V_2Y\cos\omega t - U_{2}g(1-\cos\omega t) - (V_1^2+V_2^2)\sin^2\omega t$$

При $t>0$, $Y<0$, $x=-U_1\cos\omega t$ найдем (2.14)

$$\frac{\partial\varphi}{\partial y} = -2QhV_1\sum_{n=1}^{\infty}\frac{\sin[\gamma_n(Y+h)/h]}{\Gamma(\gamma_n, Q)\cos\gamma_n}\sin\omega t +$$

$$+ 2QhV_1\frac{\operatorname{sh}[\gamma_s(Y+h)/h]}{\Gamma(\gamma_s, Q)\operatorname{ch}\gamma_s}\cos\omega t + V_2\sin\omega t$$

Как известно $\partial\varphi / \partial x = V_1 \sin \omega t$. При $t = 0$, $x = -U_1$ имеем

$$\frac{\partial\varphi}{\partial t} = \frac{2\omega}{h} V_1 \sum_{m=1,3}^{\infty} \frac{\sin CY}{C^2} + \omega V_2 Y \tag{2.15}$$

Обозначая через p^* динамическое давление жидкости, а через ρ ее плотность, имеем формулу

$$\frac{p^*}{\rho} = -\frac{\partial\varphi}{\partial t} - \frac{1}{2}\left[\left(\frac{\partial\varphi}{\partial x}\right)^2 + \left(\frac{\partial\varphi}{\partial y}\right)^2\right]$$

Подставим p^* в виде $p_1^* + p_2^*$, т. е. $p^* = p_1^* + p_2^*$, где p_1^* — обозначает совокупность слагаемых, не содержащих множителя V_2, а p_2^* — остальные слагаемые. Формулы (1.37) и (1.38) показывают, что p_1^* сильно возрастает, если ξ и η увеличиваются и $\xi \to \eta$, ибо при этом в выражении $\operatorname{ch}\gamma = \operatorname{ch} p \cos q - i \sin q \operatorname{sh} p$ имеет место $p \to 0$, а $q \to {}^1/_2\pi$.

Из формулы (1.45) вытекает, что в этом случае p_1^* быстро растет с увеличением ξ, потому что при этом $\gamma'_n \to {}^1/_2\,\pi$, причем давление максимального достигнет в момент времени, при котором движущаяся жидкость встречается с мгновенно остановившейся плотиной. Из формул (2.13) и (2.14) видно, что в этом случае p_1^* быстро растет при возрастании ω, так как при этом $\gamma_n \to {}^1/_2\pi$.

Из полученных результатов следует, что вертикальные колебания земной поверхности оказывают значительное влияние на нагрузку плотины как при разрушительном, так и при сильном землетрясении; действительно при этом могут иметь место соотношения $U_2\omega^2 \geqslant g$, $U_2\xi^2 \geqslant g$, $U_2\eta^2 \geqslant g$ или $U_2\xi\eta \geqslant g$, и, следовательно, p_2^* может быть больше статического давления $p^\circ = \rho g Y$. Давление p_1^* также может превзойти значение p° при некоторых определенных η, ξ, ω. Полученные выше формулы позволяют построить графики распределения динамического давления жидкости вдоль плотины, соответствующего каждому случаю.

Задача о динамическом давлении жидкости на плотину, вызванном ее колебаниями по закону $V = V_0 \cos \omega t$, была рассмотрена в работе [4].

Поступила 17 XII 1960

ЛИТЕРАТУРА

1. Лейбензон Л. С. О натуральных периодах колебаний плотины, подпирающей реку. Уч. зап. МГУ, 1935, № 2
2. Уразбаев М. Т. Сейсмостойкость гидроупругих систем. Строительная механика и расчет сооружений, 1959, вып. 5
3. Напетваридзе Ш. Г. Гидродинамическое давление при сейсмическом воздействии. Тр. Ин-та строительства АН ГрузССР, Тбилиси, 1955.
4. Чень Чжень-чен. О динамическом давлении жидкости на плотину при землетрясении. ПММ, 1961, т. XXV, вып. 1
5. Сретенский Л. Н. О направленном излучении волн из области, подверженной внешнему давлению. ПММ, 1956, т. XX, вып. 3
6. Войт С. С. Волны на поверхности жидкости, возникающие от перемещающейся периодической системы давлений. ПММ, 1957, т. XXI, вып. 1
7. Черкесов Л. В. О волнах на поверхности жидкости. Изв. АН СССР, ОТН, серия механика и машиностроение, 1959, вып. 2.

F-2·4

1975 年 11 月　　中国科学　　第 6 期

地面波动所激起而作用于水坝上的流体动压力

陈振诚

摘　要

在地震区，要使建成的水坝既能抵抗地震的剧烈振动而不毁坏，又要使坝体结构布局和建筑材料用量合理，就必须研究地震所激起的水动压力问题。本文导出了相应的流体动载荷和流体自由表面涌高的计算公式，较全面地分析了在地震时各种可能出现在坝面上的流体动压力。文中论证了可能出现的共振现象，指出对于空间问题，在某些情况下，重力和流体自由表面重力波对流体动载荷的影响必须加以考虑，并提出了地震流体动压力空间问题模拟试验的相似准则。本文最后还研究了三角形河谷和半圆形河谷的一些问题。

一、问题的提出

关于地震所激起的水动压力问题，前人曾做过一些研究。但是和资料 [1,2] 相类似，他们都假定，因地震引起的地面运动只沿河流的一个方向发生。这样就把问题归结为平面问题，从而能较简便地解决它。但事实上，在地震波的冲击下地面有起伏波动，因此地面运动是在任何方向都可能发生的，这就是说实际的问题是空间问题，要解决它就困难复杂得多。现在研究并解决这个问题。

本文假定大地在地震波的作用下是一个可以起伏波动的地层，带有水坝的河流处在这个地层中。在直角座标系中以条件 $0 \leqslant x \leqslant \infty$, $0 \leqslant y \leqslant h$, $-l \leqslant z \leqslant l$ 来表示。河流中充满理想可压缩流体，其压缩系数为 $K = 211 \times 10^6$ 公斤/米^2. 由于K很大，因此，其密度 ρ 的变化可以略去不计。坝和流体的接触面处于 $x = 0$ 的平面中，$y = 0$ 和 $y = h$ 则分别为处于流体下的地面和流体的自由表面。假定，在 $t < 0$ 时，地面是静止的，当 $t \geqslant 0$ 时，地面由于地震而引起了波动。其波长为某一有限值 λ，波速为 v。在行波的冲击下，坝体沿河流方向出现平移振动的同时还将出现转动振动，河底出现起伏的波动，河岸两壁出现振动，整个河床将出现平移和转动振动。这些振动迫使河床中的流体运动。假定，流体的运动是无旋的。由于地面波动的波幅是一阶的小量，同样地，平移振动和转动振动的位移振幅也是一阶小量。因此，从资料[4]可以确信，对于水下地面波动的边界条件可以不在波面上，而在 $y = 0$ 的平面上满足。而坝体绕坝与流体的接触面和河底交线为轴线的转动振动可以认为是绕 $x = 0$, $y = 0$ 轴线转动。河底绕自己中心线的转动可以认为是绕 $y = 0$, $z = 0$轴线转动。而河岸绕它和河底的交线的转动振动，可以认为是绕 $y = 0$, $z = l$ 及 $y = 0$, $z = -l$ 轴线的转动振动。在这些假

本文 1974 年 1 月 10 日收到。

定下所得解的结果是可用的．由于河岸两壁的振动在 z 方向有波的反射，因此需要考虑重力波对流体动载荷的影响．

假定，ξ_1, η_1, ν_1 分别为流体质点在 x, y, z 方向的位移．引入函数 $\phi(x, y, z, t)$．令

$$\frac{\partial \xi_1}{\partial t}=\frac{\partial \phi}{\partial x},\quad \frac{\partial \eta_1}{\partial t}=\frac{\partial \phi}{\partial y},\quad \frac{\partial \nu_1}{\partial t}=\frac{\partial \phi}{\partial z}.$$

设流体压力为 p，并假定 ξ_1, η_1, ν_1 为小量，可略去其二次以上的微商，则流体的运动方程为：

$$\frac{\partial^2 \xi_1}{\partial t^2}=-\frac{1}{\rho}\frac{\partial p}{\partial x},\quad \frac{\partial^2 \eta_1}{\partial t^2}=-\frac{1}{\rho}\frac{\partial p}{\partial y},\quad \frac{\partial^2 \nu_1}{\partial t^2}=-\frac{1}{\rho}\frac{\partial p}{\partial z},$$

设

$$p=-K\left(\frac{\partial \xi_1}{\partial x}+\frac{\partial \eta_1}{\partial y}+\frac{\partial \nu_1}{\partial z}\right).$$

从上列各式可以导出问题的方程：

$$\frac{\partial^2 \phi}{\partial x^2}+\frac{\partial^2 \phi}{\partial y^2}+\frac{\partial^2 \phi}{\partial z^2}=c^2\frac{\partial^2 \phi}{\partial t^2},\ c^2=\frac{\rho}{K}. \tag{1.1}$$

从问题的提法可知，问题的初始条件是 $t=0$ 时，在 $0\leqslant x\leqslant\infty$, $y=h$, $-l\leqslant z\leqslant l$ 面上

$$\frac{\partial \phi}{\partial t}=0. \tag{1.2}$$

问题的边界条件为：

$t\geqslant 0$ 时，在 $x=0$, $0\leqslant y\leqslant h$, $-l\leqslant z\leqslant l$ 面上，

$$\frac{\partial \phi}{\partial x}=(V_1+\Omega_1 y)\cos\omega_1 t, \tag{1.3}$$

在 $0\leqslant x\leqslant\infty$, $y=0$, $-l\leqslant z\leqslant l$ 面上，

$$\frac{\partial \phi}{\partial y}=V_2\cos(\sigma x+\xi)\cos\omega_3 t+\Omega_3(z+\chi)\cos\omega_3 t, \tag{1.4}$$

在 $0\leqslant x\leqslant\infty$, $0\leqslant y\leqslant h$, $z=\pm l$ 面上，

$$\frac{\partial \phi}{\partial z}=(-\Omega_4 y\mp V_4+V_3)\cos\omega_3 t, \tag{1.5}$$

在 $0\leqslant x\leqslant\infty$, $y=h$, $-l\leqslant z\leqslant l$ 面上，

$$\frac{\partial^2 \phi}{\partial t^2}+g\frac{\partial \phi}{\partial y}=0, \tag{1.6}$$

在 $x\to\infty$ 处，　$|\phi|<\infty$，　(1.7)

没有从 $x=\infty$ 向 $x=0$ 方向传来的反射波．　(1.8)

函数 $\phi(x, y, z, t)$ 是这样定义的：在 $t<0$ 时，$\phi(x, y, z, t)\equiv 0$；在 $t\geqslant 0$ 时，在整个充满流体的空间域中，$\phi(x, y, z, t)\equiv\phi(x, y, z, t)$；在无流体的空间域中，$\phi(x, y, z, t)\equiv 0$．

以上各式中 V_1 为坝体沿河流方向平移振动的速度振幅；Ω_1 为坝体绕 $x=0$, $y=0$ 轴转动的角速度振幅；V_2 为地面波动的速度振幅；Ω_3 为河底绕 $y=0$, $z=0$ 轴转动的角速度振幅；V_4 则为当河底转动振动时相对于座标而言的河宽变动速度振幅；Ω_4 则为河岸两壁绕 $y=0$, $z=-l$, 及 $y=0$, $z=l$ 轴转动的角速度振幅．将后面这三个振动分量相加起来即为整个河床绕 $y=0$, $z=0$ 轴的转动振动．因河床的实际宽度是不变的，于是，$\Omega_4=\Omega_3$, $V_4=\Omega_3 l\cdot\mathrm{tg}\,[\mu_3\sin\omega_3 t]\approx\Omega_3 l\mu_3\sin\omega_3 t$．但是，为了解题及分析研究时的清晰以及引用方便起见，拟保留

各该符号的项而不加以归并. V_3 为河岸两壁沿 x 方向平移振动的速度振幅. ω_1, ω_3 为各相应振动的圆频率. $\mu_3 = \Omega_3/\omega_3$ 为角位移振幅.

σ, ξ, χ 为实常量, 其中 $\sigma = 2\pi/\lambda$, λ 为地震波的波长. ξ 为与坝体在地震波段上所处的位置相关的量. 例如在 $\xi = n\pi$, $n = 0, 2, 4, 6, \cdots$ 时,地表面沿 x 在 y 方向以余弦的规律波动,水坝处在其波峰顶点,而在 $n = 1, 3, 5, \cdots$ 时, 水坝处在其波谷的最低点上. 当 $\xi = \frac{m\pi}{2}$ $(m = 1, 3, 5, \cdots)$ 时,地表面沿 x 在 y 方向以正弦的规律波动, 水坝处在其波峰波谷之间线段的中点上. 在 $0 < \xi < \frac{\pi}{2}$, $\frac{\pi}{2} < \xi < \pi$ 时, 地表面沿 x 在 y 方向以余弦波和正弦波叠加的形式波动,水坝处在峰、谷之间线段的某点上振动. 其余类推. χ 为与河床转动时的转动轴所处位置相关的量. 例如,当 $\chi = 0$ 时,河床绕 $y = 0$, $z = 0$ 轴转动振动; 在 $\chi = -l$ 时, 河床绕 $y = 0$, $z = l$ 轴转动振动; 当 $-l < \chi < 0$ 时, 河床绕 $y = 0$, $0 < z < l$ 间的某轴转动振动. 其余类推. g 为重力加速度, t 为时间.

二、问题的解法

根据上述问题的提出,就可以把问题的求解归结为寻找满足上述方程(1.1)和条件(1.2)—(1.8)式的函数 $\psi(x, y, z, t)$. 现在,首先来研究

1. 当 $\xi = 0$, $\chi = 0$ 的情况. 令

$$\psi(x, y, z, t) = \psi_1(x, y, z, t) + \psi_2(x, y, z, t) + \psi_3(x, y, z, t), \tag{2.1}$$

并给出满足方程(1.1)和条件(1.2)的

$$\psi_1(x, y, z, t) = \Psi_1(x, y, z)\cos\omega_1 t, \quad \psi_2(x, y, z, t) = \Psi_2(x, y, z)\cos\omega_3 t,$$
$$\psi_3(x, y, z, t) = \Psi_3(x, y, z)\cos\omega_3 t, \tag{2.2}$$

此处

$$\Psi_1(x, y, z) = \sum_{m=1,3}^{\infty} A(m)\cos C_m y e^{-a_m z} + \int_0^{\infty} B(k)\,\mathrm{ch}\, by\cos kx dk,$$

$$\Psi_2(x, y, z) = \frac{1}{2\pi i}\int_{C_0-i\infty}^{C_0+i\infty} C(\nu)[\beta\cos\beta(y-h) + Q_3\sin\beta(y-h)]e^{\nu x}d\nu$$
$$+ \int_0^{\infty} D(\alpha)\cos\alpha y e^{-vx}d\alpha + \int_0^{\infty} E(k)\mathrm{ch}by\cos kx dk,$$

$$\beta = \sqrt{\nu^2 + H^2},\ v = \sqrt{\alpha^2 - H^2},\ b = \sqrt{k^2 - H^2},$$

$$\Psi_3(x, y, z) = \sum_{m=1,3}^{\infty}\int_0^{\infty} F(m, k)\cos C_m y\mathrm{ch}q_m z\cos kx dk + \Psi_{31}(x, y, z) + \Psi_{32}(x, y, z),$$

$$\Psi_{31}(x, y, z) = \sum_{m=1,3}^{\infty}\int_0^{\infty} G(m, k)\cos C_m y\mathrm{sh}q_m z\cos kx dk$$
$$+ \int_0^{\infty}\sum_{n=1,2}^{\infty}[H(n, k)\mathrm{sh}r_n(y-h) + I(n, k)\mathrm{ch}r_n y]\sin D_n z\cos kx dk,$$

$$\Psi_{32}(x, y, z) = \sum_{n=1,2}^{\infty}\int_0^{\infty} J(n, k)\cos R_n z\mathrm{ch}S_n y\cos kx dk,\ R_n = \frac{n\pi}{l},\ n = 1, 2, 3, \cdots.$$

式中 $C_m = m\pi/2h$, $m = 1, 3, 5, \cdots$; C_0 为某一实常量; ν 为复数; $Q_3 = \omega_3^2/g$, $D_n = (2n -$

$-1)\pi/2l$, $\alpha_m=\sqrt{C_m^2-H^2}$, $q_m=\sqrt{C_m^2+k^2-H^2}$, $r_n=\sqrt{D_n^2+k^2-H^2}$, $S_n=\sqrt{R_n^2+k^2-H^2}$, $H=c\omega$.

在下列方程和关系式成立时，(2.1)式就能满足边界条件(1.3)—(1.6)式.

$$-\sum_{m=1,3}^{\infty}A(m)\alpha_m\cos C_m y=V_1+\Omega_1 y,\quad \mathscr{H}(k,Q_1)=b\,\mathrm{sh}\,bh-Q_1\mathrm{ch}\,bh,\tag{2.3}$$

$$\int_0^{\infty}B(k)\mathscr{H}(k,Q_1)\cos kx\,dk=\sum_{m=1,3}^{\infty}A(m)C_m\sin M\,e^{-\alpha_m x},\quad M=\frac{m\pi}{2},\tag{2.4}$$

$$\frac{1}{2\pi i}\int_{C_0-i\infty}^{C_0+i\infty}C(\nu)\beta\mathscr{K}(\nu,Q_3)e^{\nu x}d\nu=V_2\cos\sigma x,\quad \mathscr{K}(\nu,Q_3)=\beta\sin\beta h+Q_3\cos\beta h,\tag{2.5}$$

$$\int_0^{\infty}D(\alpha)v\cos\alpha y\,d\alpha=\frac{1}{2\pi i}\int_{C_0-i\infty}^{C_0+i\infty}C(\nu)\nu[\beta\cos\beta(y-h)+Q_3\sin\beta(y-h)]d\nu,\tag{2.6}$$

$$\int_0^{\infty}E(k)\mathscr{H}(k,Q_3)\cos kx\,dk=\int_0^{\infty}D(\alpha)\mathscr{K}(\alpha,Q_3)e^{-vx}d\alpha,\tag{2.7}$$

$$\sum_{m=1,3}^{\infty}\int_0^{\infty}F(m,k)q_m\mathrm{sh}\,q_m l\cos C_m y\cos kx\,dk=-V_4,\tag{2.8}$$

$$\sum_{m=1,3}^{\infty}\int_0^{\infty}G(m,k)q_m\mathrm{ch}\,q_m l\cos C_m y\cos kx\,dk=-\Omega_4 y+V_5,\tag{2.9}$$

$$\sum_{n=1,2}^{\infty}\int_0^{\infty}H(n,k)r_n\,\mathrm{ch}\,r_n h\sin D_n z\cos kx\,dk=\Omega_3 z,\tag{2.10}$$

$$\int_0^{\infty}\cos kx\left\{\sum_{n=1,2}^{\infty}\sin D_n z[I(n,k)f_1(n)+H(n,k)r_n]-\sum_{m=1,3}^{\infty}G(m,k)C_m\mathrm{sh}\,q_m z\sin M\right\}dk=0,\tag{2.11}$$

$$\sum_{n=1,2}^{\infty}\int_0^{\infty}J(n,k)f_2(n)\cos R_n z\cos kx\,dk=\sum_{m=1,3}^{\infty}\int_0^{\infty}F(m,k)C_m\sin M\,\mathrm{ch}\,q_m z\cos kx\,dk.\tag{2.12}$$

式中

$$Q_1=\omega_1^2/g,\quad \mathscr{H}(k,Q_3)=b\,\mathrm{sh}\,bh-Q_3\mathrm{ch}\,bh,\quad \mathscr{K}(\alpha,Q_3)=\alpha\sin\alpha h+Q_3\cos\alpha h.$$

$$f_1(n)=r_n\,\mathrm{sh}\,r_n h-Q_3\,\mathrm{ch}\,r_n h,\quad f_2(n)=S_n\,\mathrm{sh}\,S_n h-Q_3\,\mathrm{ch}\,S_n h.$$

解出上列积分方程和关系式，经整理化简，可得(2.1)中所有未知函数的解析表示式：

$$A(m)=\frac{2}{C_m\alpha_m}\left[\frac{\Omega_1}{M}-\left(\Omega_1+\frac{V_1}{h}\right)\sin M\right],\quad B(k)=\frac{2}{\pi}\sum_{m=1,3}^{\infty}\frac{\alpha_m C_m A(m)\sin M}{(k^2+\alpha_m^2)\mathscr{H}(k,Q_1)},$$

$$C(\nu)=\frac{\nu V_2}{(\sigma^2+\nu^2)\beta\mathscr{K}(\nu,Q_3)},\quad D(\alpha)=\frac{1}{i\pi^2}\int_{C_0-i\infty}^{C_0+i\infty}C(\nu)\frac{\mathscr{K}(\alpha,Q_3)-\mathscr{K}(\nu,Q_3)}{v(\alpha^2-\beta^2)}\nu\beta\,d\nu,$$

$$E(k)=\frac{2}{\pi}\int_0^{\infty}\frac{vD(\alpha)\mathscr{K}(\alpha,Q_3)}{(k^2+v^2)\mathscr{H}(k,Q_3)}d\alpha,\quad F(m,k)=-\frac{2V_4\delta(k)\sin M}{M\,q_m\mathrm{sh}\,q_m l},$$

$$I(n,k)=-\frac{1}{f_1(n)}\left[r_n H(n,k)+\frac{(-1)^n}{l}\sum_{m=1,3}^{\infty}2\frac{C_m q_m G(m,k)\mathrm{ch}\,q_m l}{(D_n^2+q_m^2)\sin M}\right],\quad \delta(k)=\frac{2}{\pi}\lim_{\chi_1\to\infty}\frac{\sin k\chi_1}{k},$$

$$G(m,k)=-\frac{2\delta(k)}{Mq_m\mathrm{ch}\,q_m l}\left[(\Omega_4 h-V_5)\sin M-\frac{\Omega_4 h}{M}\right],$$

$$H(n,k)=\frac{2(-1)^{n-1}\delta(k)l\Omega_3}{N^2 r_n\,\mathrm{ch}\,r_n h},\quad N=\frac{(2n-1)\pi}{2},\quad J(n,k)=-\frac{4V_4\delta(k)}{hlf_2(n)}\sum_{m=1,3}^{\infty}\frac{\cos n\pi}{R_n^2+q_m^2}.$$

把上列结果代入相应的式中之后，就可以看到(2.1)式所表示的 $\psi(x, y, z, t)$ 在整个自己的定义域内处处收敛. 因此，条件(1.7)式是满足的.

将(2.1)式对 t 微分后，可以写出在坝和流体接触面上，即相当于 $x = 0$ 处的

$$\frac{\partial\psi}{\partial t} = \frac{\partial\psi_1}{\partial t} + \frac{\partial\psi_2}{\partial t} + \frac{\partial\psi_3}{\partial t}, \tag{2.13}$$

式中

$$\frac{\partial\psi_1}{\partial t} = -\omega_1\Psi_1(0, y, z)\sin\omega_1 t, \quad \frac{\partial\psi_2}{\partial t} = -\omega_2\Psi_2(0, y, z)\sin\omega_2 t,$$

$$\frac{\partial\psi_3}{\partial t} = -\omega_3\Psi_3(0, y, z)\sin\omega_3 t.$$

在对 $\Psi_1(0, y, z)$, $\Psi_2(0, y, z)$, $\Psi_3(0, y, z)$ 做积分运算时，展开

$$\cos\beta(y-h) = \prod_{r=0}^{\infty}\left(1 - \frac{4\beta^2(y-h)^2}{(2r+1)^2\pi^2}\right), \quad \sin\beta(y-h) = \beta(y-h)\prod_{r=1}^{\infty}\left(1 - \frac{\beta^2(y-h)^2}{r^2\pi^2}\right),$$

$$\operatorname{ch} b(y-h) = \prod_{r=0}^{\infty}\left(1 + \frac{4b^2(y-h)^2}{(2r+1)^2\pi^2}\right), \quad \operatorname{sh} b(y-h) = b(y-h)\prod_{r=1}^{\infty}\left(1 + \frac{b^2(y-h)^2}{r^2\pi^2}\right),$$

$$\mathscr{H}(k, Q_1) = b^2h\prod_{r=1}^{\infty}\left(1+\frac{b^2h^2}{r^2\pi^2}\right) - Q_1\prod_{r=0}^{\infty}\left(1+\frac{4b^2h^2}{(2r+1)^2\pi^2}\right), \quad \operatorname{ch} by = \prod_{r=0}^{\infty}\left(1+\frac{4b^2y^2}{(2r+1)^2\pi^2}\right).$$

以类似的形式展开 $\mathscr{K}(\nu, Q_3)$, $\mathscr{H}(k, Q_3)$, $\mathscr{K}(\alpha, Q_3)$, $f_1(n)$, $f_2(n)$ 等.

图 1a 为方程 $\mathscr{K}_1(\nu, Q_3) = 0$ 在复平面上的虚根 γ_i' 的分布示意图. 图 1c 为 $\nu < H$ 时可能出现的二个实根 $\pm\gamma_i''$. 此处 $\mathscr{K}_1(\nu, Q_3) = \beta_1\sin\beta_1 h + Q_3\cos\beta_1 h$, $\beta_1 = \sqrt{\nu^2 - H^2}$. γ_n 为 $\mathscr{K}(\nu, Q_3) = 0$的实根，见图 1b，但要把该图的 y' 轴换成 $-x'$，把 x' 换成 y' 轴. γ_i 为同一方程在 $\nu > H$ 时的虚根，γ_m 则为 $|\nu| < H$ 时的实根，它们在复平面上的分布见图 1f，但要把该图的 y' 轴换成 x'，把 x' 换成 $-y'$. 在 γ_m 可能不出现，或可能出现一对时，见图 1d, 1e，但也应如图 1f 那样变换坐标轴. 如 γ_m 出现，则成对地落在变换后的 $-x'$ 轴上. 图 1b 为方程

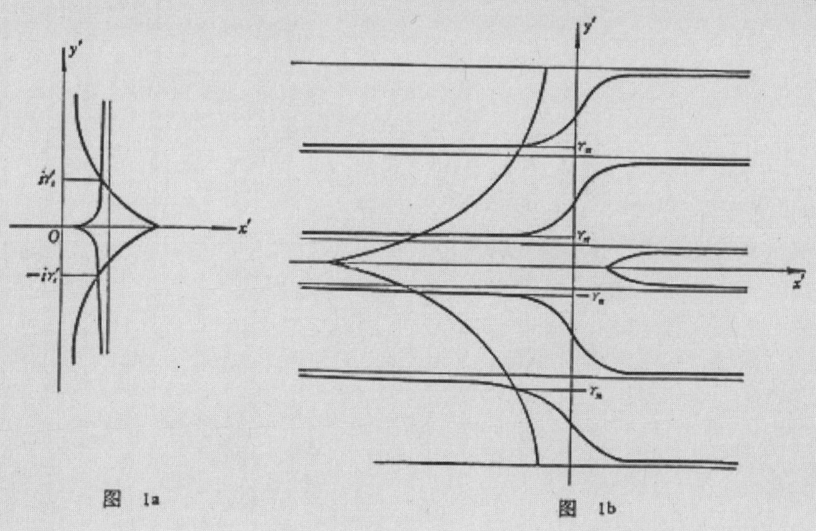

图 1a　　图 1b

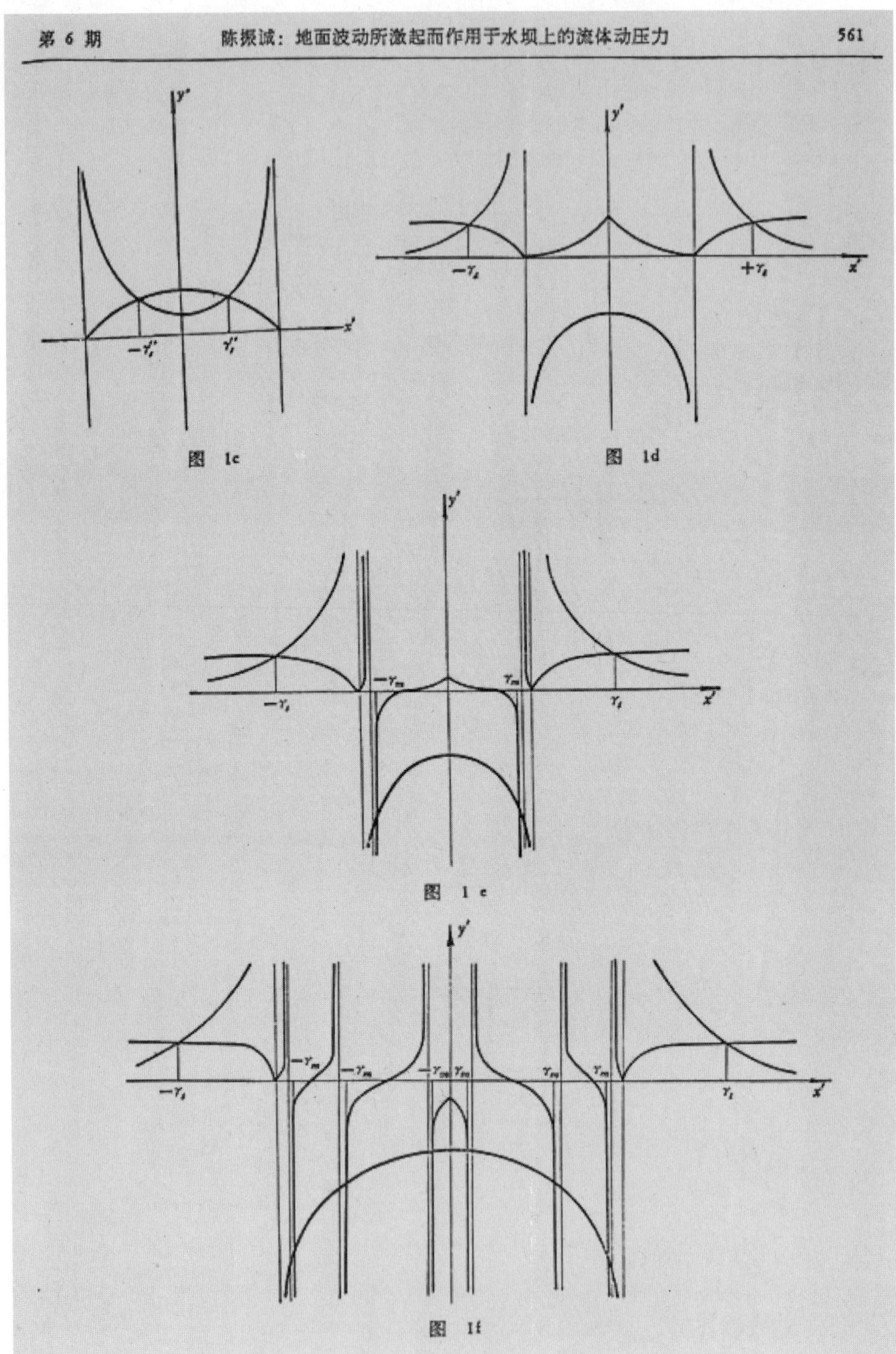

图 1c

图 1d

图 1e

图 1f

$\mathscr{H}(k, Q_1)=0$, $\mathscr{H}(k, Q_3)=0$ 的虚根 γ_n 的分布示意图. 图 1f 则为此方程实根分布情况, γ_m 是 $k<H$ 时可能出现的实根. 这时 γ_m 可能不出现, 如图 1d, 也可能出现一对, 如图 1e, 也可能出现若干对, 如图 1f. 根据具体计算确定这些根. 应该指出, 图 1 自变量轴的坐标原点值为 $\pm Hh$.

按下列步骤求 $\Psi_2(0, y, z)$ 的积分: 1) 第一项按图 2 所示的环路积分. 2) 第二项先对变数 ν 按图 2 所示的环路积分. 3) 第三项为三重积分, 先对变数 k 按图 3 所示的环路积分. 然后

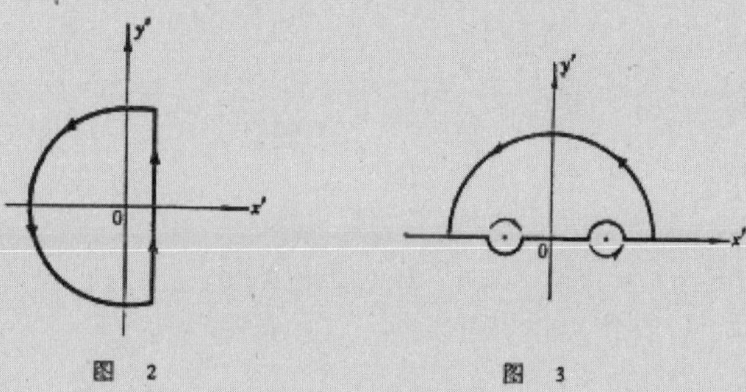

图 2 图 3

把所得结果中与第二项相关的一项先对 ν 积分, 另一项则先对 α 积分, 最后对 ν 积分. 积分、求和、简化后, 可以导出

$$\frac{\partial\psi_2}{\partial t}=-\omega_3 hV_2\left[\frac{\beta'\mathrm{ch}\beta'(y-h)+Q_3\mathrm{sh}\beta'(y-h)}{h\beta'\mathscr{H}(\beta', Q_3)}+\sum_{n=1,2}^{\infty}\frac{\gamma_{nQ}\cos(\gamma_n y/h)}{(\sigma'^2+\gamma_n^2)\mathscr{T}(\gamma_n)}\right.$$
$$\left.+2\sum_{m=1}^{r'}\frac{(\gamma_m^2+\tau)\cos(\gamma_m y/h)}{(\sigma_1^2+\gamma_m^2)\mathscr{T}(\gamma_m)}+2\frac{(\gamma_s^2-\tau)\mathrm{ch}(\gamma_s y/h)}{(\sigma'^2-\gamma_s^2)\mathscr{T}(\gamma_s)}\right]\sin\omega_3 t, \tag{2.14}$$

式中

$$\beta'=\sqrt{\sigma^2-H^2},\ \sigma'=\beta' h,\ \mathscr{H}(\beta', Q_3)=Q_3\mathrm{ch}\beta' h-\beta'\mathrm{sh}\beta' h,\ \mathscr{T}(\gamma_s)=\gamma_s^2+(1-Q_3h)Q_3h,$$
$$\mathscr{T}(\gamma_m)=\gamma_m^2-(1-Q_3h)Q_3h,\ \mathscr{T}(\gamma_n)=\gamma_n^2-(1-Q_3h)Q_3h,\ \gamma_{nQ}=\gamma_n^2+Q_3^2h^2,$$
$$\sigma_1=\sqrt{\sigma^2h^2-H^2h^2},\ \tau=Q_3^2h^2.$$

$\Psi_1(0, y, z)$ 的积分运算按图 3 所示的环路进行. 积分及求和、化简的最后结果为:

$$\frac{\partial\psi_1}{\partial t}=-2\omega_1 h^2\left[\sum_{n=1,2}^{\infty}\frac{\mathscr{R}_1(V, \gamma_n)\cos(\gamma_n y/h)}{\gamma_n H_n\mathscr{T}(\gamma_n)\cos\gamma_n}\right]\sin\omega_1 t,\ H_n=\sqrt{1-H^2h^2/\gamma_n^2}, \tag{2.15}$$

$$\mathscr{R}_1(V, \gamma_n)=\mathscr{R}_1(V)+\Omega_1(\sec\gamma_n-1),\ \mathscr{R}_1(V)=(\Omega_1 h+V_1)Q_1.$$

对 $\Psi_3(0, y, z)$ 进行积分运算, 级数求和之后, 得

$$\frac{\partial\psi_3}{\partial t}=2h\omega_3\left\{\sum_{m=1,3}^{\infty}\frac{\cos C_m y}{M^2K_m}\sin M\left[V_4\frac{\mathrm{ch}\,G_m z}{\mathrm{sh}\,G_m l}+\left(h\Omega_4-V_3-\frac{h\Omega_4}{M\sin M}\right)\frac{\mathrm{sh}\,G_m z}{\mathrm{ch}\,G_m l}\right]\right.$$
$$\left.+\frac{\Omega_3}{lh}\sum_{n=1,2}^{\infty}\frac{\sin D_n z\ \mathrm{sh}\,G_n(y-h)}{(-1)^n K_n D_n^3\ \mathrm{ch}\,G_n h}+\psi_{(\xi)}(y, z)\right\}\sin\omega_3 t, \tag{2.16}$$

$$\psi_{(\xi)}(y,z)=\psi_{(\xi)_1}(y, z)+\psi_{(\xi)_2}(y, z),\quad \psi_{(\xi)_1}(y, z)=\frac{V_4}{lh}\sum_{n=1,2}^{\infty}\frac{\cos n\pi\cos R_n z}{S_n f_2'(n)\ \mathrm{cth}\,S_n h}\mathrm{ch}\,S_n y,$$

$$\psi_{(\zeta)_2}(y, z) = \frac{1}{lh}\sum_{n=1,2}^{\infty}\frac{\sin D_n z \operatorname{ch} G_n y}{(-1)^n f_1'(n)}\left[\left(\frac{\Omega_3}{D_n^2}+\frac{\Omega_4}{G_n^2}\right)\operatorname{sech} G_n h-\frac{\Omega_4}{G_n^2}+(\Omega_4 h - V_3)\frac{\operatorname{th} G_n h}{G_n}\right],$$

$$K_m = \sqrt{1-H^2/C_m^2},\ K_n=\sqrt{1-H^2/D_n^2},\ G_m = C_m K_m,\ G_n = D_n K_n,$$

$$S_n = \sqrt{R_n^2 - H^2},\ f_1'(n) = Q_3 \operatorname{ch} G_n h - G_n \operatorname{sh} G_n h,\ f_2'(n) = S_n \operatorname{sh} S_n h - Q_3 \operatorname{ch} S_n h.$$

相应的流体表面波方程为:

$$\zeta(x, z, t) = -\frac{1}{g}\frac{\partial\psi}{\partial t}\Big|_{y=h} = \zeta_1(x, z, t)+\zeta_2(x, z, t)+\zeta_3(x, z, t), \tag{2.17}$$

$$\zeta_1(x, z, t) = \frac{\omega_1}{g}\Psi_1(x, h, z)\sin\omega_1 t,\quad \zeta_2(x, z, t) = \frac{\omega_3}{g}\Psi_2(x, h, z)\sin\omega_3 t,$$

$$\zeta_3(x, z, t) = \frac{\omega_3}{g}\Psi_3(x, h, z)\sin\omega_3 t.$$

在计算 $\Psi_2(x, h, z)\sin\omega_3 t$ 的第一项积分时，按资料[4]中处理(2.18)式的方法绕道虚轴上的极点. 计算第三项时，先对 k 积分，采用此法绕道实轴上的极点，其后对 α 积分. 计算 $\Psi_1(x, h, z)\sin\omega_1 t$ 对 k 积分时也采用相同的方法绕道实轴上的极点. 把积分的结果求和化简之后,有

$$\begin{aligned}\zeta_1(x, z, t) = \frac{2\omega_1}{g}h\Bigg\{&\sum_{m=1}^{r'}\frac{(1-\sec\gamma_m)\Omega_1-\mathscr{R}_1(V)}{-H_{\gamma_m}\mathscr{T}(\gamma_m)}\cos(H_{\gamma_m}x-\omega_1 t)\\ &+\sum_{n=1}^{\infty}\frac{\mathscr{R}_1(V, \gamma_n)\exp(-H_{\gamma_n}x)}{H_{\gamma_n}\mathscr{T}(\gamma_n)}\sin\omega_1 t\\ &-\frac{\cos(H_{\gamma_t}x-\omega_1 t)}{H_{\gamma_t}\mathscr{T}(\gamma_t)}[(1-\operatorname{sech}\gamma_t)\Omega_1-\mathscr{R}_1(V)]\Bigg\},\end{aligned}$$

$$H_{\gamma_n} = \sqrt{\frac{\gamma_n^2}{h^2}-H^2},\quad H_{\gamma_t} = \sqrt{\frac{\gamma_t^2}{h^2}+H^2}, \tag{2.18}$$

$$\begin{aligned}\zeta_2(x, z, t) = \frac{\omega_3}{g}V_3 h\Bigg\{&\frac{-\sin(\sigma x-\omega_3 t)}{2h\mathscr{K}(\beta', Q_3)}-\frac{\gamma_t^2\sin(H_{\gamma_t}x-\omega_3 t)}{(\sigma'^2-\gamma_t^2)\mathscr{T}(\gamma_t)\operatorname{ch}\gamma_t}\\ &-\sum_{m=1}^{r'}\frac{\gamma_m^2\sin(H_{\gamma_m}x-\omega_3 t)}{(\sigma_1^2+\gamma_m^2)\mathscr{T}(\gamma_m)\cos\gamma_m}+\sum_{n=1}^{\infty}\frac{\gamma_n^2\exp(-H_{\gamma_n}x)}{(\sigma'^2+\gamma_n^2)\mathscr{T}(\gamma_n)\cos\gamma_n}\sin\omega_3 t\Bigg\},\end{aligned} \tag{2.19}$$

$$\gamma'\text{为正整数},\ H_{\gamma_m} = \sqrt{H^2-\frac{\gamma_m^2}{h^2}}.$$

以上各式中相应于 ψ_1 的 γ_n 与 $Q_1 h$ 相关,而相应于 ψ_2, ψ_4 中的 γ_n 与 $Q_3 h$ 相关,在 $Q_1 \neq Q_3$ 时两者并不相等. 在具体求值时请注意其差别.

应该注意到,如果方程 $\mathscr{H}(k, Q_1)=0$, $\mathscr{H}(k, Q_3)=0$ 在 $k<H$时，不出现除 $\pm\gamma_t$ 以外的实根,即如图 1d 所示的情况,则(2.18), (2.19)式中相应于 γ_m 的项均为零. 把 $\Psi_3(x, h, z)$ 做相应的积分运算之后,可得

$$\zeta_3(x, z, t) = -\frac{2\omega_3}{g}h\left\{\frac{\operatorname{ch} S_n h}{\operatorname{ch} S_n y}\psi_{(\zeta)_1}(y, z)+\frac{\operatorname{ch} G_n h}{\operatorname{ch} G_n y}\psi_{(\zeta)_2}(y, z)\right\}\sin\omega_3 t. \tag{2.20}$$

2. 当 $\xi=\frac{\pi}{2}$, $\chi=-l$ 的情况：给出满足方程(1.1)和条件(1.2)式的函数

$$\psi(x,y,z,t)=\psi_1(x,y,z,t)+\psi_4(x,y,z,t)+\psi_5(x,y,z,t), \tag{2.21}$$

此处

$$\psi_4(x,y,z,t)=\Psi_4(x,y,z)\cos\omega_3 t,\quad \psi_5(x,y,z,t)=\Psi_5(x,y,z)\cos\omega_3 t,$$

$$\Psi_4(x,y,z)=-\frac{2\sigma V_2}{\pi}\int_0^\infty \frac{b\,\mathrm{ch}\,b(y-h)+Q_3\,\mathrm{sh}\,b(y-h)}{b(\sigma^2-k^2)\mathscr{H}(k,Q_3)}\cos kx\,dk, \tag{2.22}$$

$$\Psi_5(x,y,z)=\sum_{m=1,3}^{\infty}\int_0^\infty L(m,k)\cos C_m y\,\mathrm{ch}\,q_m(z-l)\cos kx\,dk+\Psi_{31}(x,y,z)$$

$$+\frac{1}{2}\Psi_{32}(x,y,z)+\int_0^\infty T(k)[b\,\mathrm{ch}\,b(y-h)+Q_3\,\mathrm{sh}\,b(y-h)]\cos kx\,dk. \tag{2.23}$$

对于情况 (2) 应将条件 (1.5) 式的第二项改写为：在 $0\leqslant x\leqslant\infty$, $0\leqslant y\leqslant h$, $z=-l$ 面上，$\frac{\partial\phi}{\partial z}=V_4\cos\omega_3 t$；在 $0\leqslant x\leqslant\infty$, $0\leqslant y\leqslant h$, $z=l$ 面上，$\frac{\partial\phi}{\partial z}=0$. 满足相应的条件后，得 $L(m,k)=-2V_4\delta(k)\sin M/Mq_m\,\mathrm{sh}\,2q_m l$, $T(k)=l\Omega_3\delta(k)/b\mathscr{H}(k,Q_3)$. 按图 3 所示的环路对 $\Psi_4(0,y,z)$ 进行积分计算，并对 $\Psi_5(0,y,z)$ 做相应的积分运算、求和、化简，有

$$\frac{\partial\psi_4}{\partial t}=-2\sigma h^2\omega_3 V_2\sum_{n=1,2}^{\infty}\frac{\gamma_{n0}\cos(\gamma_n y/h)}{\gamma_n(\sigma''^2+\gamma_n^2)\mathscr{T}(\gamma_n)H_n}\sin\omega_3 t,\ \sigma''=\beta''h,\ \beta''=\sqrt{\sigma^2-H^2}, \tag{2.24}$$

$$\frac{\partial\psi_5}{\partial t}=\frac{\partial\psi_3}{\partial t}+\Big\{2hV_4\sum_{m=1,3}^{\infty}\frac{\cos C_m y\sin M}{K_m M^2\,\mathrm{sh}\,G_m l}\Big[\frac{\mathrm{ch}\,G_m(z-l)}{2\,\mathrm{ch}\,G_m l}-\mathrm{ch}\,G_m z\Big]$$

$$-\frac{V_4}{\pi}\sum_{n=1,2}^{\infty}\frac{\cos R_n z}{nf_2'(n)K_R}\mathrm{th}S_n h\,\mathrm{ch}\,S_n y\cos n\pi+l\Omega_3[H\cos H(y-h)$$

$$+Q_3\sin H(y-h)]/HW_H\Big\}\omega_3\sin\omega_3 t, \tag{2.25}$$

此处

$$W_H=H\sin Hh+Q_3\cos Hh,\ K_R=\sqrt{1-H^2/R_n^2}.$$

采用对 $\Psi_2(x,h,z)\sin\omega_3 t$ 运算时相同的途径，绕道实轴上的极点，把(2.22)式的 $\Psi_4(x,h,z)\sin\omega_3 t$ 对 k 进行积分，并对 $\Psi_5(x,h,z)$ 进行相应的积分运算之后，最后有

$$\zeta_4(x,z,t)=\frac{2\omega_3}{g}\sigma hV_2\Big\{\frac{\cos(\sigma x-\omega_3 t)}{2\sigma h\mathscr{K}(\beta'',Q_3)}+\frac{\gamma_r^2\cos(H_{\gamma_r}x-\omega_3 t)}{H_{\gamma_r}(\sigma''^2-\gamma_r^2)\mathscr{T}(\gamma_r)\mathrm{ch}\gamma_r}$$

$$-\sum_{m=1}^{r'}\frac{\gamma_m^2\cos(H_{\gamma m}x-\omega_3 t)}{H_{\gamma m}(\sigma''^2+\gamma_m^2)\mathscr{T}(\gamma_m)\cos\gamma_m}-\sum_{n=1,2}^{\infty}\frac{\gamma_n^2\exp(-H_{\gamma_n}x)\sin\omega_3 t}{H_{\gamma_n}(\sigma''^2+\gamma_n^2)\mathscr{T}(\gamma_n)\cos\gamma_n}\Big\}, \tag{2.26}$$

$$\zeta_5(x,z,t)=\zeta_3(x,z,t)$$

$$+\frac{\omega_3 V_4}{\pi g}\sum_{n=1,2}^{\infty}\frac{\cos n\pi\cos R_n z}{nf_2'(n)K_R}\mathrm{sh}\,S_n h\sin\omega_3 t-\frac{l\Omega_3}{gW_H}\omega_3\sin\omega_3 t. \tag{2.27}$$

当 $\xi=0$, $\chi=$ '; $\xi=\frac{\pi}{2}$, $\chi=0$ 以及 $\xi\neq0$, $\chi\neq0$ 而等于某些常数时，可以从 (1) 和 (2)两种情况的结果作相应的组合而导出其解答.

当地面在 x, y 平面内的 y 方向以行波 $V_2(t)=V_2\cos(\sigma x-\omega_3 t)$ 运动时，可展开 $V_2(t)=V_2\cos\sigma x\cos\omega_3 t+V_2\sin\sigma x\sin\omega_3 t$，并令 $V_2(t)$ 所激起的 $\psi_2^*=\psi_{21}+\psi_{22}$，则条件 (1.4) 式中的第一项将以 $\frac{\partial\psi_2^*}{\partial y}=\frac{\partial\psi_{21}}{\partial y}+\frac{\partial\psi_{22}}{\partial y}=V_2\cos\sigma x\cos\omega_3 t+V_2\sin\sigma x\sin\omega_3 t$ 代替．从此，相应地有 $\psi_{21}=\psi_2(x,y,z,t)$, $\psi_{22}=\Psi_4(x,y,z)\sin\omega_3 t+\int_0^\infty A(k)\operatorname{ch}by\cos kx\sin\sqrt{bg\operatorname{th}bh}\,t\,dk$，式中的 $A(k)$ 由 ψ_{22} 代入条件(1.2)式确定之．

从上列 $\zeta(x,z,t)$ 的表达式可以看到，条件(1.8)式是满足的．到此，我们完成了全部数学分析，找到了所提问题的唯一准确解．

引入流体动压力 p^* 的表示式

$$p^*=-\rho\frac{\partial\psi}{\partial t}+\rho g\zeta, \tag{2.28}$$

式中 $\zeta=\zeta(0,z,t)$．根据上述相关的公式即可算出各该情况下，分布在坝面上的流体动压力．

三、流体动压力的分析

1. 当 $H\to 0$ 时，即相当于流体为理想不可压缩的情况，此时将各相应的 ψ 写成 φ，并对 $x=0$ 处的 $\frac{\partial\varphi}{\partial t}$ 进行相应的积分运算，则有

$$\frac{\partial\varphi_1}{\partial t}=-2\omega_1 h^2\sum_{n=1,2}^{\infty}\frac{\cos(\gamma_{n0}y/h)}{\gamma_{n0}\mathscr{T}(\gamma_{n0})\cos\gamma_{n0}}\mathscr{R}(V,\gamma_{n0})\sin\omega_1 t, \tag{3.1}$$

式中 γ_{n0} 为方程 $\gamma_{n0}\operatorname{tg}\gamma_{n0}=-Q_1h$ 之根．在 Q_1h 不大时，其求根法见资料 [5]，在 Q_1h 较大时，见资料[4]，此时令 $\gamma_{n0}=N+\delta_n$，并应注意到，在对 n 求和时，不论 δ_n 如何地小都不能略去它，而取 $\delta_n=N\varepsilon_1$, $(\varepsilon_1=1/Q_1h)$. $\mathscr{T}(\gamma_{n0})=\gamma_{n0}^2-(1-Q_1h)Q_1h$, $\mathscr{R}(V,\gamma_{n0})=\mathscr{R}_1(V)+\Omega_1(\sec\gamma_{n0}-1)$.

$$\frac{\partial\varphi_2}{\partial t}=-\omega_3 V_2\left\{\frac{\sigma\operatorname{ch}\sigma(y-h)+Q_3\operatorname{sh}\sigma(y-h)}{\sigma\mathscr{K}(\sigma,Q_3)}+\frac{2h(\gamma_{n0}'^2-\tau)\operatorname{ch}(\gamma_{n0}'y/h)}{(\sigma^2h^2-\gamma_{n0}'^2)\mathscr{T}(\gamma_{n0}')}+\bar{\varphi}\right\}\sin\omega_3 t, \tag{3.2}$$

$\mathscr{K}(\sigma,Q_3)=Q_3\operatorname{ch}\sigma h-\sigma\operatorname{sh}\sigma h$, $\mathscr{T}(\gamma_{n0}')=\gamma_{n0}'^2+(1-Q_3h)Q_3h$, γ_{n0}' 为方程 $\gamma_{n0}'\operatorname{th}\gamma_{n0}'=Q_3h$ 之根． $\bar{\varphi}=h\sum\limits_{n=1,2}^{\infty}(\gamma_{n0}'^2+\tau)\cos(\gamma_{n0}'y/h)/(\sigma^2h^2+\gamma_{n0}'^2)\mathscr{T}(\gamma_{n0}')$.

$$\begin{aligned}\frac{\partial\varphi_3}{\partial t}=2\omega_3\sin\omega_3 t\Bigg\{&h\sum_{m=1,3}^{\infty}\frac{\cos C_m y}{M^2}\sin M\left[\left(h\Omega_4-V_3-\frac{h\Omega_4}{M}\sin M\right)\frac{\operatorname{sh}C_m z}{\operatorname{ch}C_m l}+V_4\frac{\operatorname{ch}C_m z}{\operatorname{sh}C_m l}\right]\\&-\frac{\Omega_3}{l}\sum_{n=1,2}^{\infty}\frac{\sin D_n z\operatorname{sh}D_n(y-h)}{(-1)^{n-1}D_n^3\operatorname{ch}D_n h}+\varphi_{(\zeta)}(y,z)\Bigg\},\\&\varphi_{(\zeta)}(y,z)=\varphi_{(\zeta)_1}(y,z)+\varphi_{(\zeta)_2}(y,z),\end{aligned} \tag{3.3}$$

$$\varphi_{(\zeta)_1}(y,z)=-\sum_{n=1,2}^{\infty}\frac{\sin D_n z\operatorname{ch}D_n y}{(-1)^n N f_3(n)}\left\{(\Omega_4h-V_3)\operatorname{th}D_n h+\frac{l}{N}[(\Omega_3+\Omega_4)\operatorname{sech}D_n h-\Omega_4]\right\},$$

$$\varphi_{(\zeta)_2}(y,z)=\frac{V_4}{\pi}\sum_{n=1,2}^{\infty}\frac{\cos n\pi}{nf_4(n)}\operatorname{th}R_n h\cos R_n z\operatorname{ch}R_n y,\quad \begin{aligned}f_3(n)&=D_n\operatorname{sh}D_n h-Q_3\operatorname{ch}D_n h,\\ f_4(n)&=R_n\operatorname{sh}R_n h-Q_3\operatorname{ch}R_n h,\end{aligned}$$

$$\frac{\partial\varphi_4}{\partial t}=-2\sigma h^2\omega_3 V_2\sum_{n=1,2}^{\infty}\frac{(\gamma_{n0}'^2+\tau)\cos(\gamma_{n0}'y/h)}{\gamma_{n0}'(\sigma^2h^2+\gamma_{n0}'^2)\mathscr{T}(\gamma_{n0}')}\sin\omega_3 t, \tag{3.4}$$

γ_{n0}' 为方程 $\gamma_{n0}'\operatorname{tg}\gamma_{n0}'=-Q_3h$ 之根，

$$\frac{\partial \varphi_5}{\partial t}=\frac{\partial \varphi_3}{\partial t}+\left\{2hV_4\sum_{m=1,3}^{\infty}\frac{\cos C_m y\sin M}{M^2\operatorname{sh}C_m l}\left[\frac{\operatorname{ch}C_m(z-l)}{2\operatorname{ch}C_m l}-\operatorname{ch}C_m z\right]+l\Omega_3(y-h)\right.$$
$$\left.-\frac{V_4}{\pi}\sum_{n=1,2}^{\infty}\frac{\cos R_n z}{nf_4(n)}\operatorname{th}R_n h\operatorname{ch}R_n y\cos n\pi\right\}\omega_3\sin\omega_3 t. \tag{3.5}$$

对 $y=h$ 处的 $\frac{\partial\varphi}{\partial t}$ 进行相应的积分运算，并注意按前述途径对 k, ν 积分，可最后写出

$$\zeta_1^0(x,z,t)=\frac{2\omega_1h^2}{g}\left\{\frac{\cos\left(\frac{\gamma_{10}}{h}x-\omega_1 t\right)}{-\gamma_{10}\mathscr{T}(\gamma_{10})}[(1-\operatorname{sech}\gamma_{10})\Omega_1-R_1(V)]\right.$$
$$\left.+\sum_{n=1}^{\infty}\frac{\exp(-\gamma_{n0}x/h)}{\gamma_{n0}\mathscr{T}(\gamma_{n0})}R(V,\gamma_{n0})\sin\omega_1 t\right\}, \tag{3.6}$$

$$\zeta_2^0(x,z,t)=\frac{hV_2}{g}\omega_3\left[\frac{-\sin(\sigma x-\omega_3 t)}{2h\mathscr{K}(\sigma,Q_3)}-\frac{\gamma_{10}'^2\sin(\gamma_{10}'x/h-\omega_3 t)}{(\sigma^2h^2-\gamma_{10}'^2)\mathscr{T}(\gamma_{10}')\operatorname{ch}\gamma_{10}'}+\xi_{\gamma_n}\sin\omega_3 t\right], \tag{3.7}$$

$$\zeta_3^0(x,z,t)=-\frac{2\omega_3}{g}\left[\varphi_{(\zeta)_1}(y,z)\frac{\operatorname{ch}D_n h}{\operatorname{ch}D_n y}+\varphi_{(\zeta)_2}(y,z)\frac{\operatorname{ch}R_n h}{\operatorname{ch}R_n y}\right]\sin\omega_3 t, \tag{3.8}$$

$$\zeta_4^0(x,z,t)=2\frac{\omega_3}{g}\sigma h^2V_2\left\{\frac{\cos(\sigma x-\omega_3 t)}{2\sigma h^2\mathscr{K}(\sigma,Q_3)}+\frac{\gamma_{10}'\cos(\gamma_{10}'x/h-\omega_3 t)}{(\sigma^2h^2-\gamma_{10}'^2)\mathscr{T}(\gamma_{10}')\operatorname{ch}\gamma_{10}'}\right.$$
$$\left.+\sum_{n=1}^{\infty}\frac{\gamma_{n0}'\exp(-\gamma_{n0}'x/h)\sin\omega_3 t}{(\gamma_{n0}'^2+\sigma^2h^2)\mathscr{T}(\gamma_{n0}')\cos\gamma_{n0}'}\right\}, \tag{3.9}$$

$$\zeta_5^0(x,z,t)=\zeta_3^0(x,z,t)+\frac{\omega_3V_4}{\pi g}\sum_{n=1,2}^{\infty}\frac{\cos n\pi}{nf_4(n)}\cos R_n z\operatorname{sh}R_n h\sin\omega_3 t-\frac{l\Omega_3}{\omega_3}\sin\omega_3 t. \tag{3.10}$$

$$\gamma_n=\gamma_{n0}',\quad \xi_{\gamma_n}=\sum_{n=1,2}^{\infty}\frac{\gamma_n^2\exp(-\gamma_n x/h)}{(\sigma^2h^2+\gamma_n^2)\mathscr{T}(\gamma_n)\cos\gamma_n},$$

γ_{10} 为方程 $\gamma_{10}\operatorname{th}\gamma_{10}=Q_1h$ 之根.

引入无量纲的压力系数符号 $P_\eta=p_{0\eta}^*/\rho\omega_\chi V_\eta h$; $P_\eta'=p_{0\eta}^{*\prime}/\rho\omega_\chi\Omega_\eta h^2$; $\eta=1,2,3,4,5$; $\chi=1,3,5$; $p_{0\eta}^*$, $p_{0\eta}^{*\prime}$ 分别为相应于各该 η, 相当于平移，转动振动所激起的流体动压力振幅.

把(2.28)式中的 ψ 改写成 φ, ξ 改写成 ζ^0, 并令(3.1)—(3.10)式中的 $V_1=V_2=V_4=0$, $\Omega_1=\Omega_3=\Omega_4=0$, 可得相当于河岸两壁平移振动时出现在坝面上的流体动压力系数以及 $x=0$ 处的流体自由表面涌高

$$P_3=2\sum_{m=1,3}^{\infty}\frac{\operatorname{sh}C_m z\cos C_m y}{M^2\operatorname{ch}C_m l}\sin M-2\sum_{n=1,2}^{\infty}\frac{\sin D_n z\operatorname{th}D_n h}{(-1)^nNf_3^*(n)}\left(\frac{\operatorname{ch}D_n y}{\operatorname{ch}D_n h}+1\right), \tag{3.11}$$

$$\zeta^0(0,z,t)=\frac{2\omega_3V_3}{g}\sin\omega_3 t\sum_{n=1,2}^{\infty}\frac{\sin D_n z\operatorname{th}D_n h}{(-1)^{n-1}Nf_3^*(n)}h. \tag{3.12}$$

在(3.11)式的第二项中，当条件 $f_3^*(n)=D_nh\operatorname{th}D_nh-Q_3h\Rightarrow 0$ 满足时，相当于流体在被迫振动的同时，还存在着自由表面而有本身的自振，当这两种振动的频率趋于一致时，将出现共振现象. 在现实中，由于坝体及流体在运动时的能量耗散，在共振条件下，流体动压力并不无限增大，但是，会出现某一个大值. 用模型试验能证实这种情况. 令 Δ 为一个小量，则 $D_n\operatorname{th}D_nh-Q_3=\Delta$ 的现实可能性是存在的. 例如有这样一系列的 Δ 值；使得 $\left|\frac{\zeta}{h}\right|\leqslant 0.1$, 这时上述的理论解是

成立的．现在，来研究(3.11)式的第二项，假定 $h=100$ 米，$l=314$ 米．如果 $\zeta_{max}=5$ 米，则 $\zeta_{max}/h=0.05$．从 (3.12) 式可算出位移振幅 $u_3=0.002$ 米，$\omega=6\dfrac{1}{秒}$ 或 $\omega\approx10\dfrac{1}{秒}$．这些情况是实际存在的．这时从 (3.11) 式第二项可知，在坝的一端顶部可能出现数值为 10 吨/米² 的最大压力，而在 $\dfrac{l}{2}$ 处顶部的压力为 7.07 吨/米²．如果 $\zeta_{max}=0.5$ 米，则最大压力将为 1 吨/米²．还可以从另一个实例来看，当 $\omega_3V_3=0.3g$，$\zeta_{max}=0.5$ 米，$h=20$ 米时，在 $\dfrac{3h}{4}=15$ 米高度处由流体自由表面重力波所引起的扭转力矩为由 $\boldsymbol{V}_3$ 所引起总力矩的 26%；当 $h=10$ 米时，在 7.5 米高度处则为总力矩的 52%．从这些实例可以看到，对于空间问题，需要考虑重力和流体自由表面波对流体动载荷的影响．对于低坝，则更应考虑这一因素．

从(3.1)—(3.10)式还可以看到，当 $Q_\chi h$ 较大并且 ζ_{max} 为无穷小量时，重力对 $\boldsymbol{P}_\eta$ 值的影响可以略去．不过，$\zeta_{max}\to0$ 的情况只在振动最初某一阶段或其他某一小段时间中有可能出现．根据这种特点和资料 [4] 中的论据，可以看到，如果按准确度的要求，使 $Q_\chi h$ 值落在合适的范围内，并使 ζ_{max} 相应地小的时候，来测量试验数据，则可以认为所得模拟试验结果已排除了重力加速度 g 对流体动压力的影响．例如要模拟周期 $T=0.1$ 秒的振动试验，而准确度要求为 1‰，则当 $h\geqslant2.5$ 米，$\zeta_{max}\leqslant0.5\times10^{-6}$ 米时，即可排除 g 对 p^* 的影响．如果准确度要求为 1%，则 $h\geqslant0.25$ 米，$\zeta_{max}\leqslant0.5\times10^{-5}$ 米时，即可不考虑 g．从此，得到模型试验中排除重力对流体动压力影响的模拟相似准则为：

1) 使得 Qh 足够地大．2) 使得 ζ_{max} 足够地小．它们大、小的具体值，根据工程实际上的准确度要求而确定之．

令 $\boldsymbol{V}_1=\boldsymbol{V}_3=\boldsymbol{V}_4=0$，$\boldsymbol{\Omega}_1=\boldsymbol{\Omega}_3=\boldsymbol{\Omega}_4=0$，找出 $\boldsymbol{P}_2=\boldsymbol{P}_{2\cos\sigma x}+\boldsymbol{P}_{2\sin\sigma x}$，此处 $\boldsymbol{P}_{2\cos\sigma x}$ 为地面以 $\boldsymbol{V}_2(t)=\boldsymbol{V}_2\cos\sigma x\cos\omega_3t$ 波动时激起的流体动压力的压力系数，$\boldsymbol{P}_{2\sin\sigma x}$ 则为 $\boldsymbol{V}_2(t)=\boldsymbol{V}_2\sin\sigma x\cos\omega_3t$ 时的压力系数．当 Q_3h 较大时，

$$\boldsymbol{P}_{2\cos\sigma x}=\frac{\sigma\,\mathrm{ch}\,\sigma(y-h)+Q_3\,\mathrm{sh}\,\sigma(y-h)}{\sigma h\mathscr{K}(\sigma,Q_3)},\quad \boldsymbol{P}_{2\sin\sigma x}=2\sigma h\sum_{n=1}^{\infty}\frac{\cos(\gamma'_{n0}y/h)}{\gamma'_{n0}(\sigma^2h^2+\gamma'^2_{n0})}. \tag{3.13}$$

在地面波动的波长 $\lambda\to\infty$ 时，$\boldsymbol{P}_2\to(h-y)/h$．这与资料 [4] 所给的结果是一致的．根据(3.13)式作出在 $y=0$ 处的 $\boldsymbol{P}_{2\cos\sigma x}$，$\boldsymbol{P}_{2\sin\sigma x}$ 与 σh 的关系曲线，见图 4．前者以实线表示，后者以虚线表示．图 5 指出了 $\boldsymbol{P}_2$ 与波速 $v=\omega_3/\sigma$ 的关系．地面波动的实际情况可能是一个有不同

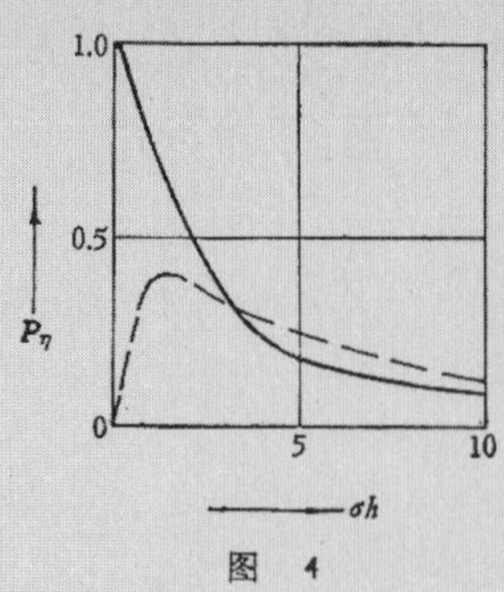

图 4

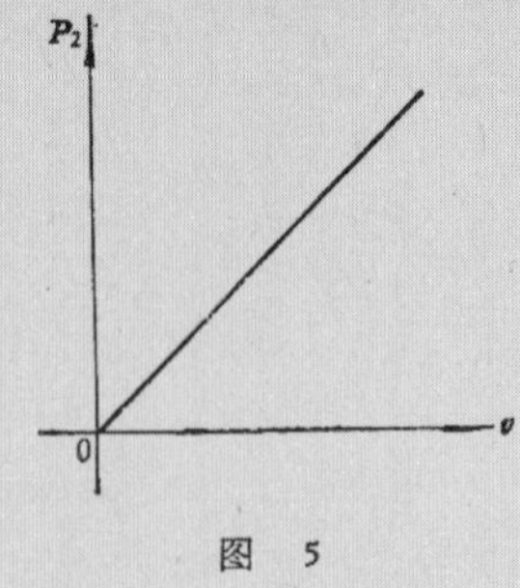

图 5

波长，不同圆频率的级数的总和．那么，实际的 P_2 值就应该依据这个级数来确定．

作为例子，取 $h = 100$ 米，$l = 314$ 米，假定 $Q_Z h$ 较大．根据前述有关公式可以算出各相应的压力系数 $P_\eta(y, z)$，其结果列于表 1 中．表中的第(一)项相当于 M. Westergaard[1] 和 Л. С. Лейбензон[2] 的解所能给出的 $P_\eta(y, z)$，其他各项都是本文提出的 $P_\eta(y, z)$．把各 P_η 值

表 1． P_η，P'_η 沿坝面分布图表

项别	流体动压力来因	速度振幅	P_η 或 P'_η 沿坝面分布图	$P_{\eta\max}$ 或 $P'_{\eta\max}$ 值	备注
(一)	坝体沿河流方向振动	V_1	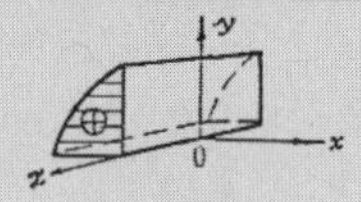	$P_{1\max} = 0.74$	$P_{\eta\max}$，$P'_{\eta\max}$ 值在 $y = 0$，$z = l$ 处
(二)	坝体绕 z 轴转动振动	Ω_1	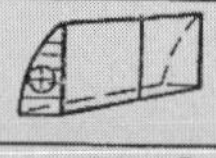	$P'_{1\max} = 0.20$	同 上
(三)	河岸两壁沿 z 方向平移振动	V_3	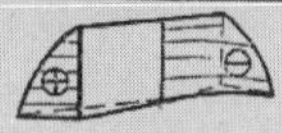	$P_{3\max} = 0.74$	同 上
(四)	河床绕 x 轴转动振动 (I)	V_4	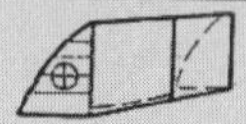	$P_{4\max} = 0.74$	1. 同 上 2. 河床转动振动的 P 值应为三者之组合
		Ω_4		$P'_{4\max} = 0.20$	
		Ω_3		$P'_{3\max} = 0.83$	
(五)	河床绕 $y = 0$，$z = -l$ 轴转动振动 (II)	V_4	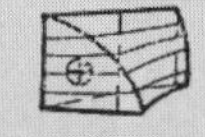	$P_{4\max} = 0.74$	同 上
		Ω_4	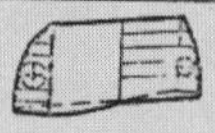	$P'_{4\max} = 0.20$	
		Ω_3		$P'_{3\max} = 1.83$	
(六)	地面余弦波动	V_2	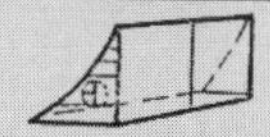	$P_{2\max} = 0.76$	这是 $\sigma h = 1$，而 $h = 100$ 米的情况
(七)	地面正弦波动	V_2		$P_{2\max} = 0.42$	同 上
(八)	流体自由表面重力波波动	V_1 Ω_1 V_2			
		Ω_3 V_3 Ω_4			
		V_4			

与第(一)项相比较，就可以看到，在一定情况下考虑本文所提出并证实的河岸两壁振动，河床、坝体的转动振动，地面波动的波长、波速等等对流体动压力的影响是必要的.

2. 当 $H \to C_0$，此处 C_0 为某一不能忽略的实常量. 此时 ω 与 h, l 同时相当地很大，但不等式 $K_m^2 > 0$, $K_n^2 > 0$, $K_R^2 > 0$ 仍然成立，相应的流体动压力分布在定性上与本节中相应的各项相同，见(3.1)—(3.10)式. 但需根据第二节中所导出的相应公式(2.14)—(2.27)作定量上的修正.

令 $\boldsymbol{V}_1 = \boldsymbol{V}_2 = 0$, $\boldsymbol{\Omega}_1 = 0$，当 ω 与 h, l 同时相当地很大到. 使得 $K_m \to 0$, $K_n \to 0$，并且 $\zeta(0, z, t)$ 相当小时，可将(2.16)式中的小量项略去而简化为：

$$\frac{\partial \phi_3}{\partial t} = -2\omega_3 \left\{ \sum_{m=1,3}^{\infty} \frac{\cos C_m y}{M \sin M} \left[\boldsymbol{V}_3 z - \frac{h^2 \boldsymbol{V}_4}{l M^2 K_m^2} - h \boldsymbol{\Omega}_4 z \left(1 - \frac{\sin M}{M}\right) \right] + l \boldsymbol{\Omega}_3 (h - y) \sum_{n=1,2}^{\infty} \frac{\sin D_n z}{N^2 (-1)^n} \right\} \sin \omega_3 t. \tag{3.14}$$

从此式可以看到可能出现的共振现象. 共振条件是 $\boldsymbol{H} = C_m$.

当 ω 与 h, l 同时相当地很大到，使得 $K_m^2 < 0$, $K_n^2 < 0$，并且 $\zeta(0, z, t)$ 相当地小时，可将(2.16)式中的小量项略去而简化成

$$\frac{\partial \phi_3}{\partial t} = -2\omega_3 \left\{ h \sum_{m=1,3}^{\infty} \frac{\cos C_m y}{M^2 K_m^*} \sin M \left[\left(\boldsymbol{V}_3 - h \boldsymbol{\Omega}_4 \left\{1 - \frac{\sin M}{M}\right\} \right) \frac{\sin G_m^* z}{\cos G_m^* l} + \boldsymbol{V}_4 \frac{\cos G_m^* z}{\sin G_m^* l} \right] - \frac{\boldsymbol{\Omega}_3}{l} \sum_{n=1,2}^{\infty} \frac{\sin D_n z \sin G_n^* (y - h)}{(-1)^n D_n^3 K_n^* \cos G_n^* h} \right\} \sin \omega_3 t, \quad K_m^* = \sqrt{\frac{H^2}{C_m^2} - 1}, \quad K_n^* = \sqrt{\frac{H^2}{D_n^2} - 1}, \tag{3.15}$$

$G_m^* = C_m K_m^*$, $G_n^* = D_n K_n^*$. 从(3.15)式可知，在 $G_m^* l \to \frac{\tau_1 \pi}{2}$, $G_n^* h \to \frac{\tau_1 \pi}{2}$, $(\tau_1 = 1, 3, 5, \cdots)$; $G_m^* l \to \tau' \pi$, $(\tau' = 1, 2, 3, \cdots)$ 时，将出现另一些共振现象. 从(2.14)—(2.16), (2.24), (2.25)式，可以引出 $\mathscr{K}(\beta', \mathcal{Q}_3) \to 0$, $H_n \to 0$, $W_H \to 0$ 等等另一些共振条件. 这些共振是由于流体的可压缩性造成的.

(3.14), (3.15) 式中以 $\boldsymbol{V}_3$ 为系数的项，提供相应于河岸两壁的平移振动所激起的流体动压力. 以 $\boldsymbol{\Omega}_3$, $\boldsymbol{\Omega}_4$, $\boldsymbol{V}_4$ 为系数的诸项的组合，提供相当于河床转动振动所激起的流体动压力. 作为例子，取 $h = 100$ 米，$l = 100$ 米，$T = 0.2$ 秒做数值计算. 假定 $\zeta(0, z, t)$ 为可以略去的小量，根据(2.28)式以及(3.15)式的四项，可作出 $\boldsymbol{P}_\eta$ 沿坝面的分布图，见图 6 和图 7，图 6 为河

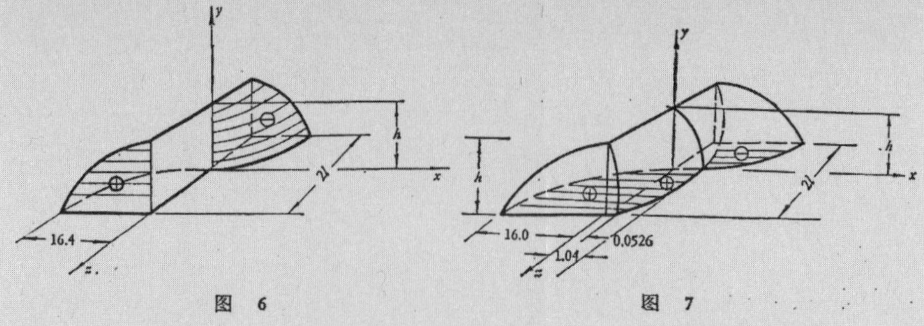

图 6　　　　图 7

岸平移振动所激起的流体动载荷，而图 7 则表示河床转动振动所造成的流体动压力. 从这些 $\boldsymbol{P}_\eta$ 值可以看到，当 ω, h, l 同时相当地很大时，考虑流体可压缩性是必要的. 因为,这时它可能对流体动压力沿坝面的分布带来定量,甚至是定性上的重大影响.

四、坝基弹性振动激起的流体动载荷

当坝基非刚性而坝宽较大时,地面在 x 方向的位移运动可能是不均匀的. 另一种情况是,由于水坝建筑在弹性地基上,而地震不规则振动所激起的流体动压力沿坝纵向的不均匀分布,势必引起坝体绕 $x=0$, $z=$ 常数轴的转动振动. 这些振动都相应地激起流体动压力. 现在,我们来寻找这种压力的分布规律.

令条件(1.3)—(1.5)式中的 $\boldsymbol{V}_1=\boldsymbol{V}_2=\boldsymbol{V}_3=\boldsymbol{V}_4=0$, $\boldsymbol{\Omega}_1=\boldsymbol{\Omega}_3=\boldsymbol{\Omega}_4=0$, 并以 $\dfrac{\partial\phi_6}{\partial x}=\boldsymbol{\Omega}_5 z\cos\omega_5 t$ 代替条件(1.3)式. 找出一个满足这样代替后的条件 (1.2)—(1.8) 式及方程(1.1)的函数 $\phi_6(x, y, z, t)$ 即为这个问题的解. 写出满足(1.1)—(1.6)式的

$$\phi_6(x, y, z, t)=\boldsymbol{\Psi}_6(x, y, z)\cos\omega_5 t, \tag{4.1}$$

$$\boldsymbol{\Psi}_6(x, y, z)=\sum_{n=1,2}^{\infty}\sum_{m=1,3}^{\infty}R(m, n)\cos C_m y\sin D_n z\exp(-b_{m,n}x)$$

$$+\sum_{n=1,2}^{\infty}\int_0^{\infty}S(n,k)\sin D_n z\cos kx\operatorname{ch}\alpha_n y\,dk,\quad b_{m,n}=\sqrt{C_m^2+D_n^2-\boldsymbol{H}^2},$$

$$\alpha_n=\sqrt{D_n^2+k^2-\boldsymbol{H}^2},\quad f_5(n,k)=\alpha_n\operatorname{sh}\alpha_n h-Q_5\operatorname{ch}\alpha_n h,\quad Q_5=\omega_5^2/g,$$

$$R(m,n)=\frac{4l\boldsymbol{\Omega}_5(-1)^n}{MN^2b_{m,n}}\sin M,\quad S(n,k)=\frac{2}{\pi}\sum_{m=1,3}^{\infty}R(m,n)\frac{C_m b_{m,n}\sin M}{f_5(n,k)(k^2+b_{m,n}^2)}.$$

展开

$$f_5(n,k)=h\alpha_n^2\prod_{r=1}^{\infty}\left(1+\frac{\alpha_n^2h^2}{r^2\pi^2}\right)-Q_5\prod_{r=0}^{\infty}\left(1+\frac{4\alpha_n^2h^2}{(2r+1)^2\pi^2}\right).$$

按图 3 所示的环路分别对 $\boldsymbol{\Psi}_6(0, y, z)$ 及 $\boldsymbol{\Psi}_6(x, h, z)\ \sin\omega_5 t$ 进行相应的积分运算、求和、化简,得 $x=0$ 处的

$$\left.\begin{aligned}&\frac{\partial\phi_6}{\partial t}=4l\omega_5Q_5h^2\boldsymbol{\Omega}_5\sum_{n=1,2}^{\infty}\frac{(-1)^n\sin D_n z}{N^2}\sum_{q=1,2}^{\infty}\frac{\cos(\gamma_q y/h)}{\mathscr{T}_q\cos\gamma_q}\sin\omega_5 t,\\&\mathscr{T}_q=\mathscr{T}(\gamma_q)\sqrt{\gamma_q^2+D_n'^2},\ \mathscr{T}(\gamma_q)=\gamma_q^2-\tau_5,\ \mathscr{T}(\gamma_s)=\gamma_s^2+\tau_5.\end{aligned}\right\}\tag{4.2}$$

流体自由表面波方程为:

$$\zeta_6(x,z,t)=4\frac{\omega_5}{g}lQ_5h^2\boldsymbol{\Omega}_5\sum_{n=1,2}^{\infty}\frac{(-1)^{n-1}\sin D_n z}{N^2}\left\{\frac{\cos(\gamma_{sD}x-\omega_5 t)}{\mathscr{T}(\gamma_s)\sqrt{\gamma_s^2-D_n'^2}}\right.$$

$$\left.+\sum_{q=1,2}^{\infty}\frac{\exp(-\gamma_{qD}x)}{\mathscr{T}_q}\sin\omega_5 t+\sum_{m=1}^{r'}\frac{\cos(\gamma_{mD}x-\omega_5 t)}{\mathscr{T}(\gamma_m)\sqrt{-\gamma_m^2-D_n'^2}}\right\},\ D_n'^2=(D_n^2-\boldsymbol{H}^2)h^2, \tag{4.3}$$

式中 γ_q 为方程 $f_5(n,k)=0$ 的虚根，γ_s 为实根，γ_m 为 $k^2+D_n^2-\boldsymbol{H}^2<0$ 时可能出现的实根. 如果不出现这种实根,见图 1d, 则相应于 γ_m 的项为零. 式中的 $\tau_5=(1-\theta_5 h)\theta_5 h$,

$$\gamma_{sD}=\sqrt{\frac{\gamma_s^2}{h^2}-D_n^2+\boldsymbol{H}^2},\ \gamma_{qD}=\sqrt{\frac{\gamma_q^2}{h^2}+D_n^2-\boldsymbol{H}^2},\ \gamma_{mD}=\sqrt{\frac{\gamma_m^2}{-h^2}-D_n^2+\boldsymbol{H}^2}.$$

$\mathscr{T}(\gamma_m)=\gamma_m^2-\tau_5$,从(4.1)—(4.3)式可以看到,条件(1.7),(1.8)式都是满足的.

当 $H\to 0$ 时，把 ψ_6 改写成 φ_6，并作相应的积分运算之后，就有

$$\frac{\partial\varphi_6}{\partial t}=4\omega_5 Q_5 h^2\Omega_5 l\sum_{n=1,2}^{\infty}\sum_{q=1,2}^{\infty}\frac{(-1)^n\sin D_n z\cos(\gamma'_q y/h)}{N^2\gamma'_{Dq}\mathscr{T}(\gamma'_q)\cos\gamma'_q}\sin\omega_5 t,\tag{4.4}$$

$$\zeta_6^0(x,z,t)=\frac{4\omega_5}{g}l\Omega_5 Q_5 h^2\sum_{n=1,2}^{\infty}\frac{\sin D_n z}{N^2(-1)^{n-1}}\left\{\frac{\cos(\gamma'_{Ds}x/h-\omega_5 t)}{\gamma'_{Ds}\mathscr{T}(\gamma'_s)}\right.$$

$$\left.+\sum_{q=1,2}^{\infty}\frac{\exp(-\gamma'_{Dq}x/h)}{\gamma'_{Dq}\mathscr{T}(\gamma'_q)}\sin\omega_5 t\right\},\ \gamma'_{Dq}=\sqrt{\gamma'^2_q+D_n^2h^2},\ \gamma'_{Ds}=\sqrt{\gamma'^2_s-D_n^2h^2}.\tag{4.5}$$

γ'_s 和 γ'_q 分别为方程 $f'_s(n,k)=b_n\,\mathrm{sh}\,b_n h-Q_5\,\mathrm{ch}\,b_n h=0$ 的实根和虚根，

$$b_n=\sqrt{k^2+D_n^2},\ \mathscr{T}(\gamma'_q)=\gamma'^2_q-(1-Q_5 h)Q_5 h,\ \mathscr{T}(\gamma'_s)=\gamma'^2_s+(1-Q_5 h)Q_5 h.$$

当 $Q_5 h$ 较大，ζ_{max} 很小时，可以略去重力和流体自由表面波对流体动载荷的影响. 于是，可将这时的流体动压力简单地写成：

$$p^*=-4\rho\omega_5 l\Omega_5\sum_{n=1,2}^{\infty}\sum_{m=1,3}^{\infty}\frac{(-1)^n\sin M}{MN^2a_{m,n}}\cos C_m y\sin D_n z\sin\omega_5 t,$$

$$a_{m,n}=\sqrt{C_m^2+D_n^2},\tag{4.6}$$

如果 $h=100$ 米，$l=314$ 米，则 $P'_{6max}=1.06$，见图 8. 与表 1 中的第(一)项相比较，就可以看出，在 $l\Omega_5\to V_1$ 时坝基弹性振动所激起的流体动压力应加以考虑.

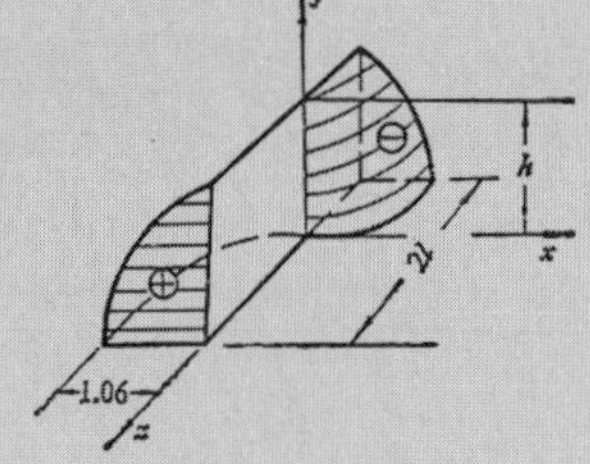

图 8

当 $H\to C_0$ 时，应依据(4.2)，(4.3)和(2.28)式来计算 p^*.

五、一个特例

当其他条件保持不变，但在 $y=h$ 处以条件 $p^*=0$ 代替条件 (1.6) 式时，可以作为特例，从上述有关各节中直接写出计算流体动压力的相应公式. 例如，从 (3.1) 式，根据资料 [4] 中 $\gamma_{n0}\to\frac{\pi}{2}$ 时对超越方程求根的分析，可写出

$$\frac{\partial\varphi_1^0}{\partial t}=-2\omega_1 h\sum_{m=1,3}^{\infty}\frac{\cos C_m y}{M^2}\sin M\left[V_1+\Omega_1 h\left(1-\frac{\sin M}{M}\right)\right]\sin\omega_1 t.\tag{5.1}$$

略去各式中与流体自由表面波有关的项，则有

$$\frac{\partial\varphi_2^0}{\partial t}=-\omega_3 V_2\frac{\mathrm{sh}\,\sigma(y-h)}{\sigma\,\mathrm{ch}\,\sigma h}\sin\omega_3 t,\tag{5.2}$$

$$\frac{\partial\varphi_3^0}{\partial t}=2\omega_3\left\{h\sum_{m=1,3}^{\infty}\frac{\cos C_m y}{M^2}\sin M\left[\left(h\Omega_4-V_3-\frac{h\Omega_4}{M}\sin M\right)\frac{\mathrm{sh}\,C_m z}{\mathrm{ch}\,C_m l}\right.\right.$$

$$\left.\left.+V_4\frac{\mathrm{ch}\,C_m z}{\mathrm{sh}\,C_m l}\right]+\frac{\Omega_3}{l}\sum_{n=1,2}^{\infty}\frac{\sin D_n z\,\mathrm{sh}\,D_n(y-h)}{(-1)^n D_n^3\,\mathrm{ch}\,D_n h}\right\}\sin\omega_3 t,\tag{5.3}$$

$$\frac{\partial\varphi_4^0}{\partial t}=-2\sigma h\omega_3 V_2\sum_{m=1,3}^{\infty}\frac{\cos C_m y}{C_m(\sigma^2h^2+M^2)}\sin\omega_3 t,\tag{5.4}$$

$$\frac{\partial\varphi_5^0}{\partial t}=-\frac{\partial\varphi_3^0}{\partial t}+\left\{2hV_4\sum_{m=1,3}^{\infty}\frac{\cos C_m y\sin M}{M^2\operatorname{sh}C_m l}\left[\frac{\operatorname{ch}C_m(z-l)}{2\operatorname{ch}C_m l}-\operatorname{ch}C_m z\right]+l\Omega_3(y-h)\right\}\omega_3\sin\omega_3 t. \tag{5.5}$$

于是(2.28)式将改写成为:

$$p^*=-\rho\frac{\partial\varphi^0}{\partial t}, \tag{5.6}$$

(4.6)式仍保持原状.

$$\frac{\partial\psi_1^0}{\partial t}=-2\omega_1 h\sum_{m=1,3}^{\infty}\frac{\cos C_m y\sin M}{M^2\sqrt{1-H_c^2}}\left\{V_1+\Omega_1 h\left(1-\frac{\sin M}{M}\right)\right\}\sin\omega_1 t, \tag{5.7}$$

$$\frac{\partial\psi_2^0}{\partial t}=-\omega_3 hV_2\left\{\frac{\operatorname{sh}\beta'(y-h)}{\beta' h\operatorname{ch}\beta' h}\right\}\sin\omega_3 t, \tag{5.8}$$

$$\frac{\partial\psi_3^0}{\partial t}=2\omega_3 h\left\{\sum_{m=1,3}^{\infty}\frac{\cos C_m y}{M^2K_m}\sin M\left[V_4\frac{\operatorname{ch}G_m z}{\operatorname{sh}G_m l}+\left(h\Omega_4\left\{1-\frac{\sin M}{M}\right\}-V_3\right)\frac{\operatorname{sh}G_m z}{\operatorname{ch}G_m l}\right]+\frac{\Omega_3}{lh}\sum_{n=1,2}^{\infty}\frac{\sin D_n z\operatorname{sh}G_n(y-h)}{(-1)^n K_n D_n^3\operatorname{ch}G_n h}\right\}\sin\omega_3 t, \tag{5.9}$$

$$\frac{\partial\psi_4^0}{\partial t}=-2\sigma h^2\omega_3 V_2\sum_{m=1,3}^{\infty}\frac{\cos C_m y\sin\omega_3 t}{M(\sigma''^2+M^2)\sqrt{1-H_c^2}},\quad H_c=Hh/M, \tag{5.10}$$

$$\frac{\partial\psi_5^0}{\partial t}=\frac{\partial\psi_3^0}{\partial t}+\left\{2hV_4\sum_{m=1,3}^{\infty}\frac{\cos C_m y\sin M}{K_m M^2\operatorname{sh}G_m l}\left[\frac{\operatorname{ch}G_m(z-l)}{2\operatorname{ch}G_m l}-\operatorname{ch}G_m z\right]+l\Omega_3\frac{\sin H(y-h)}{H\cos Hh}\right\}\omega_3\sin\omega_3 t, \tag{5.11}$$

$$\frac{\partial\psi_6^0}{\partial t}=-4lh\omega_5\Omega_5\sum_{n=1,2}^{\infty}\frac{\sin D_n z}{N^2(-1)^{n-1}}\sum_{m=1,3}^{\infty}\frac{\cos C_m y\sin M}{M\sqrt{M^2+D_n'^2}}\sin\omega_5 t, \tag{5.12}$$

这时,

$$p^*=-\rho\frac{\partial\psi^0}{\partial t}. \tag{5.13}$$

对于(5.7),(5.10)式取m始值的条件是保证$1-H_c^2>0$成立. 对于(5.12)式是$M^2+(D_n^2-H^2)h^2>0$成立. 也就是,如果$m=1$能使相应的不等式成立,则取$m=1, 3, 5, \cdots$. 如果$m=3$或$m=5$才能使不等式成立,则取$m=3, 5, 7, \cdots$,或$m=5, 7, 9, \cdots$. 从图1方程之根的分布示意,就可知这样取值的意义.

上列结果的物理意义是:在Qh较大,$\zeta_{\max}$很小的时候可以略去流体自由表面涌高对流体动压力的影响. 但是,当这二个条件不同时出现时,对于空间问题就应该如第三节中所指出的,考虑重力和流体自由表面波对流体动载荷的影响. 因此,本节所列的结果只是以前各节中所得结果的一个特殊情况.

六、地震铅直分力激起的流体动压力

1. 找出相应的解:a. 矩形河谷:在$0\leqslant x\leqslant\infty$, $0\leqslant y\leqslant h$, $-l\leqslant z\leqslant l$所围成的空间

部分充满理想可压缩流体.

令 $\lambda=\frac{2\pi}{\sigma}\to\infty$,从式(2.28)中直接引出

$$p_0^*=\rho\omega_3V_2h\frac{\sin H(h-y)}{\Xi_1\cos\Xi_1},\quad \Xi_1=Hh, \tag{6.1}$$

式中 V_2 为地震铅直分速度振幅.

流体动压力振幅系数为:

$$P_1(y,z)=\frac{p_0^*}{\rho\omega_3V_2h}=\frac{\sin H(h-y)}{\Xi_1\cos\Xi_1}, \tag{6.2}$$

图 9 表示 $P_1(y,z)$ 沿坝面的分布. 在坝底 $y=0$ 处, $P_1(0,z)=\mathrm{tg}\Xi_1/\Xi_1$. 取 $T=0.2$ 秒,当 $h=100$ 米时, $P_1=1.48$; $h=50$ 米时, $P_1=1.75$; $h=20$ 米时, $P_1=1.07$; 当 $h=80$ 米时, $P_1=3.17$; 当 $h=60$ 米时, $P_1=2.85$. 当 $H\to 0$ 时, $P_1(y,z)$ 在 y 方向的变化由曲线变成直线,与文献[4]所证实的情况完全相符.

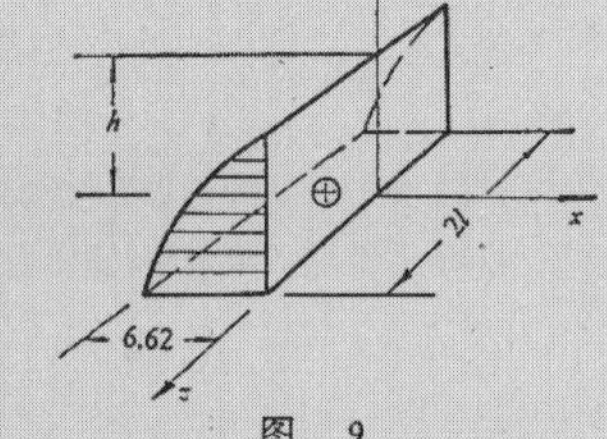

图 9

b. 二等边直角三角形河谷: 在 $0\leqslant x\leqslant\infty$, $y=-h$, $y=h$, $z=h$ 为三角形顶点的空间部分充水.

基本方程是

$$\frac{\partial^2\psi_2'}{\partial x^2}+\frac{\partial^2\psi_2'}{\partial y^2}+\frac{\partial^2\psi_2'}{\partial z^2}=c^2\frac{\partial^2\psi_2'}{\partial t^2}, \tag{6.3}$$

边界条件为:

$$\text{在 } z=0,\ -h\leqslant y\leqslant h,\ 0\leqslant x\leqslant\infty \text{ 面上;}\ \psi_2'=0, \tag{6.4}$$

$$\text{在 } z=h-y,\ 0\leqslant x\leqslant\infty \text{ 面上,}\ -\frac{\partial\psi_2'}{\partial y}-\frac{\partial\psi_2'}{\partial z}=V_2\cos\omega t, \tag{6.5}$$

$$\text{在 } z=h+y,\ 0\leqslant x\leqslant\infty \text{ 面上,}\ \frac{\partial\psi_2'}{\partial y}-\frac{\partial\psi_2'}{\partial z}=V_2\cos\omega t, \tag{6.6}$$

$$\text{在 } x=0 \text{ 处,坝面上 } \frac{\partial\psi_2'}{\partial x}=0,\ \text{在 } x\to\infty \text{ 处,}\ |\psi_2'|<\infty. \tag{6.7}$$

满足上述方程和条件的函数,

$$\psi_2'(x,y,z,t)=\frac{V_2}{\Xi_2}\sec\Xi_2\cos\frac{\Xi_2y}{h}\sin\frac{\Xi_2z}{h}\cos\omega t,\quad \Xi_2=\frac{Hh}{\sqrt{2}}, \tag{6.8}$$

相应的压力振幅系数为:

$$P_2(y,z)=\frac{\sec\Xi_2}{\Xi_2}\cos\frac{\Xi_2y}{h}\sin\frac{\Xi_2z}{h}. \tag{6.9}$$

图 10a 表示 $P_2(y,z)$ 沿坝面的分布. 在坝底 $y=0$, $z=h$ 处 $P_2(0,h)=\mathrm{tg}\Xi_2/\Xi_2$. 取 $T=0.2$ 秒,当 $h=80$ 米时 $P_2=2.28$; $h=60$ 米时, $P_2=1.45$; $h=20$ 米时, $P_2=1.00$. 图 10c 中粗实线和粗虚线构成的图表示静水压力沿坝面的分布,虚点划线为流体动压力.

c. 半圆形河谷: 在 $0\leqslant x\leqslant\infty$, $0\leqslant r\leqslant h$, $0\leqslant\theta\leqslant\pi$ 所围成的空间部分充满流体. 基本方程为:

$$\frac{\partial^2\psi_3'}{\partial r^2}+\frac{1}{r}\frac{\partial\psi_3'}{\partial r}+\frac{1}{r^2}\frac{\partial^2\psi_3'}{\partial\theta^2}+\frac{\partial^2\psi_3'}{\partial x^2}=c^2\frac{\partial^2\psi_3'}{\partial t^2}, \tag{6.10}$$

图 10a

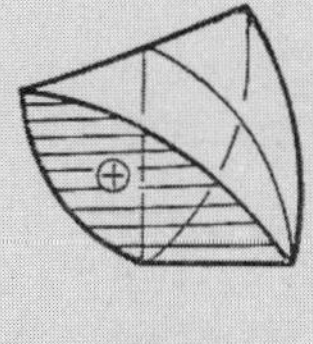

图 10b

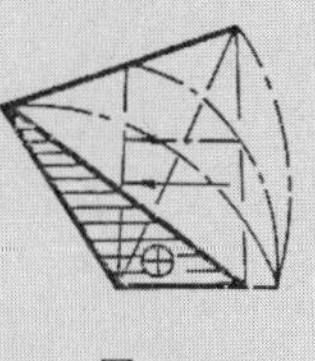

图 10c

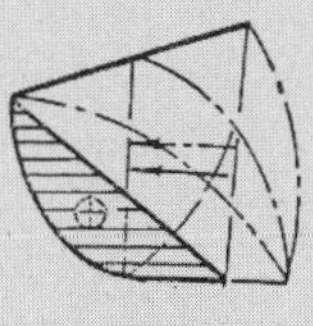

图 10d

边界条件为：

$$\text{在}\ 0\leqslant\theta\leqslant\pi,\ r=h,\ 0\leqslant x\leqslant\infty\ \text{面上},\ \frac{\partial\psi_3'}{\partial r}=V_2\sin\theta\cos\omega t, \tag{6.11}$$

$$\text{在}\begin{cases}\theta=0\\ \theta=\pi\end{cases},\ 0\leqslant r\leqslant h,\ 0\leqslant x\leqslant\infty\ \text{面上},\ \psi_3'=0.\ \text{在}\ x=0\ \text{处},\ \frac{\partial\psi_3'}{\partial x}=0.$$

在 $x\to\infty$ 处，$|\psi_3'|<\infty$.

满足上述方程和条件的

$$\psi_3'(r,\theta,x,t)=V_2h\sin\theta\frac{J_1(Hr)}{\varXi_1J_1'(\varXi_1)}\cos\omega t,\ J_1\ \text{为贝塞尔函数}. \tag{6.12}$$

相应的压力振幅系数为

$$P_3(r,\theta)=\frac{J_1(Hr)\sin\theta}{\varXi_1J_1'(\varXi_1)}, \tag{6.13}$$

在坝底 $r=h$，$\theta=\frac{\pi}{2}$ 处 $P_3\left(h,\frac{\pi}{2}\right)=J_1(\varXi_1)/\varXi_1J_1'(\varXi_1)$.

式中 $J_1'(\varXi_1)=\frac{1}{2}[J_0(\varXi_1)-J_2(\varXi_1)]$，$J_0$，$J_2$ 均为贝塞尔函数．图 10b 表示 $P_3(r,\theta)$ 沿坝面的分布．图 10d 中粗实线和粗虚线构成的图为静水压力的分布，而虚点划线则为水动压力．

2. 流体动载荷的分析

现在，我们来计算作用于坝面上的总水动压力，其系数为 C_p；对于水面线的水动力矩，其系数为 C_M；总水动力中心（总水动力的作用点），其系数为 $\bar{Y}$.

矩形河谷：

$$C_{P_1}=\frac{P_1}{2lh}=\frac{\sec\varXi_1-1}{\varXi_1^2},\quad C_{M_1}=\frac{M_1}{2lh^2}=\frac{\mathrm{tg}\,\varXi_1-\varXi_1}{\varXi_1^3},$$

$$\bar{Y}_1=\frac{y}{h}=\frac{\sin\varXi_1-\varXi_1\cos\varXi_1}{\varXi_1(1-\cos\varXi_1)},\quad P_1=\int_0^h\int_{-l}^{l}P_1(y,z)dydz,\ M_1=\int_0^h\int_{-l}^{l}(h-y)P_1(y,z)dydz.$$

二等边直角三角形河谷：

$$C_{P_2}=\frac{P_2}{h^2}=\frac{\varXi_2-\mathrm{tg}\varXi_2\cos2\varXi_2}{\varXi_2^3},$$

$$C_{M_2}=\frac{M_2}{h^3}=\frac{\mathrm{tg}\,\varXi_2-\varXi_2}{2\varXi_2^3},\quad \bar{Y}_2=\frac{z}{h}=\frac{C_{M_2}}{C_{P_2}},$$

式中

$$P_2=\int_0^h dz\int_{-b(z)}^{b(z)}P_2(y,z)dy,\quad M_2=\int_0^h zdz\int_{-b(z)}^{b(z)}P_2(y,z)dy,\ b(z)=h-z,$$

半圆形河谷:

$$C_{P_3}=\frac{2P_3}{\pi h^2}=\frac{2}{\pi J'(\Xi_1)}\sum_{m=0}^{\infty}\frac{(-1)^m\left(\frac{1}{2}\Xi_1\right)^{2m}}{m!(m+1)!(2m+3)},$$

$$C_{M_3}=\frac{2M_3}{\pi h^3}=J_2(\Xi_1)/\Xi_1^2J_1'(\Xi_1),\quad \bar{r}_{\theta=\frac{\pi}{2}}=\frac{r}{h}=C_{M_3}/C_{P_3},$$

式中

$$P_3=\int_0^{\pi}d\theta\int_0^h P_3(r,\theta)rdr,\quad M_3=\int_0^{\pi}\sin\theta d\theta\int_0^h P_3(r,\theta)r^2dr.$$

对 C_{P_1}, C_{M_1}, $\bar{Y}_1$ 作数值计算,将结果列于表 2 中. 从 C_{P_1} 可以算出,当 $\alpha=\omega V_2/g=0.1$, 0.2, 0.3 时的值,计算结果见表 3. 从表 3 可知,当 $\alpha=0.1$ 时, $\Xi_1=1.5$ 的情况下, 地面垂直

表 2

Ξ_1	C_{P_1}	C_{M_1}	$\bar{Y}_1$	Ξ_2	C_{P_2}	C_{M_2}	$\bar{Y}_2$
0.25	0.514	0.339	0.660	0.25	1.660	0.1695	0.102
0.50	0.558	0.370	0.664	0.50	1.640	0.1850	0.113
0.75	0.651	0.431	0.662	0.75	1.620	0.2160	0.133
1.00	0.850	0.557	0.656	1.00	1.650	0.2787	0.169
1.25	1.385	0.901	0.651	1.25	1.875	0.4510	0.240
1.50	5.840	3.740	0.640	1.50	4.600	1.8700	0.407

表 3

$\alpha=\frac{\omega V_2}{g}$	$\alpha=0.1$	$\alpha=0.2$	$\alpha=0.3$
Ξ_1	C_{P_1}	C_{P_1}	C_{P_1}
0.25	0.0514	0.1030	0.1542
0.50	0.0558	0.1120	0.1674
0.75	0.0651	0.1302	0.1953
1.00	0.0850	0.1700	0.2550
1.25	0.1385	0.2770	0.4155
1.50	0.5840	1.1680	1.752

振动所激起的总水动力就能大于总静水力. 如果以 50% 的 α 值来计算地面垂直振动部分的水动力, 则 $\alpha=0.2$, $\Xi_1=1.5$ 时, $C_{P_1}>C_{P_0}(0.584>0.5)$.对比表 3 的数据可以看到, 这时对坝底线($y=0$ 处)的倾覆力矩系数 $C_{M_1}>C_{M_0}$. 即$C_{M_1}=5.84\times0.36\times0.1=0.2102>C_{M_0}=0.5\times\frac{1}{3}=0.1667$, 此处 C_{P_0}, C_{M_0} 为静水总压力系数和力矩系数. 当 $\omega=60\frac{1}{秒}$, $h=36.3$ 米; $\omega=30\frac{1}{秒}$, $h=72.6$ 米; $\omega=20\frac{1}{秒}$, $h=109$ 米; $\omega=10\frac{1}{秒}$, $h=198$ 米时,都会出现 $\Xi_1=1.5$ 的情况,而这些情况是工程实际中存在的.

3. 共振条件

对于矩形河谷,当 $\cos\Xi_1\to0$ 时, 对于三角形河谷, 当 $\cos\Xi_2\to0$, 对于半圆形河谷, 当 $J'(\Xi_1)\to0$ 时,都将出现共振现象. 在给定的地震区设计水坝时,宜选择适当的蓄水深度以避免共振现象的形成. 如果在实际中不能避免共振条件的出现, 则在给定共振条件下做模型试验来校核计算的结果.

根据上述的计算和分析,可以看到, 地震铅直分加速度所激起的流体动压力、力矩等等在某些情况下,超过静水压力和力矩,在另一些条件下则有可能大于水平分加速度所激起的水动压力和力矩. 因此,正如资料[4]中所提到的,在设计中应考虑到这个因素.

*　　*　　*

令(3.1)—(3.10)式中, 除 $\boldsymbol{V}_1$ 以外的所有 $\boldsymbol{V}_\eta$, $\boldsymbol{\Omega}_\eta$ 均等于零, 根据(5.1),(5.6)式计算出 P_1 值, 并把它与资料[6]中相应的数据相比较, 可以看到,它们是较好地相符合的. 那么,建立在

同样基础上，相应于其他参变量 $\boldsymbol{V}_\eta$, $\boldsymbol{\Omega}_\eta$ 的结果也是可靠的.

资料[3]中的(4.7)式下面一行的符号 $f(m)$，应该是 $f(m) = \sin\frac{m\pi}{2} - \frac{2}{m\pi}$. 将相关各式中的级数再作一次求和化简，即得本文中相应的较简单的表示式，(4.16)式应代之以本文的(3.9)式.(4.14)式中各项的+，-号均应以本文(3.5)式中相应项的符号为准.(4.17)式等号右边各项都应乘以-1. 本文的许多公式都具有无穷级数的形式，但是，这些级数收敛很迅速. 一般取一、二项，或三项就已足够准确. 因此，计算时应用起来比较方便.

本文所提问题，虽然只分析了简谐振动的情况，而地震所激起的地面波动却是错综复杂的. 不过，通过波谱分析总可以将地面波动的规律表示为 Fourier 级数或积分的形式. 于是，本文所给结果就可能推广到一些具体的实际问题上去.

参 考 资 料

[1] Westergaard, M., *Trans. ASCE.*, 1933.
[2] Лейбензон, Л. С., *Ученые Записки МГУ*, 1935, № 2.
[3] 陈振诚，中国力学学会第一次流体力学学术讨论会论文选集，科学出版社，1963.
[4] 陈振诚，力学学报，**6**(1963), 1.
[5] 陈振诚，*ПММ*, **25** (1961), 1.
[6] Zanger, C. N., *Civ. Eng.*, **22** (1952), 4.

F—2·5　运用陈振诚积分变换寻求水动推进力的定量值

第一节　能造成水动推进力的船底浸湿面线型

对现有技术的船艇通过改进其线型，想提高航速3%都非常难做到。但是我们从改变水动力流场，能激起一些我们期盼得到的水动力和相应的水动力矩，能从根本上大幅度提高航速及其整体性能。为了达到这个诉求，我们考虑：船艇在运行中发动机所输出的功率，有一部分克服水的阻力推动船前进做有用功。而另一部分激起水流运动向两边散开成为被耗散的无用能量。如果把这部分被耗散的无用能量通过某种方法，使它转变为推动船加速前进的水动推进力做有用功，这在原理上符合物理学中的能量守恒原理，而在工程实际中是一种能大幅度提高船艇航速、高效节能的创造发明。

我们依据这项发明创造技术建成长6.3m、宽2.1m、型深0.9m的实船，空船排水量1t，用功率为200马力的舷外机推进，卫星跟踪的GPS系统实测证实，乘员为8人时，排水量为1.5t，航速为36.15节，增加乘员一倍至16人时，排水量为2t，航速非但不下降，反倒提高到37.15节。而现有技术的快艇对载重量变化的响应特别敏感。如果增加2人的载重量，航速会下降1.7节，如果增加8人的载重量，成为16人，航速就会下降6.8节，也就是下降到30.35节。

发明技术与现有船艇的技术对比：航速提高（37.15–30.35）/（30.35）≈22.4%。高效节能：空船排水量1t，乘员8人时排水量1.5t，乘员16人时1.5t+0.5t=2t，因此节能（2.0–1.5）/1.5≈33.3%。船的推进功率，保持不变为200马力，没有任何添加。这就充分证明22.4%航速的提高、33.3%的节能都是发明技术中的由耗散的无用能量转化为水动推进力的结果。

上述数据证实本发明的核心理论——激起实际存在的水动推进力能大幅度提高航速，高效节能，并且用实船实航证明了水动推进力的出现和它的实际效益。

现在阐述造成足够强大的水动推进的核心线型设计：在船底浸湿面中心线的两侧设置一对对称平行于中心线的涌浪导流槽，在两船舷设置压浪导流挡板。导流槽和导流挡板的顶部横剖面为圆弧形，其纵剖面顶线为前低后高与船底基面形成倾角，请见下列各线段的倾角。

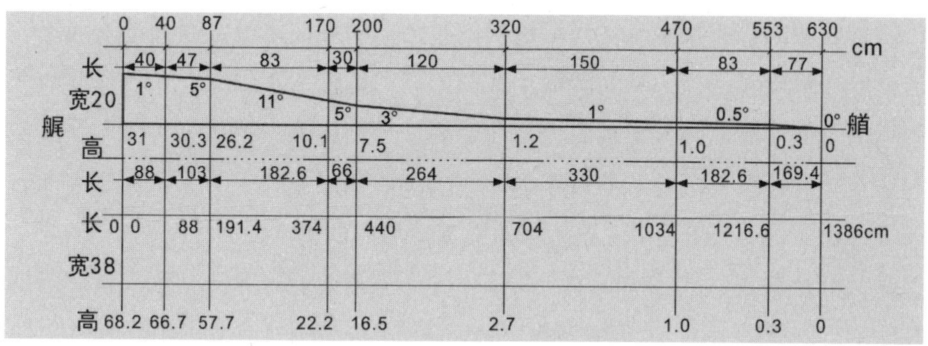

图1 涌浪导流槽的顶线布局示意图

图1中是长度为630cm，宽度为210cm，型深为90cm的快艇的涌浪导流槽的纵剖面顶线的设计，依据这项设计建成实船，实航实验成功。数据如上面的叙述。经国家船检单位审查批准，可批量生产投放市场。

——……——……——线以下的数据是以630艇为依据，缩尺比为2.2，拟放大建成1386cm的缉私、巡逻、救援快艇，推进功率拟选用2×1250马力的卧舱机，航速能达到61节，比现有技术的快艇51节提高航速19.6%。但现有技术的快艇因不可能出现本发明船艇在运行中造成的水动力流场和相应的水动推进力以及水动稳定扶正力矩。因此国内外除运动用的赛艇外，不可能有达到或超过60节的航速。

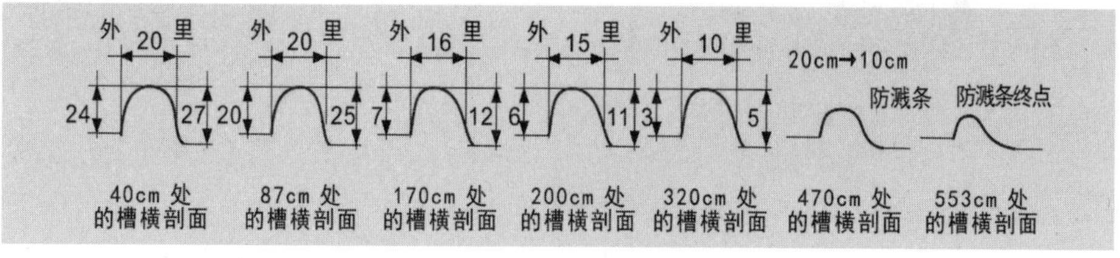

图2 涌浪导流槽从船艉到船艏各指定点处的横剖面示意图

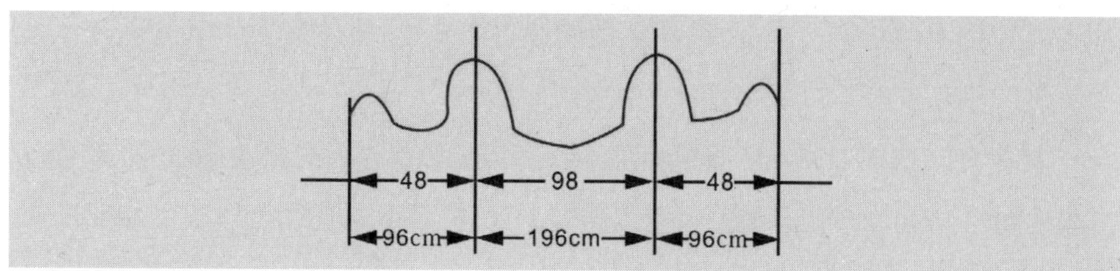

图3 涌浪导流槽和压浪导流挡板在船艉部的布局48-98-48为630艇，96-196-96为1386艇

本发明的核心技术是：当船艇前进时船艏附件的水流大部分进入涌浪导流槽和压浪导流挡板，从而降低了水面涌高而降低了水阻力，并且降低两舷附近的水面涌高而降低了水阻力。在船底，被推压的水流从侧向挤入导流槽和压浪导流挡板，汇合从前方进入导流槽和压浪导流挡板的水流一起被推向船艉部而顺畅地流出船尾。这些水流对前低后高的顶部曲面（见图1）造成足够强大的法向压力。该法向压力的水平方向分量与船行方向一致，就是名副其实的水动推进力P。法向压力的垂向分量就是水动升力L。水动推进力P对船体重心构成航向稳定扶正力矩MP，确保航行航向稳定而不偏离既定的目标。水动升力对船艇重心构成船体横向稳定扶正力矩ML和纵向稳定扶正力矩。前者确保横向稳定而克服横摇摆动，后者确保纵向稳定而克服纵摇拍击。随着航速的提高，这些力和相应的力矩迅速增大。于是出现本发明船艇行驶越快速，越是稳定安全的特殊性能。因此，加大推进功率就能突破水的速度障，把航速提高到大于60节、70节、80节，甚至更高的速度。

图4　发明船艇630（长6.3米）艇的船底构造

但是，现有技术的船艇因不可能激起本发明船艇特有的流场和相应的水动推进力P、水动升力L和水动航向稳定扶正力矩MP，水动横向稳定扶正力矩ML及水动纵向稳定扶正力矩，因此在航速大于50节之后，再加大推进功率就会出现稳定性危机，不但航速上不去，还会出现失去稳定性造成倾覆的危险。因此现有技术的快艇，除运动赛事用的小赛艇外，没有大于60节的航速，也就是说，现有技术不可能突破水的速度障。

本发明试航成功的630艇的船底构成仰透视图，请见图4。630艇敞篷实航请见图5，图6为630艇有篷实船实航照片，图7为630艇放大建成的缉私、救援、巡逻快艇。图8为1600艇的总布量图。

（1）涌浪导流槽，在船底中心线两侧；

（2）外面是压浪导流挡板。

图5　630敞篷船艇实船实航照片

舷外机200马力，乘员16人，航速37.15节。

图6　630有篷船艇实船实航照片

图7　1600（长16米）艇的船底构造，从630艇依据相似律放大获得，1600快艇的航行照片。卧舱机2300马力，乘员13人，航速62节。用于缉私、救援、巡逻、边防等

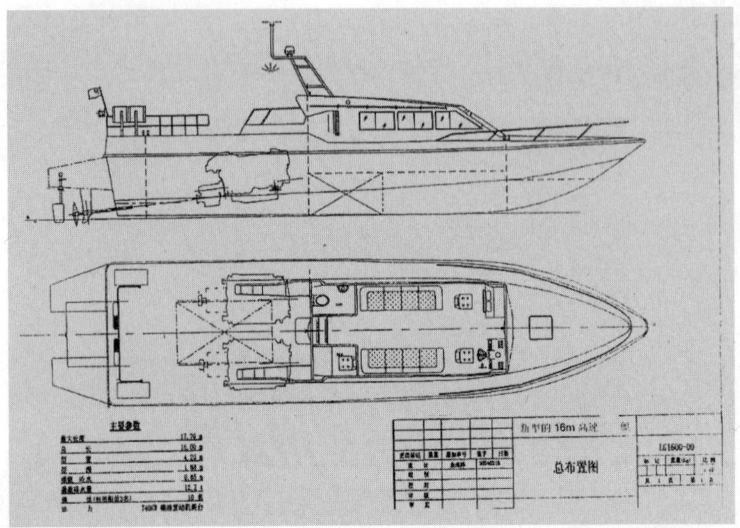

图8 1600艇的总布量图

F—2·6 运用陈振诚积分变换寻求水动推进力的定量值

第二节 水动推进力及其应用

陈振诚 陈 昕 陈 旸

（中国科学院国家天文台 流体力学小组 北京 100012）

[摘 要]考虑到三维效应和重力影响，提出研究设置导流槽的船底在水面滑行激起的流场以及作用在槽和船底浸湿面上的水动力。该导流槽的顶部曲面前低后高，对船底基面形成倾角。运用严谨的数学物理方法解决问题，求得描绘三维流场状况的解析函数，由此获得船艇前进时出现在槽顶部曲面上推船艇前进的水动推进力和向上的水动升力定量值的解析表述式。将船底浸湿面设计成设置导流槽的外形，建成实船试航，通过卫星跟踪的GPS系统实测获得的数据证明了水动推进力的存在，且它随着航速的提高而迅速增大，于是船速以及稳定性、安全性均得以大幅提高。实船设计时，可通过合理调整表述式中的物理参数，设计建造整体性能远优于常规船艇的实船。

[关键词]流体动力学；水动力学；水动推进力；水动升力；涌浪导流槽

[中图分类号]U661.1 [文献标识码]A [文章编号]1001-9855(2011)01-0010-06

Hydrodynamic propulsion and its application

Chen Zhencheng Chen Xin Chen Yang

Abstract: Taking account of the 3-D effect and the gravity impact, this paper studies the flow field which has been activated when the ship bottom with blast groove slides on the water surface and the hydrodynamic of the wetted surface of the ship bottom. The top curved surface of the blast groove is higher in fore and is lower in aft, which forms an obliquity against the bottom baseplane. The rigorous methods in mathematical physics are applied to work out the analytic function describing the 3-D flow field in order to obtain the hydrodynamic propulsive force, which appears on the top curved surface of the groove when the ship moves forward, and the quantificational analytic expression for the hydrodynamic lift. The wetted surface of the ship bottom is designed to be able to set blast groove, and the ship trails are build to prove the existences of the hydrodynamic propulsive force through the data obtaining from the satellite tracking GPS system. It augments rapidly along with the increasing ship speed, so the ship speed, stability and security all are improved greatly. In terms of the ship design, the overall design and construct performance surpasses the regular ship by rationally adjusting the physical parameters in the expressions.

Keywords: hydrokinetics; hydrodynamic; hydrodynamic propulsive force; hydrodynamic lift; swell blast groove

0 引 言

常规船艇在纵向基面对水平的攻角 θ=0 时前进，水动升力 L_0=0，船的总重量由等于排水量的水浮力承担，这种船称为排水型船。每条尺度不同的船都有各自无法超越的水的阻力峰。例如船长约 150 m，排水量约 6 000 t，吃水深度约 6 m 的常规驱逐舰或巡洋舰，推进功率约 10 万马力，航速只能达到约 30 kn。船长约 400 m，排水量约 10 万吨，吃水深度约 11 m，推进功率约 28 万马力的航空母舰，航速只能达到约 33 kn。如果对它们再加大推进功率，航速不会相应地提高，其根本原因就是它们没有能力克服水的阻力峰。排水型的集装箱船、滚装船都是这样，想提高其航速，十分困难。

为了使船行驶时能激起人们所期望的水动力，并以此来克服水的阻力峰，从而提高其航速以及整体性能，我们考虑设置特殊的船底浸湿面的外形，也就是在船底浸湿面的纵向设置一条、两条或多条涌浪导流槽，槽的顶部曲面在纵向前低后高，对船底基面形成倾角 α，α 大于纵向船底基面对水平面的攻角 θ。在两船舷设置压浪阻溅流挡板，挡板的顶部曲面也是前低后高，对船底基面形成倾角 α。导流槽向前、向后、向下敞开，挡板向前、向下、向后、侧向向外敞开。导流槽和挡板的顶部横剖面都是圆弧形。

在船底浸湿面设置对称平行于船底纵向中心线的一对导流槽，以及在两船舷设置压浪阻溅流挡板的情况下，当船前进时，船艏附近部分水流进入导流槽和压浪挡板，从而降低了船艏附近和两船舷外侧的水面涌高，降低了水阻力。在船底下面的水流受前进船底的推压，从侧向挤入导流槽和压浪挡板，会合从前方进入的水流，一同被导向艉部并顺畅地流出船尾。于是对槽和挡板纵向前低后高的顶部曲面形成足够强大的法向压力，其水平分量的方向与船行方向一致，推船前进，即为名符其实的水动推进力，其垂向分量即为水动升力。它们迫使船艇航速大幅度提高，稳定安全性大幅度增强。文中我们对前人的水动升力近似估算方法[1]做了讨论。

为了理论分析时的简要、清晰，在下一节中先考虑设置一条导流槽。

1 设置一条导流槽的水动力流场和相应的水动力

假定在半无限空间 $-\infty \leqslant x \leqslant \infty$，$-\infty \leqslant y \leqslant 0$，$-\infty \leqslant z \leqslant \infty$，域中被水充满，水的密度 ρ=常数。假定长度 $2a$、宽度 $2b$、槽宽为 $2l$、吃水深度为 δ 的船底浸湿面，以攻角 θ、速度 U 在水面滑行，槽顶部曲面对船底基面形成倾角 $\alpha(\alpha>\theta)$，见图 1。置坐标原点于船底纵向中心线和横向中心线的交点处。

图 1 中：x、y、z 为坐标系，O 为坐标原点，θ 为船底纵向基面对水平面的攻角，α 为导流槽的顶线对船底基面的倾角$(\alpha>\theta)$，$2a$ 为船底浸湿面的长度，$2b$ 为船底浸湿面的宽度，$2l$ 为导流槽横剖面的宽度，h' 为导流槽末端的高度，h 为水动推进力作用点的吃

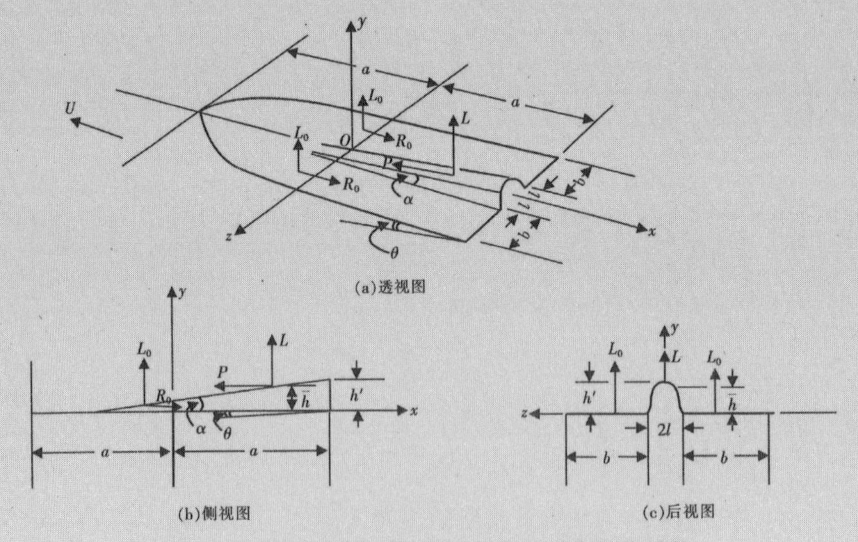

图 1　在船底纵向中心线设置导流槽的船底浸湿面直线前进时的示意图

水深度，L 为作用在导流槽顶部曲面上的水动升力，P 为作用在导流槽顶部曲面上的水动推进力。L_0 为作用在槽外两侧浸湿面上的水动升力，R_0 为作用在槽外两侧浸湿面上的水动阻力。

水的运动可以用流体速度势函数 $\Phi(x,y,z)=Ux+\varphi(x,y,z)$ 表述。其中 $\varphi(x,y,z)$ 是被扰动流体速度势函数，U 是船底浸湿面的滑行速度。

流体速度势函数满足下列的偏微分方程，它是连续方程

$$\frac{\partial^2\Phi}{\partial x^2}+\frac{\partial^2\Phi}{\partial y^2}+\frac{\partial^2\Phi}{\partial z^2}=0 \tag{1}$$

我们定义在空间域 $-\infty\leqslant x\leqslant\infty$, $-\infty\leqslant y\leqslant 0$, $-\infty\leqslant z\leqslant\infty$ 中被水充满，此处 $\Phi(x,y,z)\equiv\Phi(x,y,z)$，但是在域 $-\infty\leqslant x\leqslant\infty$, $0<y\leqslant\infty$, $-\infty\leqslant z\leqslant\infty$ 中没有水，此处 $\Phi(x,y,z)\equiv 0$。

假定在水自由表面 $-\infty\leqslant x\leqslant\infty$, $y=0$, $-\infty\leqslant z\leqslant\infty$ 处为大气压力。于是，我们可以导出水自由表面的边界条件如下式[6]

$$\frac{\partial^2\varphi}{\partial x^2}+K\frac{\partial\varphi}{\partial y}=0,\quad \text{其中 } K=\frac{g}{U^2} \tag{2}$$

假定，在浸湿面的远前方，流体的被扰动趋向于0，也就是说，在 $x\to-\infty$ 处：

$$\frac{\partial\Phi}{\partial x}=U,\quad \varphi(x,y,z)=0 \tag{3}$$

在浸湿面的远左方或远右方，流体的被扰动趋向于0，也就是说在 $z\to\infty$ 或 $z\to-\infty$ 处：

$$\varphi(x,y,z)=0 \tag{4}$$

在 $y\to-\infty$ 处：

$$\varphi(x,y,z)=0 \tag{5}$$

在船底浸湿面上的边界条件，也就是说在 $-a\leqslant x\leqslant a$, $y=-\delta$, $-b-l\leqslant z\leqslant b+l$ 面上

$$\frac{\partial\varphi}{\partial y}=-U\sin\theta \tag{6}$$

在导流槽顶部浸湿面上，也就是说在 $-a\leqslant x\leqslant a$, $y=-h$, $-l\leqslant z\leqslant l$ 面上，

$$\frac{\partial\varphi}{\partial y}=-U\sin\alpha,\ \text{其中 } h=\delta-\bar{h},\ \bar{h}=0.5889a\cdot\tan\alpha \tag{7}$$

在导流槽两边垂向壁面上，也就是在 $-a\leqslant x\leqslant a$, $-\delta\leqslant y\leqslant-(\delta-h')$, $|z|=l$ 面上，

$$\frac{\partial\varphi}{\partial z}=0 \tag{8}$$

在船底浸湿面的尾端，也就是在 $x=a$ 处，水流顺畅地流出浸湿面的尾端，也就是说，此处水流的速度为有限值，

$$\left|\frac{\partial\varphi}{\partial x}\right|<\infty,\ \left|\frac{\partial\varphi}{\partial y}\right|<\infty,\ \left|\frac{\partial\varphi}{\partial z}\right|<\infty \tag{9}$$

在 $x\to\infty$ 处流体的被扰动速度为有限值，也就是

$$\left|\frac{\partial\varphi}{\partial x}\right|<\infty,\ \left|\frac{\partial\varphi}{\partial y}\right|<\infty,\ \left|\frac{\partial\varphi}{\partial z}\right|<\infty \tag{10}$$

现在我们已经建立上述合理的物理模型和描述该模型的系列偏微分方程。在下节中我们将用严谨的数学物理方法解出那些方程，从而获得问题的唯一解析解。

2 求解方程，确定流体速度势函数

依据上节中所述的物理模型，寻找问题的解就归结为找到分别能满足上节中方程(1)和边界条件(2)~(10)的流体速度势函数 $\Phi(x,y,z)$。

我们采用一种积分变换[7-9]解决问题。

满足方程(1)，得到 $\Phi(x,y,z)=Ux+\varphi(x,y,z)$，此处

$$\begin{aligned}\varphi(x,y,z)=\int_{c_0-ik_0}^{c_0+ik_0}\cos\alpha\bar{Z}\int_{-c_1-ik_1}^{-c_1+ik_1}&\exp(-|\beta|x)\\ &\cdot[A(\alpha,\beta)ch\gamma y+D(\alpha,\beta)ch\gamma(y+\delta)\\ &+F(\alpha,\beta)ch\gamma(y+h)]d\alpha d\beta\end{aligned} \tag{11}$$

式中：$\bar{Z}=l-|z|$；$A(\alpha,\beta)$，$D(\alpha,\beta)$，$F(\alpha,\beta)$ 是未知的任意复变函数；$\gamma=\sqrt{\alpha^2-\beta^2}$；$\alpha,\beta$ 是复变数；c_0,c_1，$k_0=K\delta$，k_1 为常数。

假定：a 是参考长度；而 $x'=x/a$, $y'=y/a$, $z'=z/a$, $b'=b/a$, $\delta'=\delta/a$, $a'=a/a=1$。为了便于书写，可以把 x', y', z', b', δ' 写成 x,y,z,b,δ。

把式(11)代入式(6)，滑行船底浸湿面上的边界条件被满足，于是我们得到

$$\begin{aligned}\frac{\partial\varphi}{\partial y}=\int_{c_0-ik_0}^{c_0+ik_0}\cos\alpha\bar{Z}\int_{-c_1-ik_1}^{-c_1+ik_1}&\exp(-|\beta|x)\gamma[-A(\alpha,\beta)sh\gamma\delta\\ &+F(\alpha,\beta)sh\gamma(h-\delta)]d\alpha d\beta=-U\sin\theta\end{aligned} \tag{12}$$

把式(11)代入式(7)，导流槽顶部浸湿面上的边界条件被满足，

$$\begin{aligned}\frac{\partial\varphi}{\partial y}=\int_{c_0-ik_0}^{c_0+ik_0}\cos\alpha\bar{Z}\int_{-c_1-ik_1}^{-c_1+ik_1}&\exp(-|\beta|x)\gamma[-A(\alpha,\beta)sh\gamma h\\ &+D(\alpha,\beta)sh\gamma(\delta-h)]d\alpha d\beta=-U\sin\alpha\end{aligned} \tag{13}$$

引用一种积分变换[7-9]，从上列两式分别得到相应的下列两式，

$$-A(\alpha,\beta)sh\gamma\delta-F(\alpha,\beta)sh\gamma(\delta-h)]=-\overline{V}_1 \quad (14)$$

式中：$\overline{V}_1=V_1\Omega, V_1=U\sin\theta$。

$$-A(\alpha,\beta)sh\gamma h+D(\alpha,\beta)sh\gamma(\delta-h)=-\overline{V}_2 \quad (15)$$

式中：$\overline{V}_2=V_2\Omega, V_2=U\sin\alpha$。

式中：

$$\Omega=\frac{1}{\pi^2}\cdot\frac{k_0}{\alpha\sqrt{k_0^2+\lambda_0^2}\cos\alpha b}\cdot\frac{k_1}{\beta\sqrt{k_1^2+\lambda_1^2}\,ch\beta}\cdot\frac{1}{\gamma},$$

此处 $\lambda_0=\alpha-c_0, \lambda_1=\beta+c_1, \delta>h$，$h$ 是在导流槽顶部曲面上 P 和 L 的作用点的吃水深度。

把式(11)代入式(2)，水自由表面的边界条件被满足。我们得到

$$A(\alpha,\beta)\beta^2+D(\alpha,\beta)[\beta^2ch\gamma\delta+K\gamma sh\gamma\delta]+F(\alpha,\beta)\cdot[\beta^2ch\gamma h+K\gamma sh\gamma h]=0 \quad (16)$$

由于 $\gamma\delta$、γh 为小量，可以视 $ch\gamma\delta=1, ch\gamma h=1, sh\gamma\delta=\gamma\delta, sh\gamma h=\gamma h$；于是式(16)可简化为

$$A(\alpha,\beta)\beta^2+QD(\alpha,\beta)+RF(\alpha,\beta)=0 \quad (17)$$

式中：$Q=\beta^2+k_0\gamma^2, R=\beta^2+k_3\gamma^2, k_0=K\delta, k_3=Kh$。解联立方程(14)，(15)，(17)可以得到

$$A(\alpha,\beta)=\frac{\overline{V}_2Q-\overline{V}_1R}{N},$$

$$D(\alpha,\beta)=\frac{\overline{V}_2(R\delta-\beta^2\bar{\delta})-\overline{V}_1Rh}{N\bar{\delta}},$$

$$F(\alpha,\beta)=\frac{\overline{V}_1(Qh+\beta^2\bar{\delta})-\overline{V}_2Q\delta}{N\bar{\delta}} \quad (18)$$

式中：$N=Qsh\gamma h-Rsh\gamma\delta+\beta^2sh\gamma\bar{\delta}$，$\bar{\delta}=\delta-h$。展开 $sh\gamma h$、$sh\gamma\delta$、$sh\gamma\bar{\delta}$，略去可以被略去的高阶小量，得：

$$N=-\frac{\gamma^3}{6}\zeta_2[(G\beta)^2+\alpha^2],$$

式中：$G^2=\frac{\zeta_1-\zeta_2}{\zeta_2}, \zeta_1=\delta^3-h^3, \zeta_2=k_0h(\delta^2-h^2)$ (19)

到此，式(11)中的任意复变函数 $A(\alpha,\beta)$，$D(\alpha,\beta)$，$F(\alpha,\beta)$已被确定。

把式(18)代入式(11)，条件 8 被满足。沿指出的积分环路进行积分运算[7-9]，可以证明边界条件(3)，(4)，(5)，(9)，(10)都能满足。现在我们已经确定式(11)中 $\varphi(x,y,z)$能满足本问题所有的边界条件和方程，也就是说，本文所提问题的唯一解析解已经被找到。$\varphi(x,y,z)$是能够描述三维被扰动流场的流体速度势函数。

3 证明解的唯一性

假定，这个问题还有另一个解$\overline{\varphi}(x,y,z)$，它可以写成

$$\overline{\varphi}(x,y,z)=\int_{c_0-ik_0}^{c_0+ik_0}\cos v\overline{Z}\int_{-c_1-ik_1}^{-c_1+ik_1}\exp(-|\mu|x)[B(\mu,v)ch\xi y+E(\mu,v)ch\xi(y+\delta)+H(\mu,v)ch\xi(y+h)]d\mu dv \quad (20)$$

于是，$\Phi(x,y,z)=Ux+\varphi(x,y,z)+\overline{\varphi}(x,y,z)$ (21)

式中：μ、v 是复变数，$\xi=\sqrt{v^2-\mu^2}$；$B(\mu,v)$、$E(\mu,v)$、$H(\mu,v)$是未知复变函数。把式(21)分别代入式(6)、式(7)，得到在 $y=-\delta$ 处

$$\frac{\partial\Phi}{\partial y}=\frac{\partial\varphi}{\partial y}+\frac{\partial\overline{\varphi}}{\partial y}=-U\sin\theta \quad (22)$$

在 $y=-h$ 处，

$$\frac{\partial\Phi}{\partial y}=\frac{\partial\varphi}{\partial y}+\frac{\partial\overline{\varphi}}{\partial y}=-U\sin\alpha \quad (23)$$

分别把式(6)代入式(22)，把式(7)代入式(23)，则有

$$-U\sin\theta+\frac{\partial\overline{\varphi}}{\partial y}=-U\sin\theta \quad (24)$$

$$-U\sin\alpha+\frac{\partial\overline{\varphi}}{\partial y}=-U\sin\alpha \quad (25)$$

由式(24)导出 $\frac{\partial\overline{\varphi}}{\partial y}=0$，也就是在 $-a\leqslant x\leqslant a$，$y=-\delta$，$-b-l\leqslant z\leqslant b+l$ 面上

$$-B(\mu,v)sh\xi\delta+H(\mu,v)sh\xi(h-\delta)=0 \quad (26)$$

由式(25)导出，在$-a\leqslant x\leqslant a, y=-h, -l\leqslant z\leqslant l$ 面上，$\frac{\partial\overline{\varphi}}{\partial y}=0$ 也就是

$$-B(\mu,v)sh\xi h+E(\mu,v)sh\xi(\delta-h)=0 \quad (27)$$

把式(21)代入式(2)以满足水的自由表面的边界条件，我们得到

$$\frac{\partial^2\varphi}{\partial x^2}+K\frac{\partial\varphi}{\partial y}+\frac{\partial^2\overline{\varphi}}{\partial x^2}+K\frac{\partial\overline{\varphi}}{\partial y}=0 \quad (28)$$

把式(16)代入式(28)，可以导出$\frac{\partial^2\overline{\varphi}}{\partial x^2}+K\frac{\partial\overline{\varphi}}{\partial y}=0$，也就是

$$B(\mu,v)\mu^2+E(\mu,v)\overline{Q}+H(\mu,v)\overline{R}=0 \quad (29)$$

$$\overline{Q}=\mu^2+k_0\xi^2, \overline{R}=\mu^2+k_3\xi^2$$

解联立方程(26)、(27)、(29)，得 $B(\mu,v)=0$，$E(\mu,v)=0$，$H(\mu,v)=0$。把它们代入式(20)，我们得到

$$\overline{\varphi}(x,y,z)=0 \quad (30)$$

所以问题的解只能是

$$\Phi(x,y,z)=Ux+\varphi(x,y,z)+0 \quad (31)$$

也就是另一个解 $\overline{\varphi}(x,y,z)=0$ (32)

可见，在上节中找到的 $\Phi(x,y,z)=Ux+\varphi(x,y,z)$ 是这个问题的唯一解。本证明成立。

4 寻求作用在船底浸湿面上的水动力

船前进时，

1)作用在导流槽顶部曲面 $-a\leqslant x\leqslant a,y=-h$，$-l\leqslant z\leqslant l$ 上的法向水动压力为

$$p(x,-h,z)=-\rho U\frac{\partial\varphi}{\partial x} \quad (33)$$

从式(11)可导出，此处

$$\frac{\partial\varphi}{\partial x}=-\int_{c_0-ik_0}^{c_0+ik_0}\cos\alpha\bar{Z}\int_{-c_1-ik_1}^{-c_1+ik_1}|\beta|\exp(-|\beta|x)[A(\alpha,\beta)ch\gamma h+D(\alpha,\beta)ch\gamma\bar{\delta}+F(\alpha,\beta)]d\alpha d\beta \quad (34)$$

展开 $ch\gamma h$、$ch\gamma\bar{\delta}$，略去高阶小量，首先在复平面 α 上按图 2 所示的积分环路进行积分。图 2 中：$\alpha=\sigma+i\tau$ 是复变数，k_0 是任意实常量，c_0 是实常量，C_η 是回路的大弧，C_r 是回路的小弧。而后在复平面 β 上按图 3 进行环路积分运算。图 3 中：$\beta=\sigma+i\tau$ 是复变数，k_1 是任意常量，c_1 是常量，C_η 是回路的大弧。略去可以被略去的高阶小量，得到法向水动压力

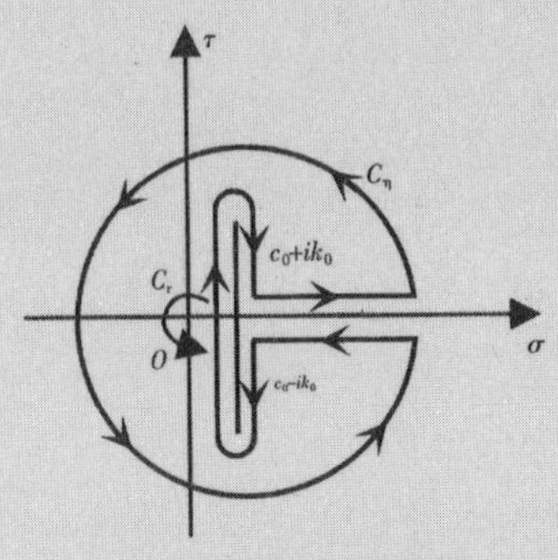

图 2 在复平面 α 上的积分回路

$$p(x,-h,z) \quad (35)$$

$$=-3\delta h\rho U\cdot\left\{\frac{V_2-V_1}{\zeta_2G^2}x+\frac{V_1h^2-V_2\delta^2}{\delta(\delta+h)}\cdot\frac{4ch\bar{k}_0\bar{Z}\exp(-\bar{G}x)}{\zeta_2G^3k_0ch\bar{k}_0bch\bar{G}}\right\}$$

此处：$k_0=K\delta$；$\bar{G}=k_0/2G$；$\bar{k}_0=\frac{k_0}{2}$。于是求得法向

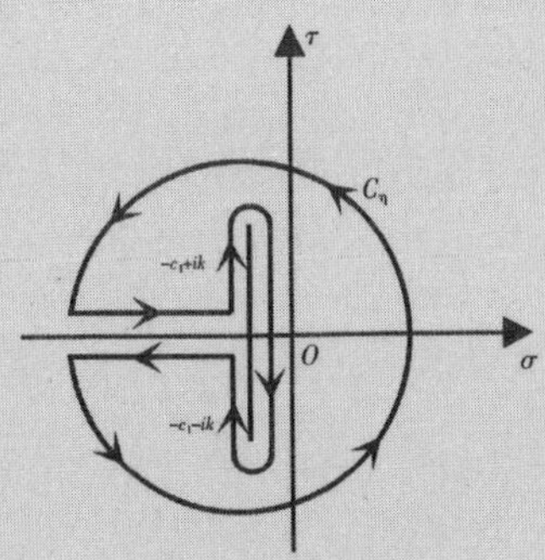

图 3 在复平面 β 上的积分回路

水动力

$$N_a=\int_{-a}^{a}2\int_{0}^{l}p(x,-h,z)dx\,dz=48a^2l\delta h\mathscr{Z}\mathscr{H}\rho U^3 \quad (36)$$

式中：$\mathscr{Z}=(\delta^2\sin\alpha-h^2\sin\theta)/\delta(\delta+h)$；

$\mathscr{H}=[h(\delta^2-h^2)/g\delta(\delta^3-h^3)^3]^{1/2}$。

所以作用在导流槽顶部曲面上，吃水深度 $-h$ 处的水动推进力 $P=N_a\sin\alpha$，

而水动升力 $L=N_a\cos\alpha$ (37)

可参见图 1 中的透视图、侧视图、后视图上标出的 P,L 。

2)作用在导流槽外两侧浸湿面 $-a\leqslant x\leqslant a,y=-\delta$，$-l-b\leqslant z\leqslant b+l$ 上的水动压力为

$$p(x,-\delta,z)=-\rho U\frac{\partial\varphi}{\partial x} \quad (38)$$

从式(11)可导出，此处的

$$\frac{\partial\varphi}{\partial x}=-\int_{c_0-ik_0}^{c_0+ik_0}\cos\alpha\bar{Z}\int_{-c_1-ik_1}^{-c_1+ik_1}|\beta|\exp(-|\beta|x)[A(\alpha,\beta)ch\gamma\delta+D(\alpha,\beta)+F(\alpha,\beta)ch\gamma\bar{\delta}]d\alpha d\beta \quad (39)$$

展开 $ch\gamma\delta$、$ch\gamma\bar{\delta}$，略去高阶小量，遵循前述的步骤，分别对 α,β 做环路积分运算，得到法向水动压力 $p(x,-\delta,z)=-3\delta h\rho U\cdot$

$$\left\{\frac{V_2-V_1}{\zeta_2G^2}x+\frac{V_1h^2-V_2\delta^2}{\delta(\delta+h)}\cdot\frac{4ch\bar{k}_0\bar{Z}\exp(-\bar{G}x)}{\zeta_2G^3k_0ch\bar{k}_0bch\bar{G}}\right\} \quad (40)$$

从而求得法向水动力，

$$N_0=\int_{-a}^{a}2\int_{l}^{l+b}p(x,-\delta,z)dx\,dz=48a^2b\delta h\mathscr{Z}\mathscr{H}\rho U^3 \quad (41)$$

于是求得作用在导流槽外两侧浸湿面上的水动升力 $L_0=N_0\cos\theta$，

而水动阻力 $R_0=N_0\sin\theta$ (42)

可参见图 1 中的透视图、侧视图、后视图上标出的 L_0,R_0。

由于在动态情况下，故很难确切测定在运动中不断变化的攻角 θ 与吃水深度 δ。因此，引入修正系数 $\eta(0<\eta\leqslant 1)$，把式(37)、(42)改写成

作用在导流槽顶部曲面上的水动推进力

$$P=48a^2 l\delta h\mathscr{Z}\mathscr{H}\eta\rho U^3\sin\alpha \quad (43)$$

而水动升力为

$$L=48a^2 l\delta h\mathscr{Z}\mathscr{H}\eta\rho U^3\cos\alpha \quad (44)$$

作用在导流槽外两侧浸湿面上的水动升力

$$L_0=48a^2 b\delta h\mathscr{Z}\mathscr{H}\eta\rho U^3\cos\theta \quad (45)$$

而水动阻力为

$$R_0=48a^2 b\delta h\mathscr{Z}\mathscr{H}\eta\rho U^3\sin\theta \quad (46)$$

修正系数 η 可以根据实际情况用实验确定之。或者用 $L+L_0=W$，W 为期盼得到的水动升力。例如：对于小艇，W=艇的总重量，这时艇进入滑行航态；对于中、大型船艇，W=部分船艇总重，这时船艇在部分滑行航态。α 为设计倾角，θ 为滑行攻角，δ 为船底浸湿面的吃水深度，U 为船底浸湿面的滑行速度。

到此，船前进时激起的水动推进力 P，水动升力 L,L_0，水动阻力 R_0 的定量值解析表达式已被找到，如式(43)~(46)所示。它们分别是船底浸湿面对水平面的攻角 θ，导流槽的顶部曲面对船底基面的倾角 α，船运动速度 U，体现重力场对流场作用的重力加速度 g，船底浸湿面的长度 a，宽度 b，导流槽的宽度 l，导流槽顶部曲面上 P,L 作用点的吃水深度 h，船底浸湿面的吃水深度 δ，水的密度 ρ 的函数。这充分体现了本文研究得到的结果，具有严谨的数学物理基础。

在下节，我们将阐述依据上述各力的合理分布，设计建造实船。在实航中卫星跟踪的 GPS 系统实测得到的准确数据与上列(43)~(46)各式得到的理论数据相对比，从而证实理论与客观实际相符合。

5 应用实例与实验验证

把上列结果，推广应用于设计建造一艘船，该船在船底纵向中心线两侧设置一对平行对称于中心线的导流槽，并且在两船舷设置压浪阻溅流挡板。槽和挡板的顶部曲面前低后高，对船底基面形成倾角 α。该船总长 6.3 m、水线长 5.8 m、宽 2.1 m，每条槽

的宽度 0.2 m、挡板宽度 0.18 m、槽和挡板末端最高处为 0.30 m，空船排水量 1 t、满载排水量 4 t，静态吃水深度 0.36 m，舷外机推进功率 147 kW(200 hp)。

当船前进时，船底浸湿面的外形会激起导流槽顶部曲面上的水动推进力 P。此处 a=2.9 m；l=0.19 m；δ=0.36 m；h=0.36−0.24=0.12 m；$\mathscr{H}$=6.573；$\mathscr{Z}$=0.101 5；θ=2°；α=8°；η=0.248 1×10^{-3}。依据式(43)得 P=106.5 kg；依据式(44)得 L=719.45 kg；依据式(45)得 L_0=1 280.19 kg；依据式(46)得 R_0=44 kg。

如果 α=15°、θ=2°，则：$\mathscr{Z}$=0.191 19；η=0.132 91×10^{-3}；L=708.15 kg；P=189.74 kg；L_0=1 291.83 kg；R_0=45.11 kg。

水动力在船体浸湿面的分布，请见图 4、图 5 所示。其中图 4 为常规船底浸湿面，图 5 为设置导流槽和压浪挡板的船底浸湿面。显然用 P、L 标出的水动力只有导流槽和挡板上才有，但图 4 常规艇上有的力，图 5 中都有。

水动推进力 P 对船艇重心构成船体航向稳定扶正力矩 M_P。

如果 α=8°、θ=2°，则：

$$\begin{aligned}M_P&=P_1\times0.49+P_2\times0.95\\&=26\times0.49+24.55\times0.95\\&=36.06\ \text{kg}\cdot\text{m}。\end{aligned}$$

如果 α=15°，θ=2°，则：

$$\begin{aligned}M_P&=48.5\times0.49+46.37\times0.95\\&=67.82\ \text{kg}\cdot\text{m}。\end{aligned}$$

式中：P_1 为导流槽的水动推进力；

P_2 为压浪挡板的水动推进力。

水动升力 L 对船艇重心构成船体横向稳定扶正力矩 M_L，抗船体横摇摆动。如果 α=8°、θ=2°，则：

$$\begin{aligned}M_L&=L_1\times0.49+L_2\times0.95\\&=90.64+165.95\\&=256.59\ \text{kg}\cdot\text{m}。\end{aligned}$$

L_1、L_2 在纵向对船艇重心构成纵向稳定扶正力矩 M_{L1}=(L_1+L_2) ×1.615=580.89 kg·m，抗船艇纵摇拍击。如果 α=15°，θ=2°，则：

$$M_L=L_1\times0.49+L_2\times0.95=253.9\ \text{kg}\cdot\text{m},$$

$$M_{L1}=(L_1+L_2)\times1.615=571.8\ \text{kg}\cdot\text{m}。$$

式中：L_1 为导流槽的水动升力；

L_2 为压浪挡板的水动升力。

从上列数据可以看到，船艇航向稳定扶正力矩、横向稳定扶正力矩、纵向稳定扶正力矩都足够强大，能在船前进时确保航向稳定而不偏离目标，确保横向稳定而克服横摇摆动，确保纵向稳定而克服纵摇拍击。从式(43)、(44)中可以看到这些水动力和水动力矩随着航速的提高与 U^3 成正比例地增大。

对比图 4、图 5 可以看到，常规艇没有 P、L，因此不可能有这种强大的稳定性保障。现在来对照试航的表现[14]，卫星跟踪的 GPS 系统实测数据显示：

逆水流行驶：乘员 8 人(排水量 1.5 t)航速 35.8 kn；乘员 16 人(排水量 2 t)，航速 36.9 kn，升速 1.1 kn。顺水流行驶：乘员 8 人，航速 36.5 kn；乘员 16 人，航速 37.4 kn，升速 0.9 kn。也就是说乘员 8 人，平均航速 36.15 kn；乘员 16 人，平均航速 37.15 kn，平均升速 1 kn。

$$\text{排水量傅汝德数 } F_\nabla=\frac{U}{\sqrt{g\sqrt[3]{\nabla}}}$$

其中 ∇ 为排水量(t=m³)；U 为航速 m/s；g=9.8 m/s² 为重力加速度。

当 F_∇>3 时，艇进入滑行航态，36.15 kn=18.6 m/s，F_∇=5.5>3；37.15 kn=19.11 m/s，F_∇=5.44>3，这时艇的总重量由水动升力承担，水的总阻力 R_S 用下式计算

$$R_S=\frac{75\times0.6}{0.515}\cdot\frac{HP}{V_S}\ (\text{kg}) \tag{47}$$

式中：V_S 航速(kn)；

HP(马力)。

$$\text{本艇 } R_S=87.38\cdot\frac{200}{37.15}=470.42\ \text{kg}。$$

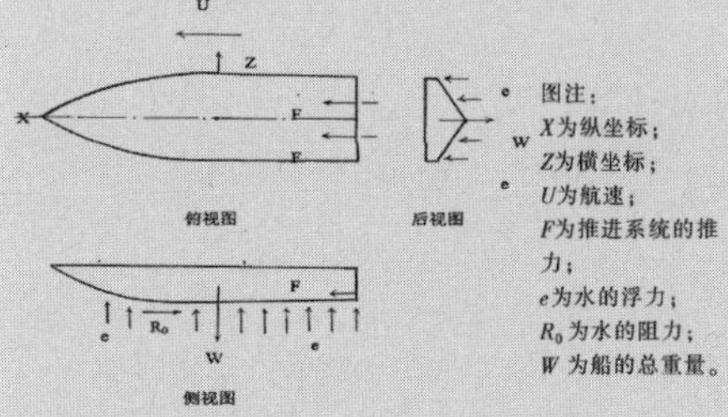

图 4 现有船艇直线前进时的受力示意图

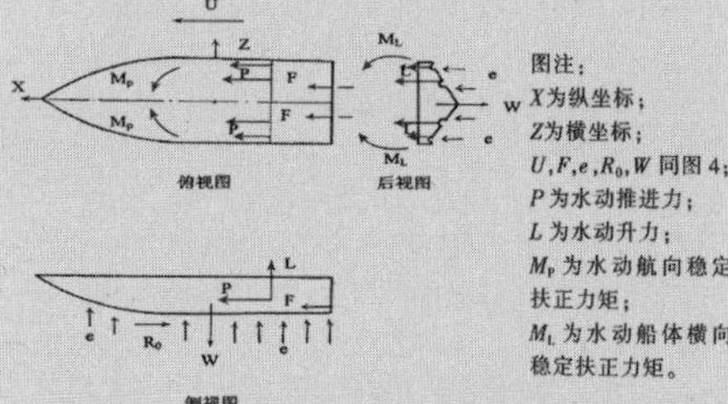

图 5 本发明船艇直线前进时的受力示意图

在常规艇上增加 2 人，航速下降 1.7 kn；如果增加 8 人，则航速下降 6.8 kn，这时常规艇

$$R_S=87.38\cdot\frac{200}{37.15-6.8}=575.82\ \text{kg。}$$

对比本艇的 470.42 kg，可以看到，本艇增加了 8 人，航速非但不下降，反倒由 36.15 kn 提升到了 37.15 kn；而常规艇却降到了 30.35 kn。其原因是 R_S 由 575.82–106.5=469.32 kg≈470.42 kg，误差(470.4–469.3)/470.4=0.002 3，所造成的结果。也就是水动推进力 P=106.5 kg，使 575.8 kg 的阻力减小 106.5 kg 而成为 470.4 kg。这就是本艇的载重量增加 100%(排水量增大 33.3%)，航速不降反升 1 kn 的根本原因。这些数据证实水动推进力的存在，并且它能大幅度提高船艇的航速。

逆水流行驶时航速提高 1.1 kn，而顺水流行驶时航速提高 0.9 kn。这是因为逆水流行驶时船体运动和水流运动之间的相对速度大于顺水流行驶时的相对速度所造成的结果。这就证明水动推进力随着航速的提高而迅速增大，如式(43)所示。这些数据表明本文的结果既有严谨的科学理论基础又符合实船实航的实验验证数据，充分证明理论与实际相符合。式(43)~式(46)计算所得的数据与实船实航实测得到的数据相符合。

6 讨 论

常规船艇在机械力的推动下会激起水动压力沿船体浸湿面的分布。从物理定性看，水动压力与船底浸湿面对水平面的攻角 θ，与体现重力场作用的重力加速度 g，船的运动速度 U，吃水深度 δ，水密度 ρ，浸湿面的尺度 a、b 等因素密切相关。也就是用数学式表述的水动压力应该是 U、θ、δ、ρ、g、a、b 等的函数，并且船底浸湿面的三维效应应予以考虑。若设置导流槽和压浪阻溅流挡板，会在槽或挡板的顶部曲面上造成水动推进压力，它应该是：U、θ、δ、ρ、g、a，b，槽顶部的吃水深度 h，槽宽度 l，槽顶部对船底基面的倾角 α 的函数。要考虑这许多因素、寻找该水动压力真实定量值的解析表述式，就必须建立描述合理模型的数学物理方程，并且用严谨的数学物理方法求解方程，才能找到真实的结果。

考虑到这些实际存在的物理因素，我们提出研究体现三维效应和重力影响设置导流槽和压浪挡板的船底浸湿面上的水动推进力。运用严谨的数学物理方法建立描绘合理模型的方程、求解方程，找到了船前进时激起而分别作用于导流槽和挡板顶部曲面上的水动推进力 P、水动升力 L、作用在导流槽和挡板外两侧的船底浸湿面上的水动升力 L_0、水动阻力 R_0 等定量值的解析表述式，详见式(43)~式(46)。

从这些解析式中人们能看到这些力是 θ、α、U、ρ、g、δ、h、a、b、l 的函数，它们体现了上述物理因素在各该力中的贡献和它们相互之间的制约关系。因此，在理论上是符合物理实际的，是严谨的。

依据这些力，我们设计并建造了实船。实航、实测的数据证实了上述力的存在，并且随着航速的提高而迅速增大。因此，经实验验证，这些表述式符合客观实际，是可靠的。人们可以看到：

(1) 本文的创新特点是运用船底浸湿面设置导流槽和压浪挡板，造成足够强大的水动推进力。也就是把水流波浪运动向船两边散开耗散的无用能量，由于把水引入导流槽和压浪挡板，通过它们顶部曲面前低后高的布局造成水动推进力做加速船前进的有用功，在物理上符合能量守恒原理。所以虽然没有加大推进功率，但航速却能大幅度提高。从而证明了水动推进力的存在以及它推船前进提高航速做有用功的事实；

(2) 在 $\theta=2°$、$\alpha=8°$时，水动推进力 P=106.5 kg、$\alpha=15°$时、P=189.7 kg，可见适当调整倾角 α，能增大 P 做有用功。也就是使无用能量更大地转化为水动推进力做有用功，从而增加航速；

(3) 船底设置导流槽和压浪阻溅流挡板，同没有槽和挡板的船底相比，槽和挡板的垂直壁面是增加的浸湿面，这将导致摩擦阻力 R_T 的增加，可能造成航速下降。

$$R_T=C_T\times A\times\frac{1}{2}\rho U^2 \tag{48}$$

式中：C_T 为摩擦系数，$C_T=\dfrac{0.455}{(\log R_N)^{2.58}}+0.5\times10^{-3}$；

A 为浸湿面积，(m²)；

雷诺数 $R_N=2aU\times10^6/1.57$。

本文实船 $\alpha=11°$、$\delta=0.36$ m、$h'=0.30$ m、雷诺数 $R_N=5.8\times19.11\times10^6/1.57=7.057\ 9\times10^7$，$\log R_N=7+\log7.057\ 9=7.848\ 8$。

$$\begin{aligned}\text{摩擦系数 } C_T&=\frac{0.455}{(\log R_N)^{2.58}}+0.5\times10^{-3}\\&=\frac{0.455}{203.51}+0.5\times10^{-3}\\&=2.735\ 7\times10^{-3}\text{。}\end{aligned}$$

槽垂直壁面的长度 ξ=1.7 m，高度 h'= 0.30 m，浸湿面积 $A_1=2\times\frac{1}{2}\times1.70\times0.30=0.51$ m²。

增加的摩擦阻力 $R_T=C_T\times A_1\times\frac{1}{2}\rho U^2=2.735\ 7\times10^{-3}\times0.51\times50\times(19.11)^2=25.48$ kg。

挡板的垂直壁面上的浸湿面积：

$A_{21}=\frac{1}{2}\times1.70\times0.10\times2=0.17\ \mathrm{m}^2$;

$A_{22}=\frac{1}{2}\times1.70\times0.09\times2=0.153\ \mathrm{m}^2$;

$A_2=A_{21}+A_{22}=0.17+0.153=0.323\ \mathrm{m}^2$。

增加的挡板垂直壁面上的摩擦阻力：

$R_{T2}=2.7357\times10^{-3}\times0.323\times50\times(19.11)^2=16.13$ kg

槽和挡板垂向壁面上造成增加的摩擦总阻力：

$R_T=25.48\times2+16.13=67.1$ kg

另一方面，对常规快艇大量增加载重，航速必然会急剧下降。但是，现在本艇实船实航的数据告诉人们，设置槽和挡板后，在推进功率不变的情况下，载重增大100%(排水量增大33.3%)航速非但不降，反而由36.15 kn提升1 kn，达到37.15 kn。如果是常规艇则由37.15 kn下降6.8 kn，达到30.35 kn。造成这种特殊现象的根本原因就在于设置了槽和挡板后能激起足够强大的水动推进力 P，请见图5和式(43)所示。$\alpha=11°$、$\theta=2°$时：

$\mathscr{Z}=[\delta^2\sin\alpha-h^2\sin\theta]/\delta\ (\delta+h)=0.140\ 21$，$\eta=0.155\ 6\times10^{-3}$，$\mathscr{H}=6.573$。于是，依据式(43)，得知作用在一条槽上的 $P_1=66.6$ kg，减去因设槽增加的摩擦阻力25.48 kg，$P_1-R_T=66.6-25.48=41.12$ kg。

有两条槽，$2\cdot(P_1-R_T)=82.24$ kg。两挡板的推力：$P_2=48\times(2.9)^2\times0.118\ 5\times0.36\times0.12\times0.140\ 21\times6.573\times0.155\ 6\times10^{-3}\times100(19.11)^3\times0.190\ 8=39.46$ kg；$P_2-R_{T2}=39.46-16.13=23.33$ kg，减去增加的摩擦阻力后，本艇还有足够强大的水动推进力：

$(P_1-R_T)+(P_2-R_{T2})=82.24+23.33=105.57$ kg。从式(47)可知，这时本艇的 $R_S=470.42$ kg，而常规艇的 $R_S=575.82$ kg。把常规艇的阻力减去因设置导流槽和压浪挡板的本艇在减去因此增加的摩擦阻力之后仍拥有的水动推进力105.57 kg，即575.82−105.57=470.25 kg，几乎等于本艇的 $R_S=470.42$ kg，误差为：(470.42−470.25)/470.25=0.000 36。也就是说，由于设置槽和挡板把常规艇的阻力575.82 kg减小了105.57 kg，而成为470.25 kg。于是航速30.35 kn就相应地提高了6.8 kn，达到37.15 kn。

对比式(48)和式(43)可见，R_T 与 U^2 成正比，P 与 U^3 成正比，在 $U>1$ 的情况下，U^3 远大于 U^2，因此航速愈高，因设置槽和挡板而提高的航速越大。

如果没有重力场对流场的作用，也就是 $g=0$，则 P 将与 U^2 成正比，那么摩擦阻力 R_T 就可能会大于 P，这时 $P_1=66.6/19.11=3.485$ kg，而摩擦阻力与 U^2 成正比，还是 $R_T=25.48$ kg，则 $P_1-R_T=3.485-25.48=-21.99$ kg。与 U^3 成正比时，$P_2=39.46$ kg，如果与 U^2 成正比，则 $P_2=39.46\div19.11=2.065$ kg，而摩擦阻力还是 $R_{T2}=16.13$ kg。$P_2-R_{T2}=-14.065$ kg，也就是说，设置导流槽和挡板后产生的水动推进力：

$P_1+P_2=3.485+2.065=5.55$ kg，

而增加的摩擦阻力却有：

$R_T+R_{T2}=25.48+16.13=41.61$ kg，

净增摩擦阻力：

$P_1+P_2-(R_T+R_{T2})=5.55-41.61=-36.06$ kg。

此时该艇的阻力增加到 $R_S=575.82+36.06=611.88$ kg，它的航速下降到 $V_S=\frac{87.38\times200}{611.88}=28.56$ kn。但是我们重复6次的实验实测，得到的航速都是37.15 kn，从来没有出现过28.56 kn，因为流场处于重力场的作用下，g不可能等于0。所以 $P>R_T$，在理论上和实际中都是事实。于是，因g不等于0，P、L 与 U^3 成正比，在理论上和实际中都是事实。

(4) 由于缺乏严谨的数学物理方法，前人采用近似方法计算水动升力系数 C_L[1]，然而乘以水的动压头 $\frac{1}{2}\rho U^2$，以及船的横向宽度 B 的平方，或船底面积 S 而得到水动升力，

$$L=\frac{1}{2}C_L\rho U^2B^2\text{，或 }L=\frac{1}{2}C_L\rho U^2S \tag{49}$$

由于水动升力 L 是物体在吃水深度 δ 以攻角 θ、速度 U 运动，并且在重力场的作用下造成的，从物理定性分析，L 的数学表述式应是 δ、θ、U、g以及运动物体的尺度 a,b 的函数。但是在式(49)L 的表述式中看不出体现 δ、θ、g的应有贡献，尤其是 θ，众所周知，如果 $\theta=0$，不可能有水动升力 L。

在不设导流槽的情况下，$l=0$，则从式(43)~式(46)可知，$P=0$、$L=0$、$\alpha=0$、$h\approx\delta$，但 $h\neq\delta$，这时：

$$\mathscr{Z}=-\frac{h^2\sin\theta}{2h^2}=-\frac{1}{2}\sin\theta,\ \mathscr{H}=\frac{1}{\delta^3\sqrt{g\delta}}。$$

则从(45)得：

$$L_0=24\frac{a^2b\eta}{\delta\sqrt{g\delta}}\rho U^3\sin\theta\cos\theta \tag{50}$$

而从(46)得：

$$R_0=24\frac{a^2b\eta}{\delta\sqrt{g\delta}}\rho U^3\sin\theta\sin\theta \tag{51}$$

式(50)中 L_0 的表述式清晰地体现了 L_0 是物理因素 δ、θ、U、g、a、b 的函数，以及它们应有的贡献和

相互之间的制约关系。在其他物理因素相同的情况下，θ 由 1°增大到 3°时，由 $(\sin3°\cos3°)/(\sin1°\cos1°)=2.995\approx3$，可知 L_0 会增大将近 3 倍。但从式(49)看不出攻角 θ 的变化对 L 有多大的影响。此外，前人采用这种近似方法计算水动升力，其误差的定量值很难确定。

7 结 语

依据上述严谨的理论和实船实航的试验验证得到下列结论：

(1) 水动推进力 P 造成的航向稳定扶正力矩、水动升力 L 造成的船体横向稳定、纵向稳定扶正力矩都会随着航速的提高相应地迅速增大。从而造成本船艇航速越高，越是稳定安全的特殊性能，使小、中型快艇能克服水的速度障，在加大推进功率时，能稳定安全地达到并超过 60 kn、70 kn、80 kn，甚至更高的航速。请见图 5 中那些标出的力 P、L 和力矩 M_P、M_L。

但是常规快艇加大推进功率、航速大于 50 kn 后，因没有图 5 中的那些水动力 P、L、水动力矩 M_P 与 M_L 的保障，就会出现稳性危机。此时若再加大推进功率，不但航速上不去，反而会失去稳性，造成倾覆的危险；

(2) 从式(43)~(46)可知，随着航速的提高，水动升力、水动推进力迅速增大，但水动阻力 R_0 却能控制 θ 值为小量而增加有限。由于 L、L_0 的增大能大幅度减小船体的吃水深度，从而大幅度提高航速。此时，再加大水动推进力 P，就能克服中、大型船舶(如集装箱船、滚装船、巡洋舰、驱逐航、航空母舰等)的水的阻力峰，从而在加大推进功率时能大幅度提高航速，由目前约 32 kn、33 kn 提高到 38 kn、40 kn，甚至更高。

但是，常规的中、大排水型舰船由于 $\theta=0$，导致 $L=0$、$L_0=0$，无力减小吃水深度，没有水动推进力 P，也就没有能力克服水的阻力峰。此时，即使再加大推进功率，航速也不会相应地有所提高；

(3) 由于水动推进力在流场中的出现，并且随着航速的提高而迅速增大。因此，在一定范围内增加载重量，排水量、航速非但不下降，反而会有所提升。继续增加载重量，航速保持不变，直到载重量达到一定值，航速才开始缓慢下降，但比常规船艇的降速要缓慢得多[15],[17]；

(4) 由于足够强大水动推进力的出现，能大幅度减小水的阻力，于是升阻比大幅度提高，船舶的整体性能相应地大幅度提高[17]；

(5) 由于水动推进力的出现使航速大幅度提高，必然相应地造成续航力的大幅度提高；

(6) 文中各项水动力表述清晰、明确。人们可以根据实际需求，调整其中除 ρ、g 之外的各项物理参数(θ、α、a、b、l、δ、h、U)，从而得到期望的设计量值，使设计建成的船舰能达到期盼得到的远优于常规船舰的整体优异性能。

[参考文献]

[1] 姜次平，邵世明.船舶阻力，升力系数[M].交通大学出版社，1985：P202，P216.

[2] Jacob W.R，Tsakonas.S.A，New procedure for solution of lifting surfare problems [T]. Journal of hydronautics，1969.3(1).

[3] Courant R. Hillert D. Methematical physics，Volume 2，partial Differential Equations[M].Interscience publishers，John wiley & sons，1962.

[4] Robinson A，Laurmann J A.Wing Theory[M]，University press Cambridge，1956.

[5] Milne-Thomsom L M.Theoretical Hydrodynamics (4th Edition) [M].

[6] 朱蔚文，张涤明.水动力学[M].高等教育出版社，1993：P17.

[7] Chen Zhen-cheng. A method to solve Boundary Value problem [J].Kexue Tongbao，Vol.26.No.1，1981：16-23.

[8] Chen Zhen-cheng and Chen Yang. Solar Force-free Magnetic fields on and above the Photosphere [J]. Appendix，An Integral Transform，Solar Physics，1989. 294-299.

[9] 陈振诚.解决流体动力学某些问题的积分变换[C].第十二届全国水动力学研讨会论文集.1998.9.

[10] Chen Zhen-cheng，The hydrodynamic pressure on sluice gate plane wetted by water in the case of free outflow[C]. Proceedings of the Second Asian congress of Fluid Mechanics，Science press，Beijing China，1983：555-557.

[11] Chen Zhen-cheng.The hydrodynamic pressure on sluice gate plane wetted by water in the case of submerged outflow[C].Proceedings of the Third Asian congress of Fluid Mechanics，Tokyo，Japan，1986：142-145.

[12] Chen Zhen-cheng，The criterion for presaging occurrence of solar flare[C].Proceedings of the Fifth Asian congress of Fluid Mechanics，Taejon Korea，1992：920-923.

[13] Sneddon，I.N.Fourier Transform，N.Y.Graw.1951.

[14] 朱珉虎.飞鳐水面航行器[J].船舶，2002，6(3).

[15] 陈振诚，陈昕.激起水动推进力的新船型[J].国际船艇，2005，9(5).

[16] 陈振诚，陈旸.水动力矩助船艇回转且抗倾覆[J].国际船艇，2006，2(1).

[17] 陈振诚，陈昕，陈旸.一种崭新的船舶运行原理[J].船舶工程，2006，8(4).

[18] Chen Zhen-cheng. Planing Vessel [C].Bulletin o. International. Bureau of WIPO，Feb.1996.

F—2·7

SOLAR FORCE-FREE MAGNETIC FIELDS ON AND ABOVE THE PHOTOSPHERE

CHEN ZHEN-CHENG and CHEN YANG

Beijing Astronomical Observatory, Chinese Academy of Sciences, Beijing, China

(Received 7 March, 1988)

Abstract. If the problem of a magnetic field being force-free with α = constant ($\alpha \neq 0$) is solved by some previously published methods, then the field obtained in the whole exterior of the Sun cannot have a finite energy content and the solution cannot be determined uniquely from only one magnetic field component given at the photosphere. A magnetic field in the volume between two parallel planes has been investigated by us (Chen and Wang, 1986).

Based on observational data we present in this paper a suitable physical model for a half-space and adopted an integral transform established by us (Chen, 1980, 1983) to solve this problem. We then obtain a unique analytical solution of the problem from only one magnetic field component (longitudinal field observed) given at the photosphere. Not only the uniqueness of the solution has been proved but also the finiteness of magnetic energy content in the half-space considered has been verified. We have demonstrated that there is no singular point in the solution. It enables us to describe analytically the configurations of magnetic fields on and above the photosphere.

1. Introduction

Magnetic field configurations and their evolutions are of great importance for solar flares, radio bursts, and other phenomena of solar activity in the solar atmosphere. Thus, when investigating the physical mechanism of solar activities, one must amass a great amount of information about the magnetic field structure throughout the solar atmosphere. However, at present, reliable and detailed firsthand information on magnetic fields obtained by observations is available only for the longitudinal field on the photosphere. In recent years, the transverse fields on the photosphere and the magnetic fields for the chromospheric level may be obtained by observation, for reference.

Therefore, in order to obtaining information about the magnetic field throughout the solar atmosphere one has, on the basis of observational data, to carry out theoretical investigations of this problem. With that object in view, some theoretical methods which are based on the assumption of a potential field, e.g., Schmidt (1964), Altschuler and Newkirk (1969), and some theoretical methods based on the supposition of a force-free field with constant α, e.g., Nakagawa and Raadu (1972), Seehafer (1978), Chiu and Hilton (1977), Alissandrakis (1981), and Elwert *et al.* (1982), have been used to solve the problem. Each author has contributed towards the solution of this problem.

However, if the problem is solved by some of the previously published methods, then it is found that a magnetic field which is force-free with α = constant ($\alpha \neq 0$) in the whole spatial domain outside the Sun cannot have a finite energy content and that such a field cannot be determined uniquely from only one magnetic field component given at the photosphere. In addition, in certain previous studies some of the fundamental

Solar Physics **119** (1989) 279–299.
© 1989 *by Kluwer Academic Publishers.*

assumptions for the boundary value may not be reasonable. A magnetic field with constant α in the volume between two parallel planes has been investigated (Chen and Wang, 1986).

Taking all such facts into consideration, based on observational data, in this paper we have, for a semi-infinite space, presented a model which approaches the real physical picture more closely. Taking reasonable boundary conditions, by means of a suitable mathematical-physical method, we have, from only the longitudinal field observed at the photosphere, obtained a unique analytical solution for this problem. We have verified the uniqueness of the solution, for the finiteness of magnetic energy content in a half-space, and we have determined that no singular point exists in the solution. In the Appendix we have clarified some theorems of an integral transform. The most distinctive features of our method and the solution presented here are illustrated in the Section 7.

2. Physical Model

We adopt the Cartesian coordinate system x, y, z. The plane $(x, y, 0)$ coincides with the photosphere. Height is set along the z-axis, which is directed toward the high solar atmosphere.

For the purpose of obtaining a clearer idea of the physical pictures of the force-free magnetic field we must first study the observational facts. Based on these observed facts we then present the physical model of the problem.

Much of observational data suggest that the distribution of the longitudinal magnetic field of sunspots on the photosphere has discretely concentrated characteristics. Its basic features are manifested by the variation with emergence of single strong sunspots with their penumbras.

Conforming to this fact, the sunspots or other magnetic features on the photosphere may be considered as the sources by which the whole magnetic field on and above the photosphere is formed. A set of analytical functions which describe, for these Sources on the photosphere, their positions, field strengths, decay rates and the regions of the same polarity can be used to express this observed magnetic field. We may write it in the following form:

$$B_z(x, y, 0) = \sum_{m=1}^{K} \Omega_m \exp(-\mu_m X_m - \nu_m Y_m) \sum_{\gamma=1}^{3} \cos(\omega_{m\gamma} X_m + \sigma_{m\gamma} Y_m), \tag{2.1}$$

where Ω_m expresses the magnetic field strength at the point $x = a_m$, $y = b_m$, $z = 0$, *i.e.*, the centre of the mth sunspot where the strength of the longitudinal component takes the maximum or minimum value. μ_m, ν_m denote the decreasing rates of the field. $\omega_{m\gamma}$, $\sigma_{m\gamma}$ express the parameters describing the extent of the magnetic region with the same polarity for the mth source. Since the boundary contour of the same polarity for the sunspot penumbra is a curve, we then take $\gamma = 1, 2, 3$. The parameters ω_{m1}, ω_{m2}, ω_{m3} and σ_{m1}, σ_{m2}, σ_{m3} are determined by the curve. If one hopes to describe the contour more exactly, then the $\gamma = 1, 2, 3, 4, \ldots$ may be taken. However, as a general rule, taking $\gamma = 1, 2$ or $\gamma = 1, 2, 3$ gives an exact enough description of the contour; in certain special cases, taking $\gamma = 1$, the basic feature of the contour is retained. $X_m = |x - a_m|$, $Y_m = |y - b_m|$. a_m, b_m denote, respectively, the centre coordinates of the mth source in the plane $(x, y, 0)$. κ denotes the total number of the sunspots or other discrete magnetic features in the active region.

The boundary condition of the problem on the photosphere is expressed by formula (2.1).

Observations show that at the centre of a single sunspot the magnetic force line is almost perpendicular to the photosphere. Hence it follows that the magnetic field for each single sunspot is symmetrically distributed with z ($X_m = 0$, $Y_m = 0$) as its symmetry axis. We can then suppose that the transverse magnetic field at the centre of mth sunspot equals zero, i.e., $B_{xm}(a_m, b_m, z) = 0$, $B_{ym}(a_m, b_m, z) = 0$. However, here, if there is another sunspot which emerges at the same time, then the total transverse field may in general be not zero. These facts enable us to establish a reasonable boundary condition as follows:

$$B_{xm}(a_m, b_m, z) = 0, \quad B_{ym}(a_m, b_m, z) = 0 \quad \text{at} \quad X_m = 0, Y_m = 0, z = z, \tag{2.2}$$

but

$$B_x(a_m, b_m, z) = \sum_{m=1}^{\kappa} B_{xm}(a_m, b_m, z) \not\equiv 0,$$

$$B_y(a_m, b_m, z) = \sum_{m=1}^{\kappa} B_{ym}(a_m, b_m, z) \not\equiv 0. \tag{2.3}$$

By use of this condition we can overcome the major difficulty in studying the problem. The difficulty is created by the non-uniqueness of the solution in many studies carried out by other authors, since the boundary conditions are insufficient.

Observations indicate that the magnetic flux with south polarity may not be equal to that with north polarity in an active region. In consideration of this fact we assume that the net magnetic flux of an active region may not be zero.

Outside the active region, if there is no other active region and no sunspot or magnetic feature, then the magnetic field decreases, but may not be zero everywhere. When two or several active regions emerge at the same time the magnetic field weakens in the area between or among the active regions, but it may be non-zero everywhere. Evidently, the magnetic field in the whole spatial domain considered has a finite energy content.

In accordance with the observed facts we suppose that when no other sunspot or magnetic feature emerges the magnetic field strength outside the active region **B** tends to decrease outwards mainly from the border of active region. **B** decays rapidly as the distance from the active region increases and reaches a large value. As a consequence, we can write another boundary condition in the following form:

$$\mathbf{B} = \sum_{m=1}^{\kappa} \mathbf{B}_m \to 0 \quad \text{when} \quad |x| \to \infty, \text{ or } |y| \to \infty, \text{ or } |x| \to \infty \text{ and } |y| \to \infty. \tag{2.4}$$

In the direction z, in general, the magnetic field decreases as the distance to the photosphere increases. Thus we assume that the magnetic field vanishes at infinity. Then the other one of boundary conditions may be written in the form:

$$\mathbf{B} = \sum_{m=1}^{K} \mathbf{B}_m \to 0 \quad \text{when} \quad z \to \infty . \tag{2.5}$$

The suppositions mentioned above are in good agreement with the observational facts.

In order to describe the force-free field in the domain considered, on the basis of the physical model as stated above, we write the equations for the mth sunspot only as follows:

$$\mathbf{J} \times \mathbf{B} = 0 , \qquad \nabla \times \mathbf{B} = \alpha \mathbf{B} . \tag{2.6}$$

The corresponding boundary conditions of the problem are written in the form:

$$\mathbf{B} \to 0 \quad \text{as} \quad |x| \to \infty, \quad -\infty < y < \infty, \quad 0 \leq z < \infty ; \tag{2.7}$$

$$\mathbf{B} \to 0 \quad \text{as} \quad -\infty < x < \infty, \quad |y| \to \infty, \quad 0 \leq z < \infty ; \tag{2.8}$$

$$\mathbf{B} \to 0 \quad \text{as} \quad -\infty < x < \infty, \quad -\infty < y < \infty, \quad z \to \infty ; \tag{2.9}$$

$$B_x(a, b, z) = B_y(a, b, z) = 0, \quad \text{at} \quad X = 0, \quad Y = 0, \quad z = z . \tag{2.10}$$

In order to simplifying the procedure in analysis we take $\gamma = 1$; then we have

$$B_z(x, y, 0) = \Omega \exp(-\mu X - \nu Y) \cos(\omega X + \sigma Y) \quad \text{when} \quad z = 0 , \tag{2.11}$$

where $X = |x - a|$, $Y = |y - b|$. The parameters $(J, B, \Omega, \mu, \nu, a, b)$ and (ω, σ) in the above expressions should carry the suffix m and m_1, respectively, for simplicity and convenience they have been omitted.

Thus far, the physical model of the problem and its mathematical equations and boundary conditions have been presented.

For the boundary value problem presented above, if the Fourier transform or Laplace transform is used in solving the integral equations obtained by satisfying the boundary condition presented in expression (2.11), then from the solution obtained we can derive that $B_z(x, y, 0) \equiv 0$ everywhere outside the active region on the photosphere. It is obvious that the result is not in good agreement with both the actual observational data and the assumptions underlying the problem. Therefore, in order to obtain a solution of the problem from which we can derive a result that reflects the actual physical picture of the force-free field in the whole spatial domain considered, we have to establish a new mathematical method (an integral transform) for solving boundary value problems of this type (Chen, 1980, 1983). Now we introduce the inverse theorems of this transform, as shown in the Appendix.

3. Procedure for Solving the Problem

In the case of a force-free magnetic field with a constant α, the magnetic induction $\mathbf{B}$ can be expressed by a scalar function $\varphi(x, y, z)$ as

$$\mathbf{B} = \nabla \times \nabla \times (\varphi \hat{e}_z) + \alpha \nabla \times (\varphi \hat{e}_z) = B_x \hat{e}_x + B_y \hat{e}_y + B_z \hat{e}_z . \tag{3.1}$$

In accordance with expression (3.1) we write the components of **B** in scalar form as

$$B_x(x, y, z) = \frac{\partial^2 \varphi}{\partial x\, \partial z} + \alpha \frac{\partial \varphi}{\partial y}, \qquad B_y(x, y, z) = \frac{\partial^2 \varphi}{\partial y\, \partial z} - \alpha \frac{\partial \varphi}{\partial x},$$

$$B_z(x, y, z) = -\frac{\partial^2 \varphi}{\partial x^2} - \frac{\partial^2 \varphi}{\partial y^2}, \tag{3.2}$$

where $\varphi = \varphi(x, y, z)$ satisfies the Helmholtz equation

$$(\nabla^2 + \alpha^2)\varphi = 0. \tag{3.3}$$

Then we may reduce the solution of the problem to finding the function $\varphi(x, y, z)$ which satisfies the equations and boundary conditions as stated above.

The function $\varphi(x, y, z)$ may be defined as that $\varphi(x, y, z) \equiv \varphi(x, y, z)$ in the spatial domain $-\infty < x < \infty$, $-\infty < y < \infty$, $0 \leq z < \infty$.

Applying the integral transform introduced in the Appendix to the solution of the partial differential equation (3.3), satisfying the boundary condition (2.11), and carrying out the transformation and its inversions, we get

$$\varphi(x, y, z) = -\frac{\Omega}{2}\left\{\frac{1}{\gamma_1^2} \exp(-\mu_1 X - \nu_1 Y - i\eta_1 z) + \right.$$

$$\left. + \frac{1}{\gamma_2^2} \exp(-\mu_2 X - \nu_2 Y + i\eta_2 z)\right\} + \int_0^\infty [A(\beta) \exp(-\lambda X - \xi Y) +$$

$$+ \Gamma(\beta) \exp(-\xi X - \lambda Y)] \sin \beta z \, d\beta, \tag{3.4}$$

where

$$\lambda = \frac{1}{\sqrt{2}}(\beta - i\alpha), \qquad \xi = \frac{1}{\sqrt{2}}(\beta + i\alpha);$$

$A(\beta)$, $\Gamma(\beta)$ are the unknown arbitrary functions. They are determined by satisfying the boundary condition (2.10) and are written as

$$A(\beta) = \frac{\Omega}{2\sqrt{2}\,\pi}\left(\frac{1}{\beta} P - \frac{i}{\alpha} Q\right), \qquad \Gamma(\beta) = \frac{\Omega}{2\sqrt{2}\,\pi}\left(\frac{1}{\beta} P + \frac{i}{\alpha} Q\right), \tag{3.5}$$

where

$$P = \frac{\nu_1 + \mu_1}{\gamma_1^2}\tau_1 + \frac{\nu_2 + \mu_2}{\gamma_2^2}\tau_2, \qquad Q = \frac{\nu_1 - \mu_1}{\gamma_1^2}\tau_1 + \frac{\nu_2 - \mu_2}{\gamma_2^2}\tau_2;$$

$$\tau_1 = \frac{\beta}{\beta^2 + \rho_1^2}, \qquad \tau_2 = \frac{\beta}{\beta^2 + \rho_2^2}; \qquad \nu_1 = \nu - i\sigma, \qquad \mu_1 = \mu - i\omega,$$

$$\nu_2 = \nu + i\sigma, \qquad \mu_2 = \mu + i\omega, \qquad \gamma_1^2 = \mu_1^2 + \nu_1^2, \qquad \gamma_2^2 = \mu_2^2 + \nu_2^2,$$

$$\eta_1 = \sqrt{\gamma_1^2 + \alpha^2}, \qquad \eta_2 = \sqrt{\gamma_2^2 + \alpha^2}, \qquad R = \sqrt[4]{q^2 + p^2},$$

$$\rho_1 = R_s + iR_c, \qquad \rho_2 = R_s - iR_c, \qquad R_s = R\sin\vartheta, \qquad R_c = R\cos\vartheta,$$

$$\vartheta = \tfrac{1}{2}\,\mathrm{arctg}\,|p/q|, \qquad p = 2(\omega\mu + \sigma\nu), \qquad q = \mu^2 + \nu^2 + \alpha^2 - \omega^2 - \sigma^2.$$

From the expressions (3.2) and (3.4) we find that each of the terms in the functions expressing $B_x(x, y, z)$, $B_y(x, y, z)$, $B_z(x, y, z)$ derived from function $\varphi(x, y, z)$ contains the multiplier factors $\exp(-\mu_1 X - \nu_1 Y)$, $\exp(-\mu_2 X - \nu_2 Y)$, $\exp(-\lambda X - \xi Y)$, and $\exp(-\xi X - \lambda Y)$, respectively. As $\mathrm{Re}\,\mu_1 > 0$, $\mathrm{Re}\,\nu_1 > 0$, $\mathrm{Re}\,\mu_2 > 0$, $\mathrm{Re}\,\nu_2 > 0$, and $\mathrm{Re}\,\lambda > 0$, $\mathrm{Re}\,\xi > 0$, and X, Y are positive reals everywhere in the whole domain considered, then obviously the conditions (2.7), (2.8) are satisfied. At first sight, in direction z, it appears that multiplier factors $\exp(-i\eta_1 z)$, $\exp(i\eta_2 z)$ may not be zero when $z \to \infty$. But, in fact, $\exp(-i\eta_1 z) = \exp[-(R_s + iR_c)z]$, $\exp(i\eta_2 z) = \exp[-(R_s - iR_c)z]$, where R_s is the non-zero positive reals. The integrand in the second term shown in formula (3.4) includes the factor $\sin\beta z$, but after carrying out the integration we obtain the combination of multiplier factors $ci[f_0(z)]$ and $si[f_0(z)]$ which will tend to zero as $z \to \infty$. In consequence, the boundary condition (2.9) is satisfied.

Therefore, function $\varphi(x, y, z)$ shown in expression (3.4) satisfies all the equations and boundary conditions of the problem. It is a unique and analytical solution of this problem. It enables us to describe clearly and conveniently the force-free magnetic field in the spatial domain considered. In the next section we will prove the uniqueness of the solution presented and demonstrate that no singular point exists in the solution.

4. Uniqueness and Non-Singularity of the Solution

As the boundary conditions are insufficient, the studies given by other authors are not unique. In accordance with the observational facts, we have added a reasonable boundary condition shown in expression (2.10). We now investigate the uniqueness of the solution given in the paper after adding this condition.

Suppose that, for this problem, there is another solution $\overline{\varphi}$, which may be written in the form

$$\overline{\varphi} = \overline{\varphi}(x, y, z) = \varphi(x, y, z) + \varphi^*(x, y, z), \tag{4.1}$$

where $\varphi(x, y, z)$ is given by formula (3.4) and $\varphi^* = \varphi^*(x, y, z)$ is an unknown arbitrary function of x, y, z. Solving Equation (3.3), we obtain φ^*, which may be written in the following form:

$$\varphi^*(x, y, z) = \iint\limits_{c_0 - i\infty}^{c_0 + i\infty} F_1(u, v) \exp(-uX - vY + i\mathfrak{B}z)\, du\, dv +$$

$$+ \iint\limits_{0}^{\infty} F_2(u, v) \cos uX \cos vY\, e^{-\mathfrak{B}^* z}\, du\, dv +$$

$$+ F_3 \left\{ \frac{1}{\gamma_1^2} \exp(-\mu_1 X - \nu_1 Y + i\eta_1 z) + \frac{1}{\gamma_2^2} \exp(-\mu_2 X - \nu_2 Y - i\eta_2 z) \right\} +$$

$$+ \int\limits_0^{\infty} [F_4(\beta) \exp(-\lambda X - \xi Y) + F_5(\beta) \exp(-\xi X - \lambda Y)] \cos \beta z\, d\beta, \quad (4.2)$$

where $F_1(u, v)$, $F_2(u, v)$, F_3, $F_4(\beta)$, and $F_5(\beta)$ are the unknown arbitrary functions which are determined by the boundary conditions (2.7)–(2.11), $\mathfrak{B} = \sqrt{u^2 + v^2 + \alpha^2}$, $\mathfrak{B}^* = \sqrt{u^2 + v^2 - \alpha^2}$.

From the expressions (4.1), (4.2) and (3.1), (3.2) we know that, in order to satisfy the boundary conditions (2.7) and (2.8), $F_2(u, v)$ must be zero. Otherwise, when $|x| \to \infty$, or $|y| \to \infty$, or $|x| \to \infty$ and $|y| \to \infty$, **B** does not tend to zero, since the integrand of the second term contains $\cos uX \cos vY$. On the other hand, the multiplier factors in the third term $\exp(i\eta_1 z) = \exp[(R_s + iR_c)z] \to \infty$, $\exp(-i\eta_2 z) = \exp[(R_s - iR_c)z] \to \infty$, when $z \to \infty$. Hence, it follows that in order to satisfy the condition (2.9) we must have $F_3 \equiv 0$. Satisfying condition (2.11) we have

$$- \iint\limits_{c_0 - i\infty}^{c_0 + i\infty} F_1(u, v)(u^2 + v^2) e^{-uX - vY} du\, dv -$$

$$- \int\limits_0^{\infty} [F_4(\beta) e^{-\lambda X - \xi Y} + F_5(\beta) e^{-\xi X - \lambda Y}] (\lambda^2 + \xi^2)\, d\beta = 0. \quad (4.3)$$

Solving this equation by means of a Laplace transform, the following expression may be deduced:

$$F_1(u, v) = \frac{-1}{4\pi^2(u^2 + v^2)} \int\limits_0^{\infty} \left[\frac{F_4(\beta)}{(u - \lambda)(v - \xi)} + \frac{F_5(\beta)}{(u - \xi)(v - \lambda)} \right] (\beta^2 - \alpha^2)\, d\beta. \quad (4.4)$$

When the conditions $B_x(a, b, z) = 0$ and $B_y(a, b, z) = 0$ as shown in (2.10) are satisfied, we derive, respectively, that

$$\int\limits_0^{\infty} [F_4(\beta)\lambda + F_5(\beta)\xi] \cos \beta z\, d\beta + \iint\limits_{c_0 - i\infty}^{c_0 + i\infty} F_1(u, v) u \exp(i\mathfrak{B}z)\, du\, dv = 0, \quad (4.5)$$

$$\int_0^\infty [F_4(\beta)\xi + F_5(\beta)\lambda]\cos\beta z\,\mathrm{d}\beta + \iint_{c_0-i\infty}^{c_0+i\infty} F_1(u,v)v\exp(i\mathfrak{B}z)\,\mathrm{d}u\,\mathrm{d}v = 0\,. \quad (4.6)$$

Using the Fourier transform, Equations (4.5) and (4.6) may result in the following expressions:

$$F_4(\beta)\lambda + F_5(\beta)\xi = \frac{2}{\pi} i \iint_{c_0-i\infty}^{c_0+i\infty} F_1(u,v)u\frac{\mathfrak{B}}{\beta^2-\mathfrak{B}^2}\,\mathrm{d}u\,\mathrm{d}v\,, \quad (4.7)$$

$$F_4(\beta)\xi + F_5(\beta)\lambda = \frac{2}{\pi} i \iint_{c_0-i\infty}^{c_0+i\infty} F_1(u,v)v\frac{\mathfrak{B}}{\beta^2-\mathfrak{B}^2}\,\mathrm{d}u\,\mathrm{d}v\,. \quad (4.8)$$

Substituting expression (4.4) into (4.7) and (4.8), respectively, we get

$$F_4(\beta)\lambda + F_5(\beta)\xi = W_1\,, \qquad W_1 = -\frac{i}{2\pi^3}\iint_{c_0-i\infty}^{c_0+i\infty} f_1(u,v)f_2(u,v)u\,\mathrm{d}u\,\mathrm{d}v\,, \quad (4.9)$$

$$F_4(\beta)\xi + F_5(\beta)\lambda = W_2\,, \qquad W_2 = -\frac{i}{2\pi^3}\iint_{c_0-i\infty}^{c_0+i\infty} f_1(u,v)f_2(u,v)v\,\mathrm{d}u\,\mathrm{d}v\,, \quad (4.10)$$

where

$$f_1(u,v) = \frac{\mathfrak{B}}{u^2+v^2}\,,$$

$$f_2(u,v) = \int_0^\infty \left[\frac{F_4(\beta)}{(u-\lambda)(v-\xi)} + \frac{F_5(\beta)}{(u-\xi)(v-\lambda)}\right]\frac{\beta^2-\alpha^2}{\beta^2-\mathfrak{B}^2}\,\mathrm{d}\beta\,. \quad (4.11)$$

The integral variables u and v have the same domain and integral range; as a result, it follows that $W_1 \equiv W_2$.

Surely, only for the case in which $F_4(\beta) = 0$ and $F_5(\beta) = 0$ are valid, will the equality $W_1 \equiv W_2$ and Equations (4.9), (4.10) be valid all together. Except for that case, expressions (4.9), (4.10) and $W_1 \equiv W_2$ are a set of inconsistent equations; evidently, they have no significance.

In consequence, after satisfying all the boundary conditions, the unknown arbitrary functions in expression (4.2) have been determined, and they may be written as follows:

$$F_1(u,v) = 0\,, \qquad F_2(u,v) = 0\,, \qquad F_3 = 0\,, \qquad F_4(\beta) = 0\,, \qquad F_5(\beta) = 0\,. \quad (4.12)$$

Therefore we have proved that $\varphi^*(x, y, z) \equiv 0$, and

$$\overline{\varphi}(x, y, z) \equiv \varphi(x, y, z). \tag{4.13}$$

The validity of Equation (4.13) enables us to be certain of the uniqueness of the solution given in this paper, and $\varphi(x, y, z)$ is the unique solution of the problem.

Function $\varphi(x, y, z)$ shown in (3.4), at first appearance, does not appear to be smooth at $x = a$, $y = b$, $z = z$, but in fact it is smooth everywhere in the whole domain considered, including the $x = a$, $y = b$, $z = z$. For a simple example, the function

$$f_1(x) = \frac{\alpha_1}{\zeta_1} \exp(-\zeta_1 |x - a|) ,$$

$$\left(f_1'(x) = \frac{\mathrm{d}f_1(x)}{\mathrm{d}x} = -\zeta_1 \exp(-\zeta_1 |x - a|) \operatorname{sign}(x - a)\right) , \tag{4.14}$$

obviously has no derivative at $x = a$, because $f_1'(a - 0) = \zeta_1$, but $f_1'(a + 0) = -\zeta_1$, it is not smooth. But the function

$$f_2(x) = \frac{\alpha_1}{\zeta_1} \exp(-\zeta_1 |x - a|) \cos(\omega_1 |x - a|) - \exp(-\alpha_1 |x - a|) ,$$

$$\left(f_2'(x) = \frac{\mathrm{d}f_2(x)}{\mathrm{d}x} = \left\{\left[-\alpha_1 \cos(\omega_1 |x - a|) - \frac{\alpha_1 \omega_1}{\zeta_1} \sin(\omega_1 |x - a|)\right] \times \right.\right.$$
$$\left.\left. \times \exp(-\zeta_1 |x - a|) + \alpha_1 \exp(-\alpha_1 |x - a|)\right\} \operatorname{sign}(x - a)\right) , \tag{4.15}$$

clearly has the derivative $f_2'(a - 0) = f_2'(a + 0) = 0$ at $x = a$, cf. the diagrams shown in Figure 1, where $\zeta_1 > 0$, $\alpha_1 > 0$, $\omega_1 > 0$ are positive reals.

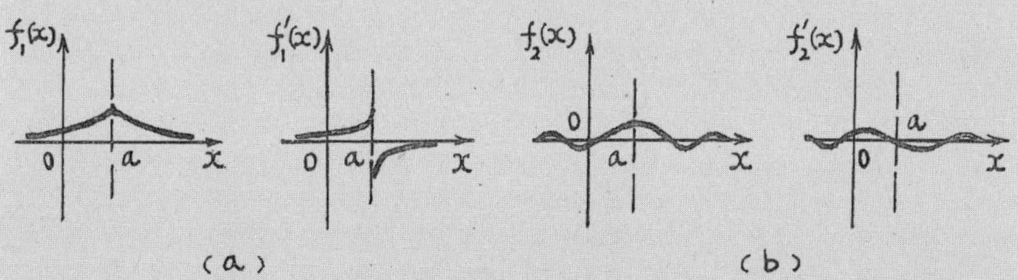

Fig. 1. (a) The curve of the function $f_1(x)$ and the curves of the function $f_1'(x)$. (b) The curves of the functions $f_2(x)$ and $f_2'(x)$.

Similar to what has been mentioned above, the function $\varphi(x, y, z)$ contains the factors $\mathfrak{E}_1 = \mathfrak{E}_1(x, y, z) = \exp(-\mu_1 X - \nu_1 Y - i\eta_1 z)$, $\mathfrak{E}_2 = \mathfrak{E}_2(x, y, z) = \exp(-\mu_2 X - \nu_2 Y + i\eta_2 z)$, $\mathfrak{E}_3 = \mathfrak{E}_3(x, y) = \exp(-\lambda X - \xi Y)$, $\mathfrak{E}_4 = \mathfrak{E}_4(x, y) = \exp(-\xi X - \lambda Y)$, but at $x = a$, $y = b$, $z = z$ we have the derivatives:

$$\frac{\partial \varphi}{\partial x} = \varphi'_x(a-0, b-0, z) = \varphi'_x(a+0, b+0, z) = 0,$$

$$\frac{\partial \varphi}{\partial y} = \varphi'_y(a-0, b-0, z) = \varphi'_y(a+0, b+0, z) = 0,$$

$$\frac{\partial^2 \varphi}{\partial x\, \partial z} = \varphi''_{xz}(a-0, b-0, z) = \varphi''_{xz}(a+0, b+0, z) = 0,$$

$$\frac{\partial^2 \varphi}{\partial y\, \partial z} = \varphi''_{yz}(a-0, b-0, z) = \varphi''_{yz}(a+0, b+0, z) = 0,$$

$$\frac{\partial^2 \varphi}{\partial x^2} = \varphi''_{xx}(a-0, b-0, z) = \varphi''_{xx}(a+0, b+0, z) = f_1(z),$$

$$\frac{\partial^2 \varphi}{\partial y^2} = \varphi''_{yy}(a-0, b-0, z) = \varphi''_{yy}(a+0, b+0, z) = f_2(z).$$

Then, in accordance with formulae (3.2) we have $B_x(a, b, z) = 0$, $B_y(a, b, z) = 0$, $B_z(a, b, z) = f(z)$, where $f(z) = -f_1(z) - f_2(z)$ is a definite function. $B_x(a, b, z)$ or $B_y(a, b, z)$ has a definite value, which equals zero, respectively. The facts just mentioned indicate that although, as for each single factor, the $\mathfrak{E}_1$, $\mathfrak{E}_2$, $\mathfrak{E}_3$, or $\mathfrak{E}_4$ has no derivatives at $x = a$, $y = b$, $z = z$, get the function $\varphi(x, y, z)$ has derivatives when these factors are combined as shown in formula (3.4). The current components are

$$J_x(a, b, z) = \alpha(\nabla \times \mathbf{B})_x = \alpha\left(\frac{\partial B_z}{\partial y} - \frac{\partial B_y}{\partial z}\right) =$$

$$= \alpha\left[\frac{\partial}{\partial y}\left(\frac{\partial^2 \varphi}{\partial z^2} + \alpha^2 \varphi\right) - \frac{\partial}{\partial z}\left(\frac{\partial^2 \varphi}{\partial z\, \partial y} - \alpha\frac{\partial \varphi}{\partial x}\right)\right] = 0,$$

$$J_y(a, b, z) = \alpha(\nabla \times \mathbf{B})_y = \alpha\left(\frac{\partial B_x}{\partial z} - \frac{\partial B_z}{\partial x}\right) =$$

$$= \alpha\left[\frac{\partial}{\partial z}\left(\frac{\partial^2 \varphi}{\partial z\, \partial x} + \alpha\frac{\partial \varphi}{\partial y}\right) - \frac{\partial}{\partial x}\left(\frac{\partial^2 \varphi}{\partial z^2} + \alpha^2 \varphi\right)\right] = 0,$$

$$J_z(a, b, z) = \alpha(\nabla \times \mathbf{B})_z = \alpha\left(\frac{\partial B_y}{\partial x} - \frac{\partial B_x}{\partial y}\right) =$$

$$= \alpha\left[\frac{\partial}{\partial x}\left(\frac{\partial^2 \varphi}{\partial y\, \partial z} - \alpha\frac{\partial \varphi}{\partial x}\right) - \frac{\partial}{\partial y}\left(\frac{\partial^2 \varphi}{\partial x\, \partial z} + \alpha\frac{\partial \varphi}{\partial y}\right)\right] = \alpha^2 B_z.$$

It is clear from the above demonstration that the functions expressing B_x, B_y, B_z are continuous, moreover, the partial derivatives of B_x, B_y, B_z for x, y, and z are also continuous at $x = a$, $y = b$, $z = z$. This means that the functions expressing B_x, B_y, B_z are smooth and the functions describing J_x, J_y, J_z are continuous everywhere in the domain considered, and that the magnetic field runs parallel to the current.

As a result, we have proved that no singular point exists in the solution presented here for the whole spatial domain considered.

5. The Formulae for Calculating the Configurations of Magnetic Fields on and above the Photosphere

Taking formula (3.4) into consideration, in accordance with formulae (3.2) the B_x, B_y, and B_z are derived as follows:

$$B_x = B_x(x, y, z) = -\frac{\Omega}{2}\left[\frac{i\eta_1\mu_1 S_x - \alpha\nu_1 S_y}{\gamma_1^2}\mathfrak{E}_1(x, y, z) - \frac{i\eta_2\mu_2 S_x + \alpha\nu_2 S_y}{\gamma_2^2}\mathfrak{E}_2(x, y, z)\right] - \int_0^\infty [A(\beta)(\lambda\beta S_x\cos\beta z + \alpha\xi S_y\sin\beta z)\mathfrak{E}_3(x, y) + \Gamma(\beta)(\xi\beta S_x\cos\beta z + \alpha\lambda S_y\sin\beta z)\mathfrak{E}_4(x, y)]\,d\beta, \quad (5.1)$$

$$B_y = B_y(x, y, z) = -\frac{\Omega}{2}\left[\frac{i\eta_1\nu_1 S_y + \alpha\mu_1 S_x}{\gamma_1^2}\mathfrak{E}_1(x, y, z) - \frac{i\eta_2\nu_2 S_y - \alpha\mu_2 S_x}{\gamma_2^2}\mathfrak{E}_2(x, y, z)\right] - \int_0^\infty [A(\beta)(\xi\beta S_y\cos\beta z - \alpha\lambda S_x\sin\beta z)\mathfrak{E}_3(x, y) + \Gamma(\beta)(\lambda\beta S_y\cos\beta z - \alpha\xi S_x\sin\beta z)\mathfrak{E}_4(x, y)]\,d\beta, \quad (5.2)$$

$$B_z = B_z(x, y, z) = \frac{\Omega}{2}[\mathfrak{E}_1(x, y, z) + \mathfrak{E}_2(x, y, z)] - \int_0^\infty [A(\beta)\mathfrak{E}_3(x, y) + \Gamma(\beta)\mathfrak{E}_4(x, y)](\beta^2 - \alpha^2)\sin\beta z\,d\beta, \quad (5.3)$$

where

$$S_x = \operatorname{sign}(x - a), \qquad S_y = \operatorname{sign}(y - b).$$

After substituting the formulae shown in expression (3.5) into (5.1), (5.2), and (5.3), respectively, and carrying out the corresponding integral calculations, the B_x, B_y, and B_z would be given in simplified analytical expressions.

6. Verification for Finiteness of the Magnetic Energy Content in a Half Space

Here we verify that the magnetic field, which is derived from the solution in this paper, being force free with α = constant ($\alpha \neq 0$ or $\alpha = 0$) in the semi-infinite spatial domain considered, has a finite energy content.

The magnetic energy content W within the volume considered may be written in the following form:

$$W = \frac{1}{8\pi}\iiint_v |\mathbb{B}|^2 \,\mathrm{d}v = \frac{1}{8\pi}\iiint_v \left(\sqrt{B_x^2 + B_y^2 + B_z^2}\right)^2 \mathrm{d}v =$$

$$= \frac{1}{8\pi}\int_0^{\infty}\iint_{-\infty}^{\infty} (B_x^2 + B_y^2 + B_z^2)\,\mathrm{d}x\,\mathrm{d}y\,\mathrm{d}z =$$

$$= \frac{1}{8\pi}\int_0^{\infty}\left[\iint_{-\infty}^{0} (B_x^2 + B_y^2 + B_z^2)\,\mathrm{d}x\,\mathrm{d}y + \right.$$

$$\left. + \iint_0^{\infty} (B_x^2 + B_y^2 + B_z^2)\,\mathrm{d}x\,\mathrm{d}y\right]\mathrm{d}z =$$

$$= \frac{1}{8\pi}(W_1 + W_2 + W_3 + W_4 + W_5 + W_6), \tag{6.1}$$

where

$$W_1 = \int_0^{\infty}\left(\iint_{-\infty}^{0} B_x^2\,\mathrm{d}x\,\mathrm{d}y\right)\mathrm{d}z, \qquad W_2 = \int_0^{\infty}\left(\iint_{-\infty}^{0} B_y^2\,\mathrm{d}x\,\mathrm{d}y\right)\mathrm{d}z,$$

$$W_3 = \int_0^{\infty}\left(\iint_{-\infty}^{0} B_z^2\,\mathrm{d}x\,\mathrm{d}y\right)\mathrm{d}z, \qquad W_4 = \iiint_0^{\infty} B_x^2\,\mathrm{d}x\,\mathrm{d}y\,\mathrm{d}z,$$

$$W_5 = \iiint_0^{\infty} B_y^2\,\mathrm{d}x\,\mathrm{d}y\,\mathrm{d}z, \qquad W_6 = \iiint_0^{\infty} B_z^2\,\mathrm{d}x\,\mathrm{d}y\,\mathrm{d}z.$$

Substituting $\varphi(x, y, z)$ of formula (3.4) into the first expression of formula (3.2), it follows that

$$B_x(x, y, z) = B_x = -B_{x1}(x, y, z) - B_{x2}(x, y, z), \qquad (6.2)$$

as shown in the formula (5.1).

$$B_{x1}(x, y, z) = B_{x1} = G_1 \mathfrak{E}_1(x, y, z) + G_2 \mathfrak{E}_2(x, y, z),$$

where

$$G_1 = (i\eta_1 \mu_1 S_x - \alpha \nu_1 S_y)\Omega/2\gamma_1^2, \qquad G_2 = -(i\eta_2 \mu_2 S_x + \alpha \nu_2 S_y)\Omega/2\gamma_2^2;$$

$$B_{x2}(x, y, z) = B_{x2} = \int_0^\infty [A(\beta)(\lambda\beta S_x \cos\beta z + \alpha\xi S_y \sin\beta z)\mathfrak{E}_3(x, y) +$$

$$+ \Gamma(\beta)(\xi\beta S_x \cos\beta z + \alpha\lambda S_y \sin\beta z)\mathfrak{E}_4(x, y)]\, d\beta =$$

$$= \frac{\Omega}{2\pi} \int_0^\infty \left\{ S_x \beta \left[(P - Q)\cos\alpha\chi + \right.\right.$$

$$\left. + \left(\frac{\beta}{\alpha} Q + \frac{\alpha}{\beta} P \right) \sin\alpha\chi \right] e^{-\beta\kappa} \cos\beta z +$$

$$\left. + S_y \alpha \left[(P + Q)\cos\alpha\chi + \left(\frac{\beta}{\alpha} Q - \frac{\alpha}{\beta} P \right) \sin\alpha\chi \right] e^{-\beta\kappa} \sin\beta z \right\} \mathrm{d}\beta, \qquad (6.3)$$

where

$$\chi = \frac{1}{\sqrt{2}}(X - Y), \qquad \kappa = \frac{1}{\sqrt{2}}(X + Y).$$

Carrying out corresponding integrations for β, from expression (6.3) we have

$$B_{x2} \approx \frac{\Omega}{2}(S_x + \alpha S_y)[P_1(x, y, z)\cos\alpha\chi + P_2(x, y, z)\sin\alpha\chi]. \qquad (6.4)$$

The functions $P_1(x, y, z)$, $P_2(x, y, z)$ in the formula (6.4) are expressed by the terms: some of them contain a multiplier factor $\exp[-\rho_1(z + \kappa)]$, or $\exp[-\rho_2(z + \kappa)]$, respectively, and other terms contain, respectively, the factor

$$B_{x21} = \frac{\exp(-\delta z/\kappa)}{\kappa(g^2 - \kappa^2)}, \qquad B_{x22} = \frac{\exp(-\delta z/\kappa)}{g^2 - \kappa^2},$$

or

$$B_{x23} = \frac{\exp(-\delta z/\kappa)}{\kappa^2(g^2 - \kappa^2)}.$$

The integral (where δ and g are positive real constants)

$$\int\int_0^{\infty}\int (B_{x21})^2\,dz\,dx\,dy, \quad \int\int_0^{\infty}\int (B_{x22})^2\,dz\,dx\,dy,$$

or

$$\int\int_0^{\infty}\int (B_{x23})^2\,dz\,dx\,dy,$$

respectively, has a finite value. Moreover the integral

$$\int\int_0^{\infty}\int B_{x21}\,e^{-\rho_1(z+\kappa)}\,dz\,dx\,dy, \quad \int\int_0^{\infty}\int B_{x22}\,e^{-\rho_1(z+\kappa)}\,dz\,dx\,dy,$$

or

$$\int\int_0^{\infty}\int B_{x23}\,e^{-\rho_1(z+\kappa)}\,dz\,dx\,dy,$$

respectively, has a finite value. Furthermore, from the expression (6.2) we derive that

$$B_{x1} = [G_1 \exp(i\omega X + i\sigma Y - iR_c z) + G_2 \exp(-i\omega X - i\sigma Y + iR_c z)] \times \times \exp(-\mu X - \nu Y - R_s z). \tag{6.5}$$

It is clear that function B_{x1} includes a multiplier factor $\exp(-\mu X - \nu Y - R_s z)$. These factors mentioned above result in the fact that .

$$W_4 = \int\int_0^{\infty}\int B_x^2\,dx\,dy\,dz = \frac{\Omega^2}{32\pi}\int\int_0^{\infty}\int (B_{x1}^2 + 2B_{x1}\,B_{x2} + B_{x2}^2)\,dz\,dx\,dy \tag{6.6}$$

has a finite value. In a similar manner we can prove that W_1, W_2, W_3, W_5, or W_6 has a finite value, respectively. We have then verified that W has a finite value. Therefore, a solar force-free magnetic field with constant α ($\alpha \neq 0$ or $\alpha = 0$) in a half-space has a finite magnetic energy content.

7. Discussion

One may generalize the corresponding conclusion from the above considerations. In this paper, on the basis of observations, a physical model has been presented for studying the force-free magnetic field with constant α in a half-space. The corresponding reasonable boundary conditions have been taken. A proper mathematical method has been adopted. Hence, as a result, a unique analytical solution of this problem has been obtained. From the corresponding verifications one may see that if the physical model, the corresponding boundary conditions and the mathematical method for solving the problem are suitably chosen, then a magnetic field, in a half space, being force-free with constant α ($\alpha \neq 0$ or $\alpha = 0$) may be determined uniquely from only one component of the magnetic field given by observations at the photosphere, and may have a finite magnetic energy content.

Our method and the solution presented here have the following distinctive features.

(1) A boundary value problem of solar force-free magnetic fields is represented by the discretely concentrated characteristics of longitudinal magnetic field observed on the photosphere.

(2) The solution is obtained by superposition of the fields of single sources described by the physical parameters of the corresponding sunspots (or magnetic features) on the photosphere, such as their position, strength, decay rates and the extent of regions of the same polarity. Thus, if the distribution of the sources (sunspots or magnetic features) is found by observation, then we can immediately obtain the structure of the force-free field on and above the photosphere. If the new sunspots emerge, or the distribution of sources evolves, one can obtain the corresponding magnetic field structure by changing the number of sources or their parameters obtained by observation. Therefore, the formulae derived from the solution for studying solar flares and radio bursts are convenient and effective.

(3) Inside an active region the net magnetic flux may not be zero. Outside the active region the magnetic field may not be zero everywhere, but it decays as the distance from the active region increases, at large distances the magnetic field decreases rapidly.

(4) For each sunspot the solution is represented by a simple analytical function. This is convenient in calculations, as the solution of any active region is only the summation of the functions for corresponding sunspots (or magnetic features) of the active region.

(5) In accordance with observation we have added a new suitable boundary condition, which ensures solution of the difficult 'nominal problem' of the force-free field in a half-space by making use of an integral transform established by us, and finding the unique solution of the problem. We have then overcome an important difficulty which appears in the studies performed by other authors, since their boundary conditions are insufficient.

(6) The function expressing the magnetic field **B** is smooth and the function describing the current **J** is continuous everywhere in the whole spatial domain considered. Accordingly, no singular point exists in the solution presented in the paper. It enables us to describe analytically the configurations of magnetic fields on the photosphere, in the chromosphere, low corona and high corona, to infinity where the magnetic field vanishes, when flares occur, and before or after solar flares occur.

In the next paper we will publish an actual example of the use of the method given in this paper.

Acknowledgement

We would like to thank the referee for helpful comments.

An Integral Transform

Here we list several theorems of the integral transform which is used to solve the problem, as follows.

THEOREM 1

If $f(x) \in L_1(0, \infty)$, or $f(x) \in L_1(-\infty, 0)$; and also the function $F(k_0, \zeta)$ is an integral transform of the function $f(x)$ by the kernel $S(\zeta, k_0, x)$; and if in the complex field the function $\mathfrak{F}(\zeta) = F(k_0, \zeta)R(\zeta, x)$ has the following properties: (i) in the plane with the branch cut $(c_0 - ik_0, c_0 + ik_0)$, $\mathfrak{F}(\zeta)$ has two regular branches; (ii) on opposite sides of the branch cut there is a difference in values of the regular branches of $\mathfrak{F}(\zeta)$, and (iii) when the $|\zeta|$ approaches infinity each of the branches of $\mathfrak{F}(\zeta)$ will have

$$\lim |\mathfrak{F}(\zeta)| \leq \frac{\exp[-\mathscr{L}(|l| - |x|)]}{\mathscr{L}^2} \to 0$$

when $|\zeta| = \mathscr{L} \to \infty$, where $\mathscr{L} > 0$; then for an arbitrary positive quantity c_0, the inverse image function $f(x)$ is given in terms of $F(k_0, \zeta)$ by the following integral formulae.

When $f(x)$ is an even function, we have

$$f(x) = \int_{c_0 - ik_0}^{c_0 + ik_0} F(k_0, \zeta) R_c(\zeta, x)\, d\zeta, \qquad R_c(\zeta, x) = \frac{1}{\pi i} \frac{\cosh \zeta x}{\cosh \zeta l}. \tag{A.1}$$

When $f(x)$ is an odd function,

$$f(x) = \int_{c_0 - ik_0}^{c_0 + ik_0} F(k_0, \zeta) R_s(\zeta, x)\, d\zeta, \qquad R_s(\zeta, x) = \frac{1}{\pi i} \frac{\sinh \zeta x}{\cosh \zeta l}. \tag{A.2}$$

where $-|l| \leq x \leq |l|$. $\zeta = \sigma + i\tau$ is a complex variable, and k_0 is an arbitrary real constant.

$$F(k_0, \zeta) = \int_0^{\infty} f(x) S(\zeta, k_0, x)\, dx, \quad \sigma x > 0,$$

or

$$F(k_0, \zeta) = \int_{-\infty}^{0} f(x) S(\zeta, k_0, x)\, dx, \quad \sigma x < 0;$$

$S(\zeta, k_0, x) = K_0\, e^{-\zeta x} / \sqrt{k_0^2 + \bar{\zeta}^2}$, $(K_0 = \sqrt{k_0^2 + \gamma^2} \cosh \gamma$, $\bar{\zeta} = \zeta - c_0)$; γ, the poles of the function $F(k_0, \zeta)$ in the ζ-plane.

THEOREM 2

If function $f(x) \in L_1(0, \infty)$, or $f(x) \in L_1(-\infty, 0)$; and the function $F(k_0, \zeta)$ is an integral transform of the $f(x)$ by the kernel $S(\zeta, k_0, x)$; and if in the complex domain the function $\mathfrak{R}(\zeta) = F(k_0, \zeta)Q(\zeta, x)$ has the properties (i), (ii), (iii) as stated in Theorem 1; then we have

$$f(x) = \int_{c_0 - ik_0}^{c_0 + ik_0} F(k_0, \zeta)Q_c(\zeta, x)\,\mathrm{d}\zeta, \quad \text{when} \quad f(x) \text{ is an even function}, \tag{A.3}$$

$$f(x) = \int_{c_0 - ik_0}^{c_0 + ik_0} F(k_0, \zeta)Q_s(\zeta, x)\,\mathrm{d}\zeta, \quad \text{when} \quad f(x) \text{ is an odd function}. \tag{A.4}$$

THEOREM 3

If the function $f_n \in L_1(0, \infty; 0, \infty; \ldots; 0, \infty)$, or $f_n \in L_1(-\infty, 0; -\infty, 0; \ldots; -\infty, 0)$; and F_n is the integral transform of the f_n; and if in the plane ζ_1 with the branch cut $(c_1 - ik_1, c_1 + ik_1)$, ..., in the plane ζ_n with the branch cut $(c_n - ik_n, c_n + ik_n)$, $\mathfrak{F}_n = \mathfrak{F}(\zeta_1, \zeta_2, \ldots, \zeta_n) = F_n R_1 R_2 \ldots R_n$ has the properties: (i), (ii) as indicated in Theorem 1, and (iii)

$$\lim_{|\zeta_1| = \mathscr{L}_1 \to \infty} |\mathfrak{F}_n| \le \mathfrak{D}_1 \to 0, \quad \ldots, \quad \lim_{|\zeta_n| = \mathscr{L}_n \to \infty} |\mathfrak{F}_n| \le \mathfrak{D}_n \to 0,$$

respectively; then the inverse image function f_n is given in terms of F_n by the integral formula

$$f_n = f(x_1, x_2, \ldots, x_n) = \int_{c_1 - ik_1}^{c_1 + ik_1} \cdots \int_{c_n - ik_n}^{c_n + ik_n} F_n R_1 R_2 \ldots R_n\,\mathrm{d}\zeta_1\,\mathrm{d}\zeta_2 \ldots \mathrm{d}\zeta_n. \tag{A.5}$$

When f_n is an even function of x_n, we take the R_{cn}; and when f_n is odd, the R_{sn} will be taken.

THEOREM 4

If $f(x) \in N_1(0, i\infty)$ or $f(x) \in N_1(-i\infty, 0)$; and also $T(k_0, \zeta)$ is an integral transform of $f(x)$ by the kernel $E(\zeta, k_0, x)$; moreover, if $\mathfrak{I}(\zeta) = T(k_0, \zeta)Q(\zeta, x)$, in the plane ζ with the branch cut $(ic_0 - k_0, ic_0 + k_0)$, has the properties stated in Theorem 1; then the inverse image function $f(x)$ may be given by the integral formulae

$$f(x) = \int_{ic_0 - k_0}^{ic_0 + k_0} T(k_0, \zeta)Q_c(\zeta, x)\,\mathrm{d}\zeta, \quad \text{when} \quad f(x) \text{ is even}; \tag{A.6}$$

$$f(x) = \int_{ic_0 - k_0}^{ic_0 + k_0} T(k_0, \zeta)Q_s(\zeta, x)\,\mathrm{d}\zeta, \quad \text{when} \quad f(x) \text{ is odd}. \tag{A.7}$$

THEOREM 5

If the function $f_n \in N_1(0, i\infty; 0, i\infty; \ldots; 0, i\infty)$, or $f_n \in N_1(-i\infty, 0; -i\infty, 0; \ldots; -i\infty, 0)$; in addition, the T_n is the integral transform of the f_n; and if in the plane ζ_1

with the branch cut $(ic_1 - k_1, ic_1 + k_1)$, ..., in the plane ζ_n with the branch cut $(ic_n - k_n, ic_n + k_n)$, function $\mathfrak{J}_n = \mathfrak{J}(\zeta_1, \zeta_2, \ldots, \zeta_n) = T_n Q_1 Q_2 \ldots Q_n$ has the properties: (i), (ii) as indicated in Theorem 1, and (iii)

$$\lim_{|\zeta_1| = \mathcal{L}_1 \to \infty} |\mathfrak{J}_n| \leq \mathfrak{D}_1 \to 0, \quad \ldots, \quad \lim_{|\zeta_n| = \mathcal{L}_n \to \infty} |\mathfrak{J}_n| \leq \mathfrak{D}_n \to 0,$$

respectively; then the inverse image function f_n can be expressed in terms of T_n by the integral formula

$$f_n = f(x_1, x_2, \ldots, x_n) = \int_{ic_1 - k_1}^{ic_1 + k_1} \cdots \int_{ic_n - k_n}^{ic_n + k_n} T_n Q_1 Q_2 \ldots Q_n \, d\zeta_1 \, d\zeta_2 \ldots d\zeta_n . \tag{A.8}$$

When f_n is even, we take Q_{cn}; if f_n is odd, then we take Q_{sn}.

THEOREM 6

If the function $f_n \in L_1(0, \infty; 0, \infty; \ldots; 0, \infty)$, or $f_n \in L_1(-\infty, 0; -\infty, 0; \ldots; -\infty, 0)$; and the function F_n is the integral transform of f_n; and if in the complex plane ζ_1 with the branch cut $(c_1 - ik_1, c_1 + ik_1)$, ..., in the plane ζ_n with the branch cut $(c_n - ik_n, c_n + ik_n)$, function $\mathfrak{B}_n = \mathfrak{B}(\zeta_1, \zeta_2, \ldots, \zeta_n) = F_n Q_1 Q_2 \ldots Q_n$ has, in addition to the properties (i) and (ii) referred in Theorem 1, the property (iii):

$$\lim_{|\zeta_1| = \mathcal{L}_1 \to \infty} |\mathfrak{B}_n| \leq \mathfrak{D}_1 \to 0, \quad \ldots, \quad \lim_{|\zeta_n| = \mathcal{L}_n \to \infty} |\mathfrak{B}_n| \leq \mathfrak{D}_n \to 0,$$

respectively; then the inverse image function f_n can be given in terms of F_n by the integral formula

$$f_n = f(x_1, x_2, \ldots, x_n) = \int_{c_1 - ik_1}^{c_1 + ik_1} \cdots \int_{c_n - ik_n}^{c_n + ik_n} F_n Q_1 Q_2 \ldots Q_n \, d\zeta_1 \, d\zeta_2 \ldots d\zeta_n . \tag{A.9}$$

The Q_{sn} should be taken when f_n is an odd function of x_n. If f_n is even, we should take the Q_{cn}.

THEOREM 7

If we assume $f(x) \in N_1(0, i\infty)$, or $f(x) \in N_1(-i\infty, 0)$; and that $T(k_0, \zeta)$ is an integral transform of the function $f(x)$ by the kernel $E(\zeta, k_0, x)$; in addition, in the complex plane ζ with the branch cut $(ic_0 - k_0, ic_0 + k_0)$ the function $\mathfrak{E}(\zeta) = T(k_0, \zeta)R(\zeta, x)$ has the properties (i), (ii), and (iii) as related in Theorem 1; then $f(x)$ is given by

$$f(x) = \int_{ic_0 - k_0}^{ic_0 + k_0} T(k_0, \zeta) R_c(\zeta, x) \, d\zeta , \tag{A.10}$$

when $f(x)$ is an even function; and

$$f(x) = \int_{ic_0 - k_0}^{ic_0 + k_0} T(k_0, \zeta) R_s(\zeta, x) \, \mathrm{d}\zeta \,, \tag{A.11}$$

if $f(x)$ is an odd function.

THEOREM 8

If we suppose that $f_n \in N_1(0, i\infty; 0, i\infty; \ldots ; 0, i\infty)$, or $f_n \in N_1(-i\infty, 0; -i\infty, 0; \ldots ; -i\infty, 0)$; and the function T_n is its integral transform by the kernel E_n; and also in the plane ζ_1 with the branch cut $(ic_1 - k_1, ic_1 + k_1)$, ..., in the plane ζ_n with the branch cut $(ic_n - k_n, ic_n + k_n)$, the function $\mathfrak{E}_n = \mathfrak{E}(\zeta_1, \zeta_2, \ldots, \zeta_n) = T_n R_1 R_2 \ldots R_n$ has the properties (i), (ii) as referred in Theorem 1 and (iii): $\lim|\mathfrak{E}_n| \le \mathfrak{D}_1 \to 0$ when $|\zeta_1| = \mathscr{L}_1 \to \infty, \ldots, \lim|\mathfrak{E}_n| \le \mathfrak{D}_n \to 0$ when $|\zeta_n| = \mathscr{L}_n \to \infty$; then

$$f_n = f(x_1, x_2, \ldots, x_n) = \int_{ic_1 - k_1}^{ic_1 + k_1} \cdots \int_{ic_n - k_n}^{ic_n + k_n} T_n R_1 R_2 \ldots R_n \, \mathrm{d}\zeta_1 \, \mathrm{d}\zeta_2 \ldots \mathrm{d}\zeta_n \,. \tag{A.12}$$

We should take R_{cn} when f_n is an even function, and when f_n is odd, the R_{sn} should be taken.

The notations that appear in the above theorems are:

$$Q_c(\zeta, x) = \cos \zeta x / i\pi \cos \zeta l \,, \qquad Q_s(\zeta, x) = \sin \zeta x / i\pi \cos \zeta l \,;$$

$$Q_{cn} = Q_{cn}(\zeta_n, x_n) = \cos \zeta_n x_n / i\pi \cos \zeta_n l_n \,,$$

$$Q_{sn} = Q_{sn}(\zeta_n, x_n) = \sin \zeta_n x_n / i\pi \cos \zeta_n l_n \,; \qquad |x_n| \le |l_n| \,,$$

$$R_{cn} = R_{cn}(\zeta_n, x_n) = \cosh \zeta_n x_n / i\pi \cosh \zeta_n l_n \,,$$

$$R_{sn} = R_{sn}(\zeta_n, x_n) = \sinh \zeta_n x_n / i\pi \cosh \zeta_n l_n \,; \qquad \overline{\zeta}_n = \zeta_n - c_n \,,$$

$$S_n = S(\zeta_n, k_n, x_n) = K_{on} \, e^{-\zeta_n x_n} / \sqrt{k_n^2 + \overline{\zeta}_n^2} \,,$$

$$K_{on} = \overline{\gamma}_n \cosh \gamma_n l_n \,, \qquad \overline{\gamma}_n = \sqrt{k_n^2 + \gamma_n^2} \,.$$

In addition

$$T(k_0, \zeta) = \int_0^{i\infty} f(x) E(\zeta, k_0, x) \, \mathrm{d}x, \quad \text{when} \quad \sigma x > 0$$

or

$$T(k_0, \zeta) = \int_{-i\infty}^{0} f(x) E(\zeta, k_0, x) \, \mathrm{d}x, \quad \text{when} \quad \sigma x < 0 \,.$$

$$F_n = F(\zeta_1, \zeta_2, \dots, \zeta_n) = \int_0^{\infty} \dots \int_0^{\infty} f_n S_1 S_2 \dots S_n \, \mathrm{d}x_1 \, \mathrm{d}x_2 \dots \mathrm{d}x_n,$$

when $\sigma_n x_n > 0$;

or

$$F_n = F(\zeta_1, \zeta_2, \dots, \zeta_n) = \int_{-\infty}^{0} \dots \int_{-\infty}^{0} f_n S_1 S_2 \dots S_n \, \mathrm{d}x_1 \, \mathrm{d}x_2 \dots \mathrm{d}x_n,$$

when $\sigma_n x_n < 0$;

$$T_n = T(\zeta_1, \zeta_2, \dots, \zeta_n) = \int_0^{i\infty} \dots \int_0^{i\infty} f_n E_1 E_2 \dots E_n \, \mathrm{d}x_1 \, \mathrm{d}x_2 \dots \mathrm{d}x_n,$$

when $\sigma_n x_n > 0$;

or

$$T_n = T(\zeta_1, \zeta_2, \dots, \zeta_n) = \int_{-i\infty}^{0} \dots \int_{-i\infty}^{0} f_n E_1 E_2 \dots E_n \, \mathrm{d}x_1 \, \mathrm{d}x_2 \dots \mathrm{d}x_n,$$

when $\sigma_n x_n < 0$.

γ, the poles of the function $T(k_0, \zeta)$ in the ζ-plane; γ_n, the poles of the function F_n or T_n, in the ζ_n-plane,

$$E(\zeta, k_0, x) = K_2 \, e^{i\zeta x} / \sqrt{\xi^2 - k_0^2}, \qquad K_2 = \sqrt{\gamma^2 - k_0^2} \cos \gamma l; \qquad \xi = \zeta - ic_0,$$

$$E_n = E(\zeta_n, k_n, x_n) = K_{2n} \, e^{i\zeta_n x_n} / \sqrt{\xi_n^2 - k_n^2}, \qquad \mathfrak{D}_n = \frac{\exp[-\mathscr{L}_n(|l_n| - |x_n|)]}{\mathscr{L}_n^2},$$

$$K_{2n} = \sqrt{\gamma_n^2 - k_n^2} \cos \gamma_n l_n, \qquad \xi_n = \zeta_n - ic_n, \quad n = 1, 2, \dots;$$

$\mathscr{L}_n > 0$, positive reals.

If the conditions

$$\left| \int_0^{i\infty} |f(x)| \, e^{i\zeta x} \, \mathrm{d}x \right| < \infty, \ \sigma x > 0 \quad \text{or} \quad \left| \int_{-i\infty}^{0} |f(x)| \, e^{i\zeta x} \, \mathrm{d}x \right| < \infty, \quad \sigma x < 0$$

are valid, we shall write, respectively, all the functions using the symbols $N_1(0, i\infty)$ or $N_1(-i\infty, 0)$.

When it is unnecessary to give a special explanation, in general, the $R_c(\zeta, x)$ and $R_s(\zeta, x)$ are denoted simply by $R(\zeta, x)$. In the same way, we denote $Q_c(\zeta, x)$ and $Q_s(\zeta, x)$ simply by $Q(\zeta, x)$; R_{cn} and $R_{sn}$by R_n; Q_{cn} and Q_{sn} by Q_n.

Using the corresponding inversion theorem and the inverse formulae referred above, the problem will be solved, and a unique and analytical solution will be obtained. The result derived from the solution will agree well with the actual physical picture in the whole domain considered.

References

Alissandrakis, C. E.: 1981, *Astron. Astrophys.* **100**, 197.
Altschuler, M. D. and Newkirk, G., Jr.: 1969, *Solar Phys.* **9**, 131.
Chen Zhen-cheng: 1981, *Kexue Tongbao* **26**, 16.
Chen Zhen-cheng: 1983, *Proceedings of the Second Asian Congress of Fluid Mechanics*, Science Press, Beijing, China, p. 550.
Chen Zhen-cheng and Wang Jing-xiu: 1986, *Solar Phys.* **103**, 317.
Chiu, Y. T. and Hilton, H. H.: 1977, *Astrophys. J.* **212**, 873.
Elwert, G., Müller, K., Thur, L., and Balz, P.: 1982, *Solar Phys.* **75**, 205.
Nakagawa, Y. and Raadu, M. A.: 1972, *Solar Phys.* **25**, 127.
Schmidt, H. U.: 1964, *AAS-NASA Symposium on the Physics of Solar Flares*, NASA SP-50, p. 107.
Seehafer, N.: 1978, *Solar Phys.* **58**, 215.
Seehafer, N.: 1982, *Solar Phys.* **81**, 69.
Stenflo, J. O.: 1970, in R. Howard (ed.), 'Solar Magnetic Fields', *IAU Symp.* **43**, 115.
Zwaan, C.: 1978, *Solar Phys.* **60**, 213.

F—2 · 8

THE CRITERION FOR PRESAGING OCCURRENCE OF SOLAR FLARE

THE FIFTH ASIAN CONGRESS OF FLUID MECHANICS

August 10-14, 1992 Korea

Chen Zhen-cheng

Beijing Astronomical Observatory,Chinese Academy of Sciences,
Beijing, China

ABSTRACT Applying the method to make researches on fluid mechanics refs.[1,2], one may investigate the condensation of magnetic energy and the criterion for presaging occurrence of Solar flare. Solar activities influence upon the circumstance of the earth. Study of solar activities has scientific and practical interest. In this paper we derive the formulae for calculating the configurations of magnetic fields on and above the photosphere, for studying the condensation of magnetic energy due to the vortical, displacement, squeeze, shearing motion between the sunspots or magnetic features with different polarity. The magnetic energy may be the main energy source triggering solar flares, radio bursts and other solar active phenomena. Finally, we propose a criterion given by an analytical expression,which may presage triggering off solar flares.

1. Introduction

The solar flare and other solar activities directly influence upon the earth. In fact, the Sun is a natural accelerator of charged particles, it is also a laboratory for astrophysics. For investigating various phenomena of solar activity, one must, in the first place, research the magnetic fields on and above the photosphere in an active region. But , at present, reliable and detailed firsthand information on magnetic fields obtained by observations is available only for the longitudinal field on the photosphere. Therefore, in order to obtain information about the magnetic fields throughout the solar atmosphere one has, on the basis of observational data obtained from the longitudinal component of the magnetic fields on the photosphere, to carry out theoretical investigation of this problem. For solving the problem, in previously published studies, some methods are based on the assumption of a potential field ref.[3], etc. and some methods on the force free field with constant α ref.[4],etc.. Each author has contributed towards the solution of this problem. However, as the boundary conditions are insufficient, their solutions are not unique, some of them the magnetic energy content in a half-space is infinite.

Based on the observational data, we have, for a semi-infinite space, presented a reasonable physical model. Taking reasonable boundary conditions, by means of a suitable mathematical method, we have, from only the longitudinal field observed at the photosphere, obtained a unique analytical solution for this problem. We have verified the uniqueness of the solution, the finiteness of magnetic energy content in a half-space. No singular point exists in the solution has been proved ref.[5].

2. The formulae expressing the magnetic fields throughout the solar atmosphere.

On the bases of our published paper ref.[5], the expressions of magnetic field in the spatial domain considered may be written as following form

$$B_x(x,y,z)=\sum_{m=1}^{k}B_{xm}(x,y,z),\quad B_y(x,y,z)=\sum_{m=1}^{k}B_{ym}(x,y,z),\quad B_z(x,y,z)=\sum_{m=1}^{k}B_{zm}(x,y,z).\quad (1)$$

where k denotes the total number of sunspots or magnetic features in an active region.

$$B_{xm}=B_{xm}(x,y,z)=\frac{\partial^2\varphi_m}{\partial x\partial z}+\alpha\frac{\partial\varphi_m}{\partial y},\quad B_{ym}=B_{ym}(x,y,z)=\frac{\partial^2\varphi_m}{\partial y\partial z}-\alpha\frac{\partial\varphi_m}{\partial x},$$

$$B_{zm} = B_{zm}(x,y,z) = -\frac{\partial^2\varphi_m}{\partial x^2} - \frac{\partial^2\varphi_m}{\partial y^2}. \tag{2}$$

The formulae listed below belong to the m-th sunspot or magnetic feature, but for simplicity the suffix m is omitted, that is, $\varphi_m = \varphi_m(x,y,z)$, B_{xm}, B_{ym}, B_{zm}, etc. are written as $\varphi = \varphi(x,y,z)$, B_x, B_y, B_z, etc. .

$$\varphi = \psi_1 + \psi_2,\ \psi_1 = \psi_1(x,y,z) = -\frac{\Omega}{2}\{\frac{1}{\gamma_1^2}\exp(-\mu_1 X - \nu_1 Y - i\eta_1 z) + \frac{1}{\gamma_2^2}\exp(-\mu_2 X - \nu_2 Y + i\eta_2 z)\}, \tag{3}$$

$$\psi_2 = \psi_2(x,y,z) = \int_o^\infty [A(\beta)\exp(-\lambda X - \xi Y) + \Gamma(\beta)\exp(-\xi X - \lambda Y)] sin\beta z d\beta. \tag{4}$$

$$B_x = B_{1x} + B_{2x},\ B_y = B_{1y} + B_{2y},\ B_z = B_{1z} + B_{2z}\ . \tag{5}$$

$$B_{1x} = \frac{\partial^2\psi_1}{\partial x\partial z} + \alpha\frac{\partial\psi_1}{\partial y},\ B_{2x} = \frac{\partial^2\psi_2}{\partial x\partial z} + \alpha\frac{\partial\psi_2}{\partial y}.$$

$$B_{1y} = \frac{\partial^2\psi_1}{\partial y\partial z} - \alpha\frac{\partial\psi_1}{\partial x},\ B_{2y} = \frac{\partial^2\psi_2}{\partial y\partial z} - \alpha\frac{\partial\psi_2}{\partial x}. \tag{6}$$

$$B_{1z} = -\frac{\partial^2\psi_1}{\partial x^2} - \frac{\partial^2\psi_1}{\partial y^2},\ B_{2z} = -\frac{\partial^2\psi_2}{\partial x^2} - \frac{\partial^2\psi_2}{\partial y^2}.$$

3. Triggering a solar flare due to the condensation of magnetic energy

Basing on continued observations and theoretical formulae given in the above section, we may investigate the magnetic field configurations and their evolution, may describe generally the appearance and development of the magnetic vortex, that is, describe the twisting magnetic lines, the condensation of magnetic energy. Figs. 1-4 show that the magnetic lines twist near the neutral line, where the magnetic flux may increase rapidly. The magnetic energy condenses. If it reaches certain limited value, if, among the sunspots or magnetic features with different polarity, the displacement or squeeze, shearing motion appears, then an unbalance may arouse, a strong electric field could be aroused. The particles may be accelerated. The light and heat may be given off. That means the solar flare occurs, The magnetic lines may be cracked and reconnected. The high energy is released. Therefore the Sun is a natural accelerator of charged particles, a laboratory for astrophysics.

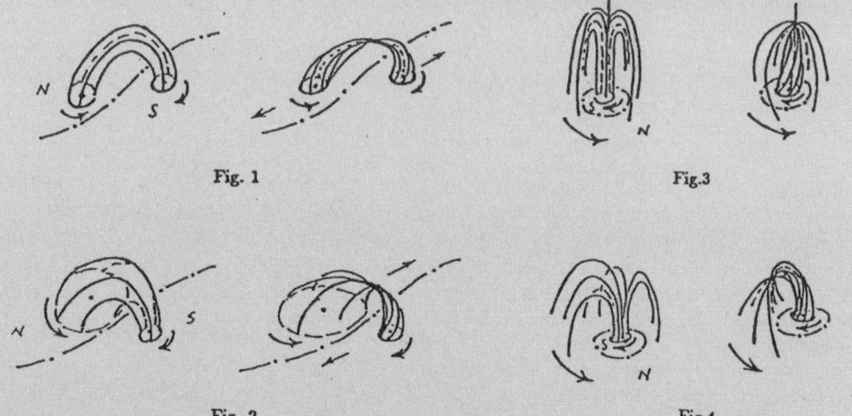

Fig. 1 Fig.3

Fig. 2 Fig.4

For the following cases we enter into detail.

1). Two sunspots with different polarity emerge at the same time:

Taking opposite direction, the relative rotation of sunspots around self-centers could twist the magnetic lines somewhere in the chromosphere or low corona, where the magnetic flux may increase rapidly. The condensation of magnetic energy appears(see Fig.1).

2). Sunspot group emerges at the photosphere:

In this case the relative rotations of sunspots with different polarity around self-centres may form easy the strong magnetic vortex somewhere in the chromosphere or corona, where the solar flare may be aroused.

3). A single sunspot emerges at the photosphere:

a). There is a single sunspot at one side of neutral line. But at the other side there are only magnetic features. Then, in the side having sunspot the magnetic line density is larger than the side having only the magnetic features. The distribution of magnetic lines in space likes a casting net, see Fig. 2. Taking opposite direction, both ends of the net rotate relatively around self-centers at the photosphere. It could twist the magnetic lines somewhere near the neutral line in the space, where the magnetic energy may condense, the solar flare may be excited.

b). A single sunspot surrounded by the magnetic features with another polarity. If the strength of magnetic field is evenly distributed outside the circular neutral line, the magnetic lines would distribute as shown in Fig.3. The relative opposite rotation between the sunspot and the magnetic features outside the circular neutral line round the same center, that is the center of the sunspot, leads to twist the magnetic lines above the sunspot,and causes the condensation of magnetic energy and the solar flare may be aroused . If the magnetic field in the left outside of the circular neutral line is stronger than the right, the condensation of magnetic energy may appear in the left as shown in Fig. 4.

4. A criterion presaging solar flares

The magnetic vorticity component in the direction x, y, z, may be written respectively as follows

$$B_{vx} = (rotB)_x = \frac{\partial B_z}{\partial y} - \frac{\partial B_y}{\partial z} = \alpha B_x, B_{vy} = (rotB)_y = \frac{\partial B_x}{\partial z} - \frac{\partial B_z}{\partial x} = \alpha B_y,$$

$$B_{vz} = (rotB)_z = \frac{\partial B_y}{\partial x} - \frac{\partial B_x}{\partial y} = \alpha B_z. \tag{7}$$

The rotation of foot point of sunspot or magnetic feature on the photosphere may impel the twist of magnetic lines somewhere near the neutral line above the photosphere, here the magnetic flux increase rapidly, that is, the condensation of magnetic energy appears. When the energy condensed reaches certain limited value which is enough for appearance of unbalance and triggering a solar flare, then the solar flare erupts.

We may define the limited value of magnetic energy as the criterion of triggering a solar flare. It may be written in the following form

$$W_{lim} = \frac{B_v^2}{8\pi\alpha^2}, \quad B_v = \sqrt{B_{vx}^2 + B_{vy}^2 + B_{vz}^2} = \alpha\sqrt{B_x^2 + B_y^2 + B_z^2}. \tag{8}$$

When the maximum magnetic energy W_{max} somewhere in the solar atmosphere reaches $W_{max} \geq W_{lim}$, the solar flare occurs. One may determine the numerical value of W_{lim} based on the observations for the occurrence of solar flares. According to the observational data for the longitudinal component of magnetic field on the photosphere and the formulae for calculating the magnetic energy given in this paper, one may presage when and where the solar flare will arouse. Its importance could be determined.

References

[1] Chen Zhen-cheng: Proceedings of the Second Asian Congress of Fluid Mechanics, Science Press, Beijing, China, 550(1983).

[2] Chen Zhen-cheng: Kexue Tongbao, 26(1), 16(1981).

[3] Schmidt, H.U.: AAS-NASA Symposium on the Physics of Solar Flares, NASA SP-50, 107(1964)
[4] Seehafer, N.: Solar Phys. 58, 215(1978)
[5] Chen Zhen-cheng and Chen Yang: Solar Phys. 119, 279(1989).

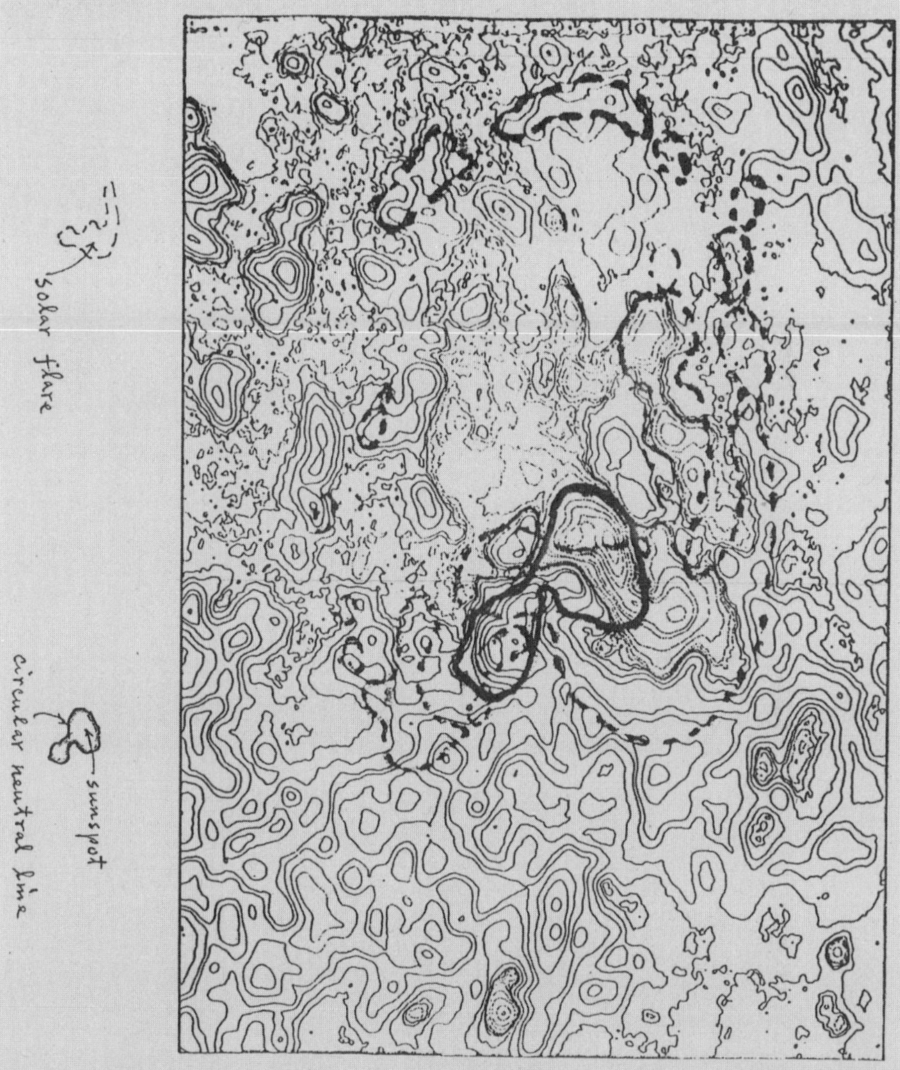

Fig.5: The observational result shows that a strong sunspot is surrounded by the magnetic features with another polarity, and a large solar flare occurs above the sunspot. It corresponds to the theoretical result as shown in section 3, 3)-b).

F—3

用中文、英文、俄文、意大利文、德文、法文、韩文、日文、西班牙文、挪威文、波兰文等发表的陈振诚原创性发明专利

F—3·1 中国的发明专利授权

证书号第1777866号

发明专利证书

发 明 名 称：一种水面交通运输工具

发 明 人：陈振诚

专 利 号：ZL 2013 1 0054313.0

专利申请日：2013年02月20日

专 利 权 人：陈振诚

授权公告日：2015年09月02日

本发明经过本局依照中华人民共和国专利法进行审查，决定授予专利权，颁发本证书并在专利登记簿上予以登记。专利权自授权公告之日起生效。

本专利的专利权期限为二十年，自申请日起算。专利权人应当依照专利法及其实施细则规定缴纳年费。本专利的年费应当在每年02月20日前缴纳。未按照规定缴纳年费的，专利权自应当缴纳年费期满之日起终止。

专利证书记载专利权登记时的法律状况。专利权的转移、质押、无效、终止、恢复和专利权人的姓名或名称、国籍、地址变更等事项记载在专利登记簿上。

局长
申长雨

第1页（共1页）

发明专利证书

发明名称：水面航行器船体

发明人：陈振诚

专利号：ZL 94 1 14846.7　国际专利主分类号：B63B 1/04

专利申请日：1994 年 8 月 13 日

专利权人：陈振诚

该发明已由本局依照中华人民共和国专利法进行审查，

决定授予专利权。

本发明已由本局依照专利法进行审查，决定于 1999 年 8 月 28 日授予专利权，颁发本证书并在专利登记簿上予以登记。专利权自证书颁发之日起生效。

本专利的专利权期限为二十年，自申请日起算。专利权人应当依照专利法及其实施细则规定缴纳年费。缴纳本专利年费的期限是每年 8 月 13 日前一个月内。未按照规定缴纳年费的，专利权自应当缴纳年费期满之日起终止。

专利证书记载专利权登记时的法律状况。专利权的转让、继承、撤销、无效、终止和专利权人的姓名或名称、国籍、地址变更等事项记载在专利登记簿上。

证书号　第 46688 号

申请号

局长　姜颖

第 1 页(共 1 页)

F—3·2 美国的发明专利授权

The Commissioner of Patents and Trademarks

Has received an application for a patent for a new and useful invention. The title and description of the invention are enclosed. The requirements of law have been complied with, and it has been determined that a patent on the invention shall be granted under the law.

Therefore, this

United States Patent

Grants to the person(s) having title to this patent the right to exclude others from making, using, offering for sale, or selling the invention throughout the United States of America or importing the invention into the United States of America for the term set forth below, subject to the payment of maintenance fees as provided by law.

If this application was filed prior to June 8, 1995, the term of this patent is the longer of seventeen years from the date of grant of this patent or twenty years from the earliest effective U.S. filing date of the application, subject to any statutory extension.

If this application was filed on or after June 8, 1995, the term of this patent is twenty years from the U.S. filing date, subject to any statutory extension. If the application contains a specific reference to an earlier filed application or applications under 35 U.S.C. 120, 121 or 365(c), the term of the patent is twenty years from the date on which the earliest application was filed, subject to any statutory extension.

Acting Commissioner of Patents and Trademarks

Attest

United States Patent [19]
Chen

[11] **Patent Number:** **5,934,218**
[45] **Date of Patent:** **Aug. 10, 1999**

[54] **PLANING VESSEL**

[76] Inventor: **Zhencheng Chen**, Room 308# Bldg. 822, Zhongguancun, Beijing 100080, China

[21] Appl. No.: **08/793,377**

[22] PCT Filed: **Jun. 30, 1995**

[86] PCT No.: **PCT/CN95/00054**

§ 371 Date: **Feb. 12, 1997**

§ 102(e) Date: **Feb. 12, 1997**

[87] PCT Pub. No.: **WO96/05096**

PCT Pub. Date: **Feb. 22, 1996**

[30] **Foreign Application Priority Data**

Aug. 13, 1994 [CN] China 94114846
Mar. 2, 1995 [CN] China 95203983

[51] **Int. Cl.**[6] **B63B 1/32**
[52] **U.S. Cl.** **114/288**; 114/290
[58] **Field of Search** 114/56, 271, 288–290; D12/300, 310–314

[56] **References Cited**

U.S. PATENT DOCUMENTS

2,938,490 5/1960 Martin 114/290
3,602,179 8/1971 Cole .
4,708,085 11/1987 Blee 114/290
4,862,817 9/1989 Hornsby, Jr. et al. 114/288
5,191,849 3/1993 Labrucherie et al. 114/290
5,231,949 8/1993 Hadley .
5,357,894 10/1994 Jacobson .
5,425,325 6/1995 Washio 114/290

FOREIGN PATENT DOCUMENTS

89102251 11/1989 China .
1106441 3/1968 United Kingdom .
WO 95/16603 6/1995 WIPO .

Primary Examiner—Ed L. Swinehart
Attorney, Agent, or Firm—Dickinson Wright PLLC

[57] **ABSTRACT**

A planing vessel has a hull and a propulsion and control system. The hull has a plane bottom formed of an equicrural triangle in the front and a rectangle at the back, two boards and one or more swell guideways. Each swell guideway has an inclined top line with a lower front and a higher back denting upwardly into and extending lengthwise throughout the bottom and paralleling its centerline. The hull also has a pair of wave-splash guards inlaid or dented one into the boards as an integrated body, a deck, a cabin and an upper construction. The planing vessel so formed can generate sufficient hydrodynamic buoyancy with reasonable distribution to quickly lift itself out of the water and enter a planing state. The planing vessel can have various fine performances, desirable speed and stability to move on rough waters.

21 Claims, 10 Drawing Sheets

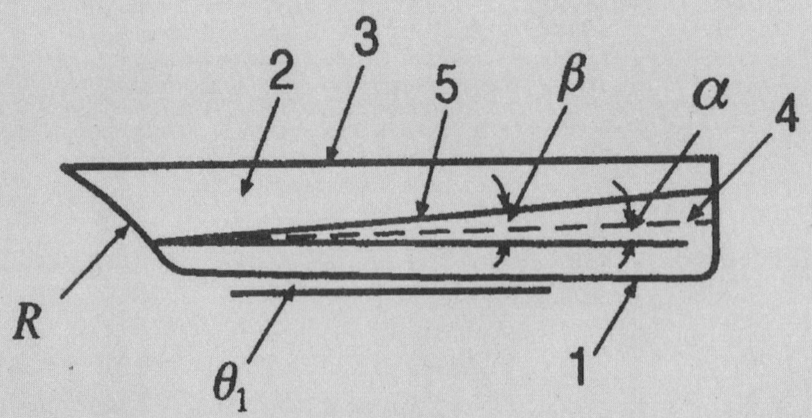

The United States of America

The Director of the United States Patent and Trademark Office

Has received an application for a patent for a new and useful invention. The title and description of the invention are enclosed. The requirements of law have been complied with, and it has been determined that a patent on the invention shall be granted under the law.

Therefore, this

United States Patent

Grants to the person(s) having title to this patent the right to exclude others from making, using, offering for sale, or selling the invention throughout the United States of America or importing the invention into the United States of America, and if the invention is a process, of the right to exclude others from using, offering for sale or selling throughout the United States of America, or importing into the United States of America, products made by that process, for the term set forth in 35 U.S.C. 154(a)(2) or (c)(1), subject to the payment of maintenance fees as provided by 35 U.S.C. 41(b). See the Maintenance Fee Notice on the inside of the cover.

Michelle K. Lee

Director of the United States Patent and Trademark Office

MAINTENANCE FEE NOTICE

If the application for this patent was filed on or after December 12, 1980, maintenance fees are due three years and six months, seven years and six months, and eleven years and six months after the date of this grant, or within a grace period of six months thereafter upon payment of a surcharge as provided by law. The amount, number and timing of the maintenance fees required may be changed by law or regulation. Unless payment of the applicable maintenance fee is received in the United States Patent and Trademark Office on or before the date the fee is due or within a grace period of six months thereafter, the patent will expire as of the end of such grace period.

PATENT TERM NOTICE

If the application for this patent was filed on or after June 8, 1995, the term of this patent begins on the date on which this patent issues and ends twenty years from the filing date of the application or, if the application contains a specific reference to an earlier filed application or applications under 35 U.S.C. 120, 121, 365(c), or 386(c), twenty years from the filing date of the earliest such application ("the twenty-year term"), subject to the payment of maintenance fees as provided by 35 U.S.C. 41(b), and any extension as provided by 35 U.S.C. 154(b) or 156 or any disclaimer under 35 U.S.C. 253.

If this application was filed prior to June 8, 1995, the term of this patent begins on the date on which this patent issues and ends on the later of seventeen years from the date of the grant of this patent or the twenty-year term set forth above for patents resulting from applications filed on or after June 8, 1995, subject to the payment of maintenance fees as provided by 35 U.S.C. 41(b) and any extension as provided by 35 U.S.C. 156 or any disclaimer under 35 U.S.C. 253.

(12) **United States Patent**
Chen

(10) **Patent No.: US 9,567,035 B2**
(45) **Date of Patent: Feb. 14, 2017**

(54) **MEANS OF WATER SURFACE TRANSPORT**

(71) Applicant: **Zhencheng Chen**, Beijing (CN)

(72) Inventor: **Zhencheng Chen**, Beijing (CN)

(*) Notice: Subject to any disclaimer, the term of this patent is extended or adjusted under 35 U.S.C. 154(b) by 0 days.

(21) Appl. No.: **14/769,105**

(22) PCT Filed: **Feb. 20, 2014**

(86) PCT No.: **PCT/CN2014/072325**
§ 371 (c)(1),
(2) Date: **Aug. 20, 2015**

(87) PCT Pub. No.: **WO2014/127723**
PCT Pub. Date: **Aug. 28, 2014**

(65) **Prior Publication Data**

US 2016/0001848 A1 Jan. 7, 2016

(30) **Foreign Application Priority Data**

Feb. 20, 2013 (CN) 2013 1 0054313

(51) **Int. Cl.**

B63B 1/16	(2006.01)
B63B 1/04	(2006.01)
B63B 3/00	(2006.01)
B63B 1/12	(2006.01)
B63B 1/20	(2006.01)

(52) **U.S. Cl.**
CPC ***B63B 1/042*** (2013.01); ***B63B 1/125*** (2013.01); ***B63B 3/00*** (2013.01); *B63B 2001/201* (2013.01); *B63B 2001/208* (2013.01)

(58) **Field of Classification Search**
CPC B63B 1/042; B63B 1/20; B63B 1/16; B63B 1/08; B63B 2001/325; B63B 2001/201
See application file for complete search history.

(56) **References Cited**

U.S. PATENT DOCUMENTS

2,515,005 A *	7/1950	Hickman	....	B63B 1/20 114/288
3,602,179 A	8/1971	Cole		
4,722,294 A	2/1988	Bruning		
5,016,552 A	5/1991	Ludlow		

(Continued)

FOREIGN PATENT DOCUMENTS

CN	1121882 A	5/1996
CN	2228055 Y	5/1996

(Continued)

Primary Examiner — Andrew Polay
(74) *Attorney, Agent, or Firm* — Ling Wu; Stephen Yang; Ling and Yang Intellectual Property

(57) **ABSTRACT**

A water surface transport means, comprising a bottom (1), boards (2), a deck (3), surge diversion grooves (4) and wave suppression diversion baffles (5), the surge diversion groove (4) being provided in a space between a bottom surface vertically recessed into the hull bottom (1) and the deck (3) and extending from the bow to the stern, with an arc-shaped transverse section and a top line of longitudinal section being lower in the front and higher in the rear; a top transverse section of the wave suppression diversion baffle (5) being arc-shaped and a top line of longitudinal section being lower in the front and higher in the rear. The water surface transport means can be configured as mono-hull, catamaran and trimaran.

5 Claims, 6 Drawing Sheets

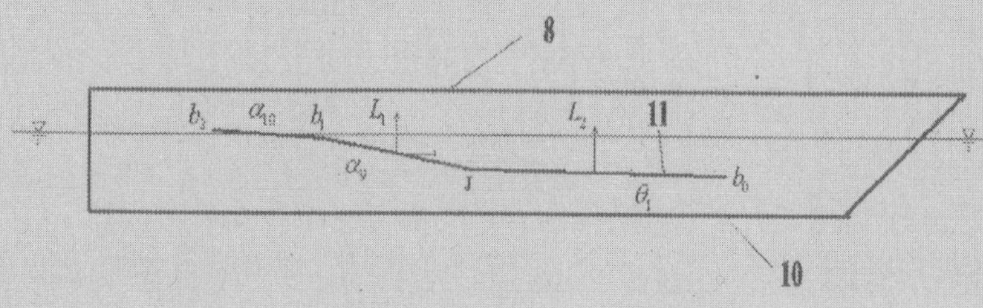

F—3·3 欧洲局（英、法、德、意大利、荷兰等11国）的发明专利授权

Europäisches Patentamt | European Patent Office | Office européen des brevets

Urkunde Certificate Certificat

Es wird hiermit bescheinigt, daß für die in der beigefügten Patentschrift beschriebene Erfindung ein europäisches Patent für die in der Patentschrift bezeichneten Vertragsstaaten erteilt worden ist.

It is hereby certified that a European patent has been granted in respect of the invention described in the annexed patent specification for the Contracting States designated in the specification.

Il est certifié qu'un brevet européen a été délivré pour l'invention décrite dans le fascicule de brevet ci-joint, pour les Etats contractants désignés dans le fascicule de brevet.

Europäisches Patent Nr. European Patent No. Brevet européen n°

0775626

Patentinhaber Proprietor of the Patent Titulaire du brevet

Chen, Zhencheng
308, 822 Block Zhongguancun
Beijing 100080/CN

München, den
Munich,
Fait à Munich, le 12.06.02

Ingo Kober

Präsident des Europäischen Patentamts
President of the European Patent Office
Président de l'Office européen des brevets

EPA/EPO/OEB Form 2031 01.96

欧洲局授权证书

(19) Europäisches Patentamt
European Patent Office
Office européen des brevets

(11) EP 0 775 626 B1

(12) EUROPEAN PATENT SPECIFICATION

(45) Date of publication and mention of the grant of the patent: 12.06.2002 Bulletin 2002/24

(21) Application number: 95923171.3

(22) Date of filing: 30.06.1995

(51) Int Cl.7: B63B 1/02, B63B 1/40, B63B 1/04

(86) International application number: PCT/CN95/00054

(87) International publication number: WO 96/05096 (22.02.1996 Gazette 1996/09)

(54) PLANING VESSEL
GLEITBOOT
VAISSEAU PLANANT

(84) Designated Contracting States:
BE DE DK ES FR GB GR IT NL PT SE

(30) Priority: 13.08.1994 CN 94114846
02.03.1995 CN 95203983

(43) Date of publication of application:
28.05.1997 Bulletin 1997/22

(73) Proprietor: Chen, Zhencheng
Beijing 100080 (CN)

授权国:
BE 比利时，DE 德国，DK 丹麦，ES 西班牙，FR 法国，GB 英国，GR 希腊，IT 意大利，NL 荷兰，PT 葡萄牙，SE 瑞典 共11国.

(72) Inventor: Chen, Zhencheng
Beijing 100080 (CN)

(74) Representative: Darby, David Thomas
Abel & Imray,
20 Red Lion Street
London WC1R 4PQ (GB)

(56) References cited:

WO-A-95/16603	CN-A- 1 036 734
GB-A- 1 108 441	US-A- 2 938 490
US-A- 3 602 178	US-A- 5 231 949
US-A- 5 357 894	

EP 0 775 626 B1

Note: Within nine months from the publication of the mention of the grant of the European patent, any person may give notice to the European Patent Office of opposition to the European patent granted. Notice of opposition shall be filed in a written reasoned statement. It shall not be deemed to have been filed until the opposition fee has been paid. (Art. 99(1) European Patent Convention).

5

F—3·4 俄罗斯的发明专利授权

РОССИЙСКАЯ ФЕДЕРАЦИЯ

ПАТЕНТ

НА ИЗОБРЕТЕНИЕ

№ 2150401

Российским агентством по патентам и товарным знакам на основании Патентного закона Российской Федерации, введенного в действие 14 октября 1992 года, выдан настоящий патент на изобретение

ГЛИССЕР

Патентообладатель(ли):

Чень Чжэнь-чен (CN)

по заявке № 97104001, дата поступления: 30.06.1995

Приоритет от 13.08.1994; 02.03.1995

Автор(ы) изобретения:

Чень Чжэнь-чен (CN)

Патент действует на всей территории Российской Федерации в течение 20 лет с **30 июня 1995 г.** при условии своевременной уплаты пошлины за поддержание патента в силе

Зарегистрирован в Государственном реестре изобретений Российской Федерации

г. Москва, ***10 июня 2000 г.***

Генеральный директор

А.Д. Корчагин

F—3·5 波兰的发明专利授权

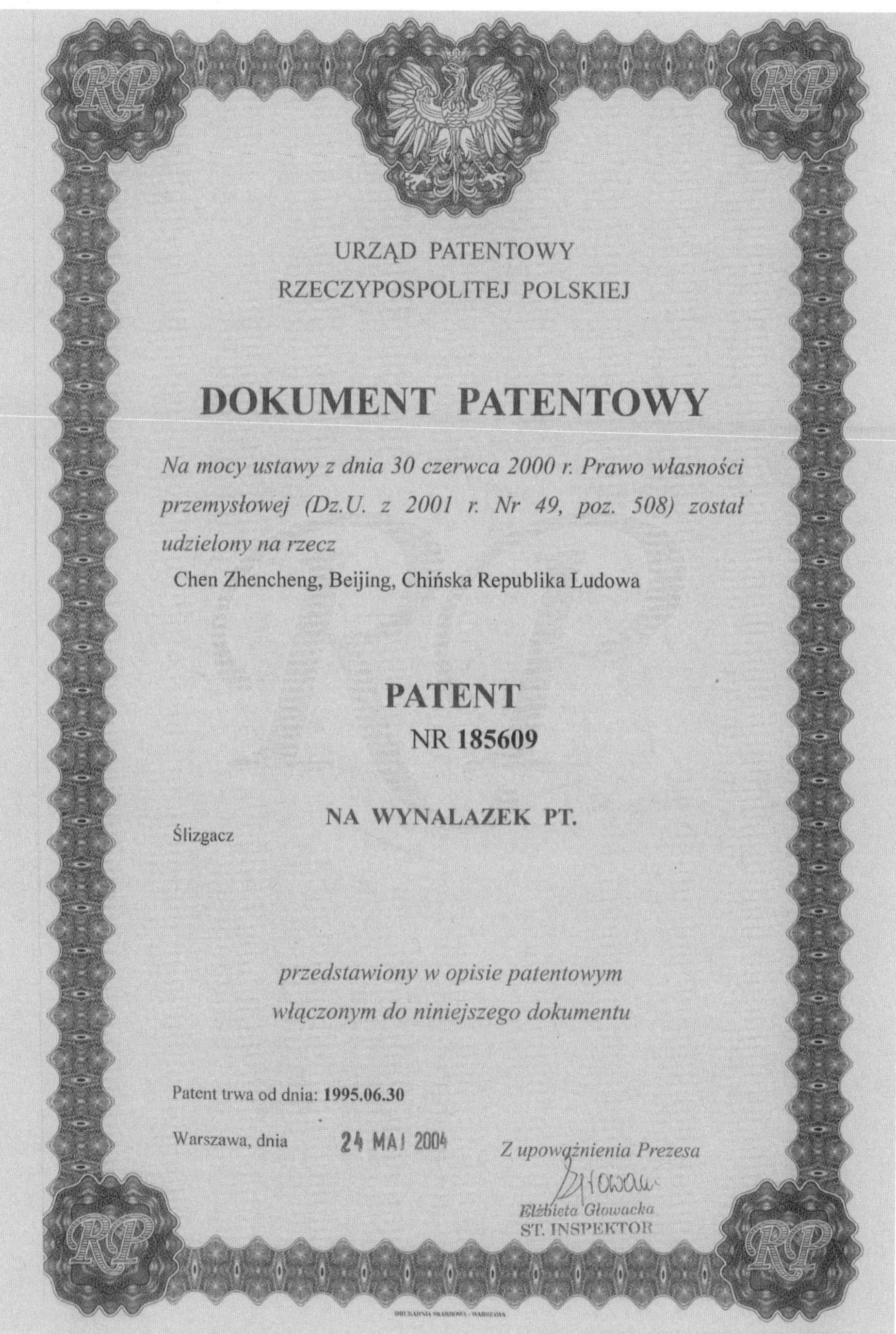

URZĄD PATENTOWY
RZECZYPOSPOLITEJ POLSKIEJ

DOKUMENT PATENTOWY

Na mocy ustawy z dnia 30 czerwca 2000 r. Prawo własności przemysłowej (Dz.U. z 2001 r. Nr 49, poz. 508) został udzielony na rzecz

Chen Zhencheng, Beijing, Chińska Republika Ludowa

PATENT

NR **185609**

NA WYNALAZEK PT.

Ślizgacz

przedstawiony w opisie patentowym włączonym do niniejszego dokumentu

Patent trwa od dnia: **1995.06.30**

Warszawa, dnia 24 MAJ 2004

Z upoważnienia Prezesa

Elżbieta Głowacka
ST. INSPEKTOR

F—3·6 日本的发明专利授权

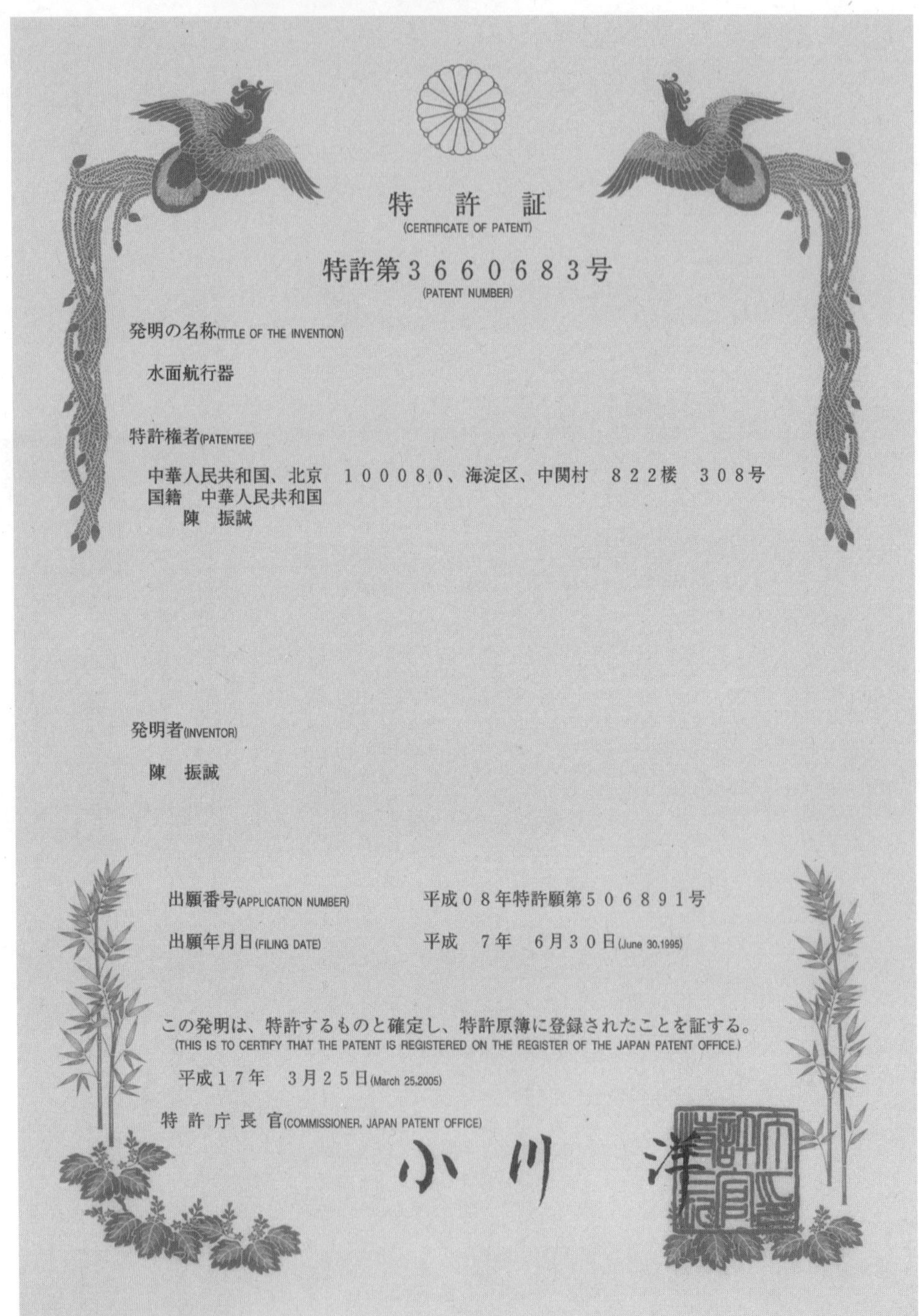

特　許　証
(CERTIFICATE OF PATENT)

特許第３６６０６８３号
(PATENT NUMBER)

発明の名称(TITLE OF THE INVENTION)

水面航行器

特許権者(PATENTEE)

中華人民共和国、北京　１０００８０、海淀区、中関村　８２２楼　３０８号
国籍　中華人民共和国
陳　振誠

発明者(INVENTOR)

陳　振誠

出願番号(APPLICATION NUMBER)　平成０８年特許願第５０６８９１号

出願年月日(FILING DATE)　平成　７年　６月３０日(June 30.1995)

この発明は、特許するものと確定し、特許原簿に登録されたことを証する。
(THIS IS TO CERTIFY THAT THE PATENT IS REGISTERED ON THE REGISTER OF THE JAPAN PATENT OFFICE.)

平成１７年　３月２５日(March 25.2005)

特 許 庁 長 官(COMMISSIONER, JAPAN PATENT OFFICE)

小 川　洋

JP 3660683 B2 2005.6.15

15頁

(19)日本国特許庁(JP)　　(12)特 許 公 報（B2）　　(11)特許番号

特許第3660683号

(P3660683)

(45)発行日　平成17年6月15日(2005.6.15)　　(24)登録日　平成17年3月25日(2005.3.25)

(51)Int.Cl.^{7}　　FＩ

Ｂ６３Ｂ　1/18　　Ｂ６３Ｂ　1/18

請求項の数 10　(全 19 頁)　(15)

(21)出願番号	特願平8-506891	(73)特許権者	
(86)(22)出願日	平成7年6月30日(1995.6.30)		陳　振誠
(65)公表番号	特表平11-508507		中華人民共和国、北京　１０００８０、海淀区、中関村　８２２楼　３０８号
(43)公表日	平成11年7月27日(1999.7.27)	(74)代理人	
(86)国際出願番号	PCT/CN1995/000054		弁理士　西教　圭一郎
(87)国際公開番号	WO1996/005096	(74)代理人	
(87)国際公開日	平成8年2月22日(1996.2.22)		弁理士　杉山　毅至
審査請求日	平成14年6月19日(2002.6.19)	(74)代理人	
(31)優先権主張番号	94114846.7		弁理士　廣瀬　峰太郎
(32)優先日	平成6年8月13日(1994.8.13)	(74)代理人	
(33)優先権主張国	中国(CN)		弁理士　竹内　三喜夫
(31)優先権主張番号	95203983.4	(72)発明者	陳　振誠
(32)優先日	平成7年3月2日(1995.3.2)		中華人民共和国、北京市　１０００８０、海淀区、中関村　８２２楼　３０８号
(33)優先権主張国	中国(CN)		

最終頁に続く

(54)【発明の名称】水面航行器

1

(57)【特許請求の範囲】

【請求項１】

船底１、舷頭２、甲板３、船室および上層構造からなっている船体と、推進操縦システムとからなる水面航行器において、

船底１は前部の二等辺三角形と後部の矩形とを組み合わせた平面船底であり、

船底１と甲板３との間に鉛直方向に凹まれたガイド・ウェイ部4を１本或いは複数本船首から船尻まで貫通させ

、

その底面のセンター・ラインは船底１のセンター・ラインに平行し（１本のガイド・ウェイ部を設ける場合、その底面のセンター・ラインと船底１のセンター・ラインとが合致する）、

ガイド・ウェイ部の断面は

形或いは

形或いは

形になって、縦方向断面は

形、上部線は前が低く、後が高くなるような勾配を有し

、

2

船体の甲板３と船底１との間の両舷頭２にウェーブ・スプラッシュ・ガード５を設け、

ウェーブ・スプラッシュ・ガード５は前が低く、後が高くなるような傾斜角を持っている差し板であるが、舷頭２の表面にはめ込むか、舷頭２の表面に凹まれて、舷頭２と一体になってもよく、

前記船底１中、三角形の２つ等辺の長さＳがＯＸ軸の投影１、矩形のＯＸ方向での長さｔとＯＺ方向での巾２ｂの寸法が、式（１）および式（２）を参照して決め、

式（１）は、$L=2\rho U^2a^2P\sin\theta$

であり、その中に、Ｐは、下記のように定義され、

F—3·7 加拿大的发明专利授权

Office de la propriété intellectuelle du Canada

Un organisme d'Industrie Canada

Canadian Intellectual Property Office

An Agency of Industry Canada

Brevet canadien / Canadian Patent

Le commissaire aux brevets a reçu une demande de délivrance de brevet visant une invention. Ladite requête satisfait aux exigences de la *Loi sur les brevets.* Le titre et la description de l'invention figurent dans le mémoire descriptif, dont une copie fait partie intégrante du présent document.

Le présent brevet confère à son titulaire et à ses représentants légaux, pour une période expirant vingt ans à compter de la date du dépôt de la demande au Canada, le droit, la faculté et le privilège exclusif de fabriquer, construire, exploiter et vendre à d'autres, pour qu'ils l'exploitent, l'objet de l'invention, sauf jugement en l'espèce rendu par un tribunal compétent, et sous réserve du paiement des taxes périodiques.

The Commissioner of Patents has received a petition for the grant of a patent for an invention. The requirements of the *Patent Act* have been complied with. The title and a description of the invention are contained in the specification, a copy of which forms an integral part of this document.

The present patent grants to its owner and to the legal representatives of its owner, for a term which expires twenty years from the filing date of the application in Canada, the exclusive right, privilege and liberty of making, constructing and using the invention and selling it to others to be used, subject to adjudication before any court of competent jurisdiction, and subject to the payment of maintenance fees.

BREVET CANADIEN **2,197,422** CANADIAN PATENT

Date à laquelle le brevet a été accordé et délivré	2005/10/04	Date on which the patent was granted and issued
Date du dépôt de la demande	1995/06/30	Filing date of the application
Date à laquelle la demande est devenue accessible au public pour consultation	1996/02/22	Date on which the application was made available for public inspection

Commissaire aux brevets / Commissioner of Patents

Canada

3258 (CIPO 91) 02/05

F—3•8 韩国的发明专利授权

특 허 증

특 허 제 0415770 호

출원 번호 제 1997-0700960 호
출 원 일 1997년 02월 13일
등 록 일 2004년 01월 07일

발명의명칭 수면 항행기

특허 권자 첸, 젠 칭

중국, 베이징 1 80, 관춘, 822, 308호

발 명 자 첸, 젠 칭

중국, 베이징 1 80, 관춘, 822, 308호

위의 발명은 특허법에 의하여 특허등록원부에 등록되었음을 증명합니다.

2004년 01월 07일

특 허 청 장

No. 216167

유 의 사 항

1. 권리 내용의 확인

특허권의 내용은 특허공보와 특허등록원부를 열람하면 구체적으로 확인할 수 있습니다.

2. 특허권의 존속기간

특허권의 설정등록이 있는 날부터 특허출원일후 20년

3. 특허료의 납부

가. 특허료를 소정기간내에 납부하지 아니하면 특허권은 소멸됩니다.

나. 제4년분 이후의 특허료는 설정등록일(출원공고된 경우 출원공고일)을 기준하여 매년 1년분씩 그 전년도에 납부하여야 합니다. 다만, 위 기간이 경과된 후에는 6월이내에 추가 납부할 수 있으며 이 경우에는 당해 특허료의 2배를 납부하여야 합니다.

다. 제4년분 이후의 특허료는 그 납부년차 순위에 따라 수년분 또는 모든 연차분을 일괄 납부할 수 있습니다.

라. 설정등록 이후의 연차특허료는 특허청 종합민원실(서울사무소 포함)에 연차특허료 납부서를 제출하여 접수증을 교부받은 후 납부용지에 납부자번호(접수번호)등을 정확히 기재한 후 접수을 다음날까지 은행·우체국 등 국고수납기관에 납부하여야 합니다.

마. 특허료는 특허권자는 물론 이해관계인이 대납할 수 있습니다.

4. 등록명의인 표시(주소·명칭)변경·경정 등록

특허권 설정등록후 주소 또는 명칭이 변경 또는 착오등록되었을 경우 등록명의인 표시(주소·명칭)변경·경정 등록을 신청하지 아니하면 불이익을 받을 우려가 있으니 유의하시기 바랍니다.

5. 특허권에 대한 권리구제

가. 특허권이 침해된 경우, 특허법에 의거 침해금지청구권, 손해배상청구권, 신용회복청구권, 부당이득반환청구권 등을 행사할 수 있습니다.

나. 특허권에 대한 분쟁이 발생한 경우, 특허청에 설치된 산업재산권분쟁조정위원회에 화해의 알선·조정을 신청할 수 있습니다.

6. 특허권의 표시·광고 요령

가. 위와 같이 등록된 특허권을 외부에 알리거나 광고하는 경우 특허 제000000호로 표기해야 합니다.

나. 실용신안, 의장, 상표로 등록된 것을 "특허 제000000호"라고 표기할 수 없으며, 허위 표기한 경우에는 관계법에 의거 처벌을 받을 수 있습니다.

7. 등록업무에 대한 보다 상세한 문의처는 다음과 같습니다.

특허청 등록과 ☎ 042-481-5237~5260, FAX 042-472-3467, 특허청 종합민원실 ☎ 042-481-5220~3
특허청 서울사무소 ☎ 02-568-8155~7 (교환: 314, 316)
주소 : ㊞302-701 대전광역시 서구 둔산동 920 (정부대전청사 4동) 특허청 등록과

* 위의 사항은 관계법령의 개정으로 그 내용이 변경될 수도 있습니다.

210mm×297mm

F—3•9 新加坡的发明专利授权

THE REGISTRY OF PATENTS
SINGAPORE

THE PATENTS ACT
(CHAPTER 221)

CERTIFICATE OF GRANT OF PATENT

In accordance with section 35 of the Patents Act, it is hereby certified that a patent having the following P-No. 46110 [WO96/05096] had been granted in respect of an invention having the following particulars:

Title	:	WATER SURFACE SHIP
Application No.	:	9705087-6
Date of Filing	:	30 June 1995
Priority Data	:	13 August 1994 - PATENT APPLICATION NO. 94114846.7(CHINA) 02 March 1995 - PATENT APPLICATION NO. 95203983.4(CHINA)
Name of Inventor(s)	:	ZHENCHENG CHEN
Name(s) and Address(es) of Proprietor(s) of Patent	:	ZHENCHENG CHEN ROOM 308# BLDG., 822 ZHONGGUANCUN, BEIJING 100080, CHINA
Date of Grant	:	16 November 1998

Dated this 16th day of November 1998.

Liew Woon Yin (Ms)
Registrar of Patents,
Singapore.

F—3·10 巴西的发明专利授权

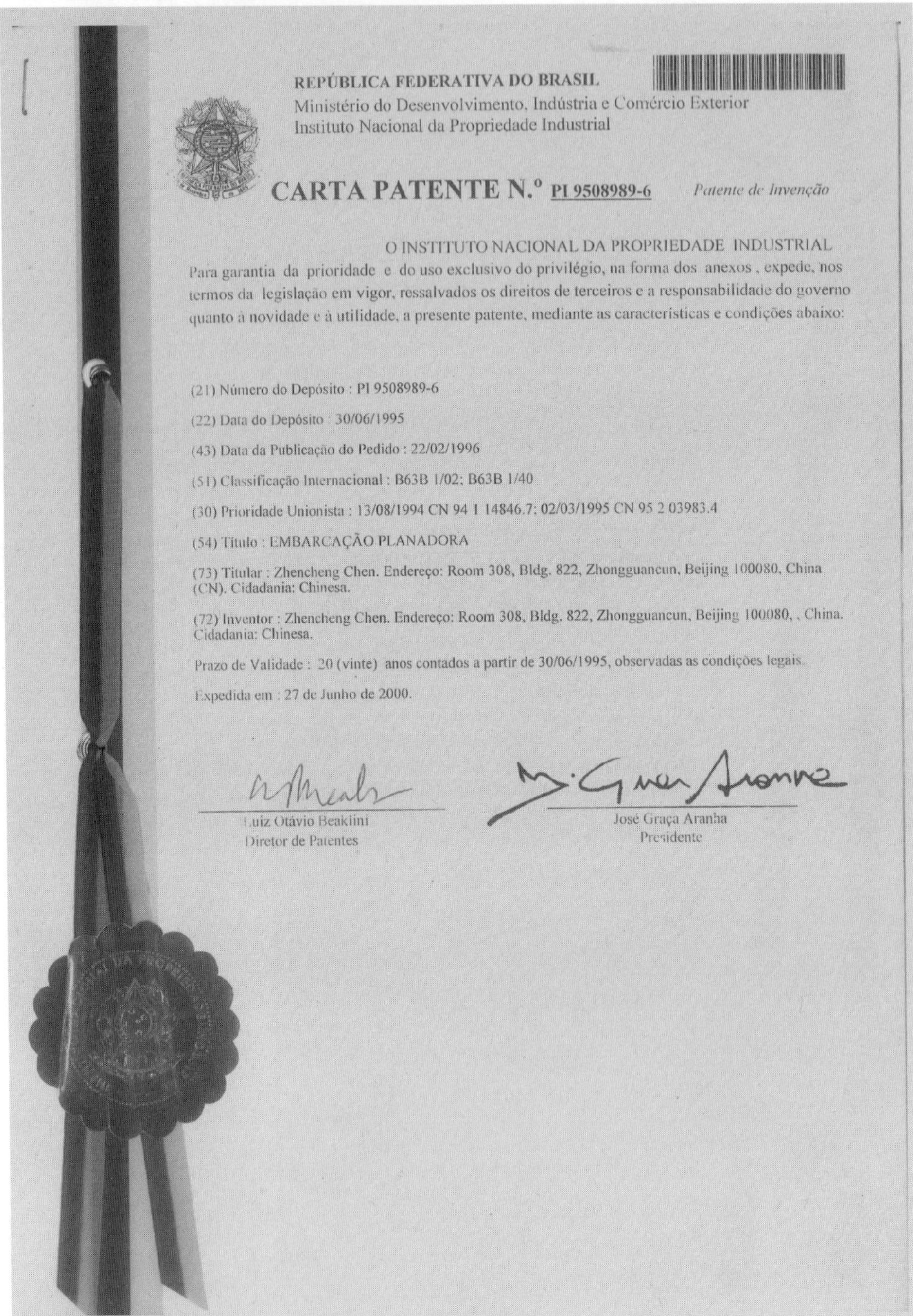

REPÚBLICA FEDERATIVA DO BRASIL
Ministério do Desenvolvimento, Indústria e Comércio Exterior
Instituto Nacional da Propriedade Industrial

CARTA PATENTE N.º PI 9508989-6 *Patente de Invenção*

O INSTITUTO NACIONAL DA PROPRIEDADE INDUSTRIAL

Para garantia da prioridade e do uso exclusivo do privilégio, na forma dos anexos, expede, nos termos da legislação em vigor, ressalvados os direitos de terceiros e a responsabilidade do governo quanto à novidade e à utilidade, a presente patente, mediante as características e condições abaixo:

(21) Número do Depósito : PI 9508989-6

(22) Data do Depósito : 30/06/1995

(43) Data da Publicação do Pedido : 22/02/1996

(51) Classificação Internacional : B63B 1/02; B63B 1/40

(30) Prioridade Unionista : 13/08/1994 CN 94 1 14846.7; 02/03/1995 CN 95 2 03983.4

(54) Título : EMBARCAÇÃO PLANADORA

(73) Titular : Zhencheng Chen. Endereço: Room 308, Bldg. 822, Zhongguancun, Beijing 100080, China (CN). Cidadania: Chinesa.

(72) Inventor : Zhencheng Chen. Endereço: Room 308, Bldg. 822, Zhongguancun, Beijing 100080, . China. Cidadania: Chinesa.

Prazo de Validade : 20 (vinte) anos contados a partir de 30/06/1995, observadas as condições legais.

Expedida em : 27 de Junho de 2000.

Luiz Otávio Beaklini
Diretor de Patentes

José Graça Aranha
Presidente

F—3·11 挪威的发明专利授权

挪威授权证书

KONGERIKET NORGE
The Kingdom of Norway

Registreringsbrev
Certificate of Registration

Patent nr.: 316265
Patent No.

I henhold til patentloven av 15 desember 1967 er Deres patent meddelt med opplysninger som angitt i vedheftet patentskrift.

This is to certify that the Norwegian Patent Office, in accordance with the Patents Act No. 9 of 15 December 1967, has granted a patent for the enclosed invention.

Jørgen Smith
direktør

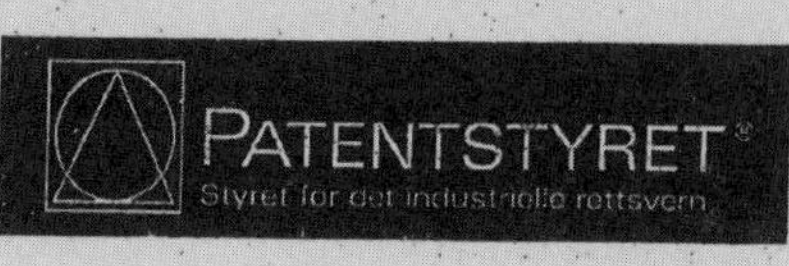

F—3·12　澳大利亚的发明专利授权

澳大利亚授权证书

Commonwealth of Australia

Letters patent

Patents Act 1990

No. 698205

STANDARD PATENT
(DUPLICATE)

I, Vivienne Joyce Thom, Commissioner of Patents, seal a duplicate of the Standard Patent granted on 11 February 1999 with the following particulars:

Name and Address of Patentee:
Zhencheng Chen , Room 308# Bldg. 822, Zhongguancun Beijing 100080 China

Name of Actual Inventor: Zhencheng Chen

Title of Invention: Planing vessel

Application Number: 27843/95

Term of Letters Patent: Twenty years commencing on 30 June 1995

Priority Details:

Number	*Date*	*Filed with*
94114846	13 August 1994	CHINA
95203983	2 March 1995	CHINA

Dated this 13 day of July 2000

V. Thom

V.J.THOM
COMMISSIONER OF PATENTS

图书在版编目(CIP)数据

陈振诚 / 陈昕编著. -- 贵阳 : 贵州人民出版社, 2018.12
（中华当代著名科学家书系）
ISBN 978-7-221-14690-8

Ⅰ. ①陈… Ⅱ. ①陈… Ⅲ. ①陈振诚－传记 Ⅳ. ①K826.11

中国版本图书馆CIP数据核字(2018)第167753号

陈振诚

主　　编　吴阶平　杨福家　吴文俊　袁隆平
　　　　　孙家栋　陈清泉　刘国光　汝　信
执行主编　唐廷友　唐　洁　赵岩青　刘忠勤
副 主 编　单天伦　张　维　马京生　马胜云
　　　　　王　霞　王建蒙　王庭槐　彭洁清
著　　者　陈　昕
责任编辑　唐　露　张　薇
出版发行　贵州出版集团　贵州人民出版社
地　　址　贵阳市观山湖区中天会展城会展东路SOHO公寓A座
开　　本　787 mm × 1 092 mm 1/16
印　　张　12.5
字　　数　170千字
版　　次　2019年7月第1版第1次印刷
印　　刷　贵州兴隆印务有限责任公司
书　　号　ISBN 978-7-221-14690-8
定　　价　30.00元

版权所有，侵权必究